The 8 Patterns
of Highly Effective Entrepreneurs

The 8
Patterns

OF
HIGHLY EFFECTIVE
ENTREPRENEURS

Brent Bowers

FOREWORD BY CARL SCHRAMM

NEW YORK   LONDON   TORONTO   SYDNEY   AUCKLAND

A CURRENCY BOOK
PUBLISHED BY DOUBLEDAY

A hardcover edition of this book was published in 2006 by Currency under the title
If at First You Don't Succeed . . . : The Eight Patterns of Highly Effective Entrepreneurs.

Published in the United States by Doubleday, an imprint of The Doubleday Broadway
Publishing Group, a division of Random House, Inc., New York.
www.currencybooks.com

CURRENCY is a trademark of Random House, Inc., and DOUBLEDAY is a registered
trademark of Random House, Inc.

All trademarks are the property of their respective companies.

Book design by Fearn Cutler de Vicq

LIBRARY OF CONGRESS CATALOGING-IN-PUBLICATION DATA
Bowers, Brent.
  The 8 patterns of highly effective entrepreneurs / Brent Bowers.
    p. cm.
  Previously published under title: If at first you don't succeed, 2006.
  Includes index.
  1. Entrepreneurship. I. Title. II. Title: Eight patterns of highly effective entrepreneurs.

  HB615.B675 2007
  658.4'21—dc22

                              2006031863

ISBN 978-0-385-51547-4

PRINTED IN THE UNITED STATES OF AMERICA

SPECIAL SALES
Currency Books are available at special discounts for bulk purchases for sales promotions or premiums. Special editions, including personalized covers, excerpts of existing
books, and corporate imprints, can be created in large quantities for special needs. For
more information, write to Special Markets, Currency Books, specialmarkets@random
house.com

10 9 8 7 6 5 4 3 2 1

FIRST PAPERBACK EDITION

For Barbara, Jennie, and Matthew, lights of my life

Acknowledgments

I am deeply grateful to Robert Wilson, my agent, for his help in honing the concept for this book; to Roger Scholl, my editor at Doubleday, for his encouragement and advice at every step of the way in the writing of it; to Barbara Bowers, my wife and fellow journalist, for painstakingly reading through my raw copy, and to all the people I interviewed in the course of my research for their openness, graciousness, and good humor.

I am indebted to the many editors I have worked with at the *New York Times* over the years, notably John Geddes, to whom I wisely latched my star many years ago; Glenn Kramon, a gentleman's gentleman whose gift for encouraging reporters and editors is legendary; Larry Ingrassia, the energetic and endlessly curious business editor; Tom Redburn, who is everything an editor should be: brilliant, decisive, plain-spoken, and savvy at poker; Jim Schachter, a modern-day Renaissance man with a wry wit and a sympathetic ear; and, above them all, David Rosenberg, a beloved editor who left this world far too early.

Heartfelt thanks also go to my fellow wordsmiths at the *Times,* without whose encouragement I would have long ago torn out what little hair remains on my head. Tim O'Brien, a bulldog reporter and gifted writer if ever there was one, buoyed my sagging spirits so many times I lost count. I appreciate more than they know the moral support that I got from Margaret Loke, Deidre Leipziger, and Joan O'Neill; the commiseration and funny stories that came my way from fellow authors Barry Meier, Walt Bogdanich, Connie Hays, Fred Brock, and Joe Sharkey; and the good humor of my cubicle mates Donna Anderson, Ken Meyn, Judith Spindler, and Jim Cobb. Kurt Eichenwald was generous to me in more ways than one.

Outside the officeplace, I relied for emotional succor on friends Henry and Tracy Gottlieb, once and future book collaborators; Barry and Pat Adler, fellow lovers of Cape Cod and the Islands; Bill and Donna Taaffe, comrades in the faith; Bela and Judi Gajary, innkeepers of the Gajary Hilton; Mack Harrell, the motorcycle preacher; and Bea Rosenberg, David's courageous mother.

And then there are those highly talented but insufficiently recognized foot soldiers of the newspaper business, with whom I have had the good fortune to work closely over the past decade: freelancers. In alphabetical order, I pay tribute to Marci Alboher, Shira J. Boss-Bicak, Charles Butler, Betsy Cummings, Abby Ellin, Christopher Elliott, Alice Feiring, Anne Field, Paul Burnham Finney, Julie Flaherty, James Flanigan, Perry Garfinkel, David Jones, David Koeppel, Jane Levere, Melinda Ligos, Sharon McDonnell, Tanya Mohn, Regan Morris, Patricia Olsen, Elizabeth Olson, Francine Parnes, Glenn Rifkin, Ellen Rosen, Weld Royal, Susan Stellin, Eve Tahmincioglu, Bob Tedeschi, Thom Weidlich, and Amy Zipkin. Quite a few of them have written books of their own, and I treasure the yarns they have recounted to me about the experience.

Finally, I would like to pay tribute to Yvette Bowers, my stepmother; Cathy Yarnelle, the high-spirited, ninety-something grande dame of my childhood; and Bruce and Bob, my brothers, fellow writers, and hiking companions.

Contents

Foreword
By Carl Schramm

The very nature of our economy is changing in profound, yet largely unseen, ways. Most of us continue to think of the economy in terms of big institutions—gigantic corporations such as General Electric and General Motors, big labor unions, and an enormous federal bureaucracy. This is old thinking. While these institutions will continue to exist, underneath them is a new economy. It is one where these institutions will become less and less important. Why? Because the new economy is not about institutions, it is about people. We no longer think of ourselves as cogs in the great institutional economy where manufacturing was king. As cogs, the typical working person did the same thing for years on end. The company and the union figured out what people got paid. The company and the union agreed as to what benefits would be. Our economy treated most people as "inputs" to be guided or "bosses" to maximize production.

Today, manufacturing is a shrinking part of our economy, much of it being done either by robots or people in other countries. Unions no longer speak for a significant share of workers. (Indeed, the only substantial part of the workforce that is organized is public employment: teachers, bus drivers, carpenters working for the parks department.) Interestingly, for all the robots and all the worries about outsourcing, we are at record levels in terms of people having jobs. Our unemployment rate is under five percent. Anyone who wants a job can have one.

And, there is so much demand for lower-skilled workers—the service workers, groundskeepers, and gardeners who keep our homes, hotels, and cities clean—that we have created a huge underground labor market for immigrants.

The people who are directing and driving the economy are the creators and innovators who guide our companies and universities. Those who are shaping our future more than any other group are the nation's entrepreneurs. These are the people who see opportunity where others see risk. They are the people who would rather work in organizations that they start. They are the highly trained people who create jobs and wealth for others as well as for themselves. They are critical to the growth of the economy. Most of the new jobs created in the United States every year are in firms less than five years old! More and more younger Americans look forward to working for themselves or working in small companies where they know the founder and share the sense of building a new and highly creative and responsive organization. These new firms operate on one common perspective—that the nation's (and increasingly the world's) consumers need the innovative product or service that they saw and developed and applied to increase human satisfaction and happiness.

Our workforce is getting skilled at quick job changes. Whereas only a few decades ago college graduates might imagine having three employers throughout their careers, today's graduates know that in the course of their first decade of work, they may be employed by five or six firms. They are building different types of résumés—résumés that proudly display failed companies and other types of dead ends, as well as the firms that are on their way to becoming household names.

There is something especially magical about this new "people economy" that is populated by what some might call a new kind of people: entrepreneurs. The entrepreneur sees the question of job security and personal economic security differently. (Our entrepreneurs are at least one, and often three, generations removed from the Great Depression. Many do not even remember the ravages of the "stagflation" economy of the late 1970s and 1980s where we saw little growth, record levels of inflation, the erosion of savings, and the fear that the Japanese economy would soon overtake us.) They do not test opportunities against the notion that they will have a long-term job and a good pension when they retire. Again and again, we watch people in their thirties and forties leave large firms to start their own firms, or to take a job with much less apparent security where they can be part of the creation of something new. We even see young entrepreneurs appear to throw away paths that would lead to certain success. We read of someone who left Berkeley before graduation because he could not wait to commercialize a new idea; or the Stanford graduate who turned down a great job at Google or a Ph.D. fellowship at M.I.T. to go to work with a friend in a new start-up; or the high school student who turned down Georgetown to skip college so that she could devote full-time attention to her new software business.

Such people are ready to take risk in ways in which their parents could never dream. The American economy, which entrepreneurs are shaping, makes it easier to take risk. Our entrepreneurs have helped rescue our economy from its last five recessions. And through their creation of jobs, they help to keep the economy at full employment. As a result, individuals who take a risk and fail find it much easier to get a job. Ironically, as our economy is increasingly driven by entrepreneurs who are taking risk, we are watching a less risky economy evolve.

Brent Bowers has written a book about these people, what they do, and how they do it. And, while he focuses on entrepreneurs and the keys to their success, he has also written a book that describes who is making the new economy and how it operates. Thus, his book is as unique as it is valuable. It achieves where so many business books fail. It provides practical insights for individuals. It answers two important questions that would-be entrepreneurs must ask: "Am I really an entrepreneur?" and "What should I do to become successful?"

Successful entrepreneurs possess, in Bowers' view, eight talents or traits that distinguish them from people who couldn't begin to dream of starting a business. But, in explaining each of the traits, Bowers also points out how failed or modestly successful entrepreneurs can improve their odds. His taxonomy is the result of exhaustive interviews of dozens of entrepreneurs. The book beautifully brings the evidence to bear on each of the aspects so that the reader is provided with a clear sense of what Bowers sees. As befits one of the nation's most talented business reporters, the book is alive with stories that illustrate each point. It is in his discussions with entrepreneurs that the author gives the reader the best of treats. The stories are compelling and are told with an inspiring touch that sticks. Without effort, the book actually relates the largest set of stories of entrepreneurial struggle and success ever in print. In doing so, it delivers what few business books ever aspire to or achieve—wisdom regarding business and decision making, within a special context: start-up firms.

Taken as a whole, this book tells yet another story. The millions of entrepreneurs succeeding and failing are building together a new kind of economy—one that is more comfortable and supportive to just such risk-taking behavior. As more and more people understand what Bowers has uncovered, we will understand a great deal more about how the economy of the future will work.

When the economic history of our time is written, its links to cultural and political history will be clearer than at any time before. The line between work and personal growth is being blurred. Entrepreneurial firms are driven, as many of Bowers' stories tell, more by a need to create a vehicle for personal creativity and fulfillment than for profit. Before the industrial revolution, many more people worked for themselves. England was, in those times, described as a mercantile society— the proverbial "nation of shopkeepers." The entrepreneurial economy that Bowers shows us here is a step back into a dazzling new future. The firms of the future will be the adjuncts of economically creative activity for millions more Americans.

The people economy, really entrepreneurial capitalism, emerges from a nation of astoundingly well-educated and technologically literate people who will do nothing less than reform democracy and the aspirations of the world's people to pursue such rewarding work in peace and security. This book will be a touchstone of our understanding and serve as a guidepost to readers and thinkers in the years ahead.

Carl Schramm is president and CEO of the Ewing Marion Kauffman Foundation.

Introduction

This is not an ordinary business book. But here's betting you'll learn more about the art of starting and running a company from the stories of the entrepreneurs you'll meet in here than from all the charts, questionnaires, and checklists in those how-to tomes no one ever seems able to finish reading. More to the point, you'll be able to answer that all-important question: Do I have what it takes to be an entrepreneur? Most people don't, and there's no shame in that. In fact, knowing that you don't might save you a lot of grief and get you on a faster track in whatever profession you're pursuing.

But if you do have what it takes, if you recognize yourself in these pages, then that revelation ought to be enough to dislodge you from the office cubicle where you have been languishing—how many years has it been now?—into a life of independence, adventure, and quite possibly riches.

If you do take the plunge, you'll be in good company. Consider the following statistics:

- There are roughly 24 million entrepreneurs in the United States, accounting for close to 11 percent of the adult population. This is the most of any nation, and their numbers are growing.
- Half of these 24 million run their businesses mostly as sidelines, and half do so as full-time professions. Somewhere between

5 million and 8 million of them employ others. Anywhere from 500,000 to 800,000 of such "employee firms" are started every year.

- Small businesses account for 51 percent of America's gross domestic product and more than two-thirds of all new jobs. From 1989 to 2004, by one estimate, they created 30 million jobs, while in the same fifteen-year period, Fortune 500 companies shed 5 million.
- In 2003, income increased 3.7 times faster for small-business owners than for people on corporate payrolls.
- The number of American colleges and universities that offer courses in entrepreneurship has soared to 1,500 from a mere sixteen in 1970.

America's grassroots capitalist culture has had a profound and lasting impact on our society. It is a wellspring of innovation. It is a lure to people the world over who flee the bureaucratic corruption and regulatory shackles of their homelands for a place in an economy that is already the world's most dynamic. And it is our nation's greatest weapon in the growing competition for world markets.

Americans are infatuated with entrepreneurs, for they are the embodiment of the American dream. "Next to Mom, apple pie, and God, the entrepreneur is the great truth about America," says Tim Mahoney, the founder of vFinance Inc. and one of the people profiled in this book.

While the dream was once open mostly to white males, today it is within reach of anyone with smarts, initiative, and fire in the belly. And sure enough, in recent years a surge of women, African Americans, Hispanics, and Asian Americans have grasped it.

So have increasing numbers of the older set, many of them willing or unwilling refugees from the management echelons of Fortune 500 companies. Such people probably wouldn't have given it a try twenty years ago. But consider this: With corporate benefits shrinking and job security evaporating, the risk of striking out on one's own is decreasing compared with the risk of staying on and being forced into an early retirement.

In the future, "everyone will either be a business owner or a temp," according to Watts Wacker, the author and futurist.

Each of the eight chapters in the book is organized around a core entrepreneurial trait, such as the knack for spotting and seizing opportunities nobody else has noticed or a compulsion to be the person in charge of running the show. As you read the stories of people who have given entrepreneurship a go, you'll see what attributes define a successful entrepreneurial personality.

As I was cautioned by one of the experts I consulted, Judith Cone of the Marion Ewing Kauffman Foundation, a $1.7 billion organization in Kansas City that does extensive research on entrepreneurship, most Americans like to think of themselves as being just like the people in this book: self-starters with high aspirations and dogged dispositions, risk takers and dreamers and pragmatists all rolled into one. Most of us do exhibit these characteristics to some extent, she says, but entrepreneurs exhibit them in the *right measure*. Here is how she puts it:

"When it comes to risk taking, on a scale of 1 to 10, people who engage in extreme sports rate a 10. Entrepreneurs like Ted Turner maybe rate a 9. But most entrepreneurs probably would be at 5 or 6. They take smart risks, not huge ones.

"On the other hand, when it comes to spotting and seizing opportunities, some highly creative people are disinclined to run to the marketplace with their ideas. They score a 1. The average person might score 2 or 3 or 4. In this category, most true entrepreneurs rate a 10. They see opportunities all the time and they seize them."

So you have to hit the right point on the spectrum for each trait?

Right, she replies. "And you have to have all the eight traits."

To be sure, no list is definitive. But almost any is revealing. In my interviews, I asked both experts and entrepreneurs what they viewed as the core characteristics that define the entrepreneurial personality. Here is a sampling of some of the responses.

- "First and foremost: hunger. It can be economic hunger or psychological hunger, but you're desperate to make something happen.

Also: luck; persistence, which can come from passion; focus, which can come from passion; energy, which can come from passion."

- "You need balls. That is the number-one ingredient. You also need intelligence. You need common sense. You need to be a visionary of sorts. You must be able to see a need and have the balls to go after it."
- "High tolerance for risk, bullheadedness, impatience with the status quo, a high energy level, and a vision of the way something should be or look like."
- "Passion. Itchiness to wear a different hat, to start a new business. Liking the rush of starting a business, of making it grow, and then the boredom of running it and moving on. Wanting to be in charge. Creativity. Being able to wing it."

All good lists, smart lists.

But I believe mine is better.

What, then, are the eight traits? First, an aptitude for spotting and seizing opportunities that nobody else has noticed. Second, a compulsion to be in charge and, tied to that, a gift for leadership. Third, a history of innovative activities dating back to childhood, usually in a family environment that encouraged that bent. Fourth, a talent for improvisation. Fifth, fierce drive, energy, and tenacity—doggedness, in other words. Sixth, enthusiasm that borders on the delusional for a product. Seventh (and as a counterpoint to such unbridled optimism), unfailing pragmatism. And eighth, a knack for viewing setbacks as opportunities, what I call the facility for "failing upward."

Does that sound like you? Then go for it!

The 8 Patterns
of Highly Effective Entrepreneurs

CHAPTER 1

Seizing Opportunities

Entrepreneurs notice things.

They spot opportunities nobody else has seen and seize them. It sounds simple enough, but it is an aptitude most people lack. Ask yourself: Would you have figured out how to make a windfall out of an aging laundry plant during a construction moratorium in Princeton, New Jersey?

J. Robert Hillier did.

Hillier, the founder of Hillier Architecture, the fifth-largest architectural firm in the United States, is always on the lookout for arcane property deals. Successful as his architecture business is, it accounts for only 10 percent of his income. The rest comes from real estate.

His first big venture was his purchase a quarter century ago of a beat-up cinderblock building that housed a dry cleaning and laundry establishment. The company was going out of business, and Hillier saw right away that once it was fixed up, it might be converted into apartments.

Trouble was, Princeton's sewer system had reached its limit, and the city had imposed a moratorium on real-estate construction until a new system could be built. Hillier, however, came up with a way around that. "I found out that the laundry pumped out 9,000 gallons of wash water a day," he recounts. "So I went to the health board and asked, 'If I buy the building and close it down permanently, could I build eleven town-houses that collectively would release only 2,200 gallons?'" They readily agreed, so he took the proposal to the zoning board, which approved it. "I sold all eleven townhouses before we broke ground, for $97,000 apiece," he says. (He can't help adding ruefully that today, they are selling for about $1 million each.)

Hillier is always keeping an eye out for angles. Not long ago, he learned that the guy who ran a repair shop for the town's garbage trucks was retiring. Hillier knew there was a lot of demand for singles housing in downtown Princeton. He also knew the building in question had big iron trusses seventeen feet high, meaning you could fit two floors in it. He bought the building, got zoning approval to turn it into tiny loft apartments, and built sixteen of them. He rented them for $2,000 a month (an average of $48 a square foot, 50 percent higher than the most expensive office space in Princeton).

"That's how entrepreneurs make money, doing little things like that, leveraging them by the multiplier effect," Hillier says. "Maybe the important attribute of the entrepreneur is working at things in an unconventional way and seeing opportunity in doing so."

You want unconventional? Greg Herro has found a business opportunity in cremated human remains that has to rate high on anybody's list of creative thinking. Herro and his buddies found a gold mine in them. Or, more accurately, a diamond mine.

Literally.

Herro's company, LifeGem, in Elk Grove Village, Illinois, extracts the carbon from the ashes of corpses and turns it into diamond jewelry. Macabre? Herro doesn't think so, and neither, clearly, do his customers.

The way he sees it, LifeGem's concept is a cosmic breakthrough in the way society disposes of corpses. In the million years or so that our species has walked the planet, humans have mostly either buried or burned their dead. Herro believes his company has come up with another alternative: bejewel your body with them.

Looking for unconventional solutions is an old habit with Herro. In high school, for example, he discovered that one of his teachers always asked questions based solely on captions under pictures. Thenceforth, he always got an A in her class.

In 2000, after selling a computer consulting company he had started seven years earlier, Herro was looking for something else to do. Then a friend, Rusty VandenBiesen, came to him with an interesting proposal. VandenBiesen had been watching a TV show about diamonds and had learned two important facts: Carbon is the building block of life, and diamonds are made out of carbon. So why, he wanted to know, couldn't they create diamonds from human carbon?

Herro bought into the idea at once. "As Einstein once said, 'If an idea does not at first seem insane, it has no hope,'" Herro points out.

Each of the four partners sank $25,000 into the venture, but it was Herro who did most of the legwork in the beginning—doing research into the technology of turning human carbon into diamonds, putting together a business plan, raising money, and recruiting a Russian-speaking associate as a contact to Russia's diamond industry—while the other three continued holding down their jobs. Today, he holds the CEO title at LifeGem (he is seen as the guy who can get things done), while his three co-founders—Rusty VandenBiesen, Rusty's brother Dean, and Herro's brother Mike—report to him.

•   •   •

The gift for detecting—and grabbing—unique moneymaking opportunities that have somehow eluded everybody else lies at the center of entrepreneurs' mental universe, according to academics and other experts. It is the most basic test of anyone's entrepreneurial mettle. If you lack it, all the drive, passion, quick-footedness, and smarts in the world won't bail you out of a life of professional servitude.

"The defining trait of entrepreneurs is that they notice things," says William J. Dennis, senior research fellow at the National Federation of Independent Business's NFIB Research Foundation in Washington, D.C. "They see opportunity. They smell it. Take the guy who came up with the absolutely simple idea of cargo containers for ships. He had been driving products to the dock and dumping them off. Somebody else would have to load them onto the ship. And he thought, 'Why not just leave the container?'"

Other examples Dennis cites include the paint roller, invented by Norman Breakey of Toronto in 1940; the Jersey barrier, the concrete separator used in narrow highway medians; and the marketing genius behind the Vermont Teddy Bear Company, who realized that you don't have to sell teddy bears as toys, you can sell them as alternatives to candy and flowers.

Tim Faley, managing director of the Samuel Zell & Robert H. Lurie Institute for Entrepreneurial Studies at the University of Michigan's Ross School of Business, has his own favorite examples. One is Henry Ford's famous inspiration to adapt the assembly line to automobiles. Another, lesser-known example is a Japanese company's development of a technology that *reduced* the range of its golf balls by half. This meant that people could give the ball the same energetic whacking on small courses as on large ones—a winner in a country with a dearth of real estate.

It is important to note that the process of exploiting untapped opportunity comes in two parts: perception and action. How many times have you come up with brilliant ideas that never went anywhere beyond dinner-table conversation or idle late-evening fantasies? "A friend of mine coined the phrase 'Entrepreneurs are dreamers who do,' and I think that is what sets them apart," says Judith Cone of the Ewing Marion Kauffman Foundation. "Simple desire, or some catalytic event, puts them on this journey of tremendous work that requires commitment, stubbornness, perseverance, and the ability to live within paradoxes."

Guy Kawasaki, the managing director of Garage Technology Ventures in Palo Alto, California, an early-stage venture capital firm for high-technology companies, has listened to hundreds of pitches over the years. He says it is not uncommon to meet Ph.D.'s "who've been thinking and thinking and thinking for years but never actually starting doing anything." The trick, he says, is to stop thinking and start doing. Tom Peters, the bestselling business writer, he notes, called this "a predisposition for action."

Like Dennis and Faley, Kawasaki says business innovators often hit pay dirt just by taking a fresh approach to the obvious. "Take Apple's iPod," he says. "It had a better industrial design" than earlier-model MP3 players, "but that isn't rocket science. The product was tightly integrated with online sales, and that wasn't anything new. Anybody could have done both things at once, but no one did."

Opportunities like this aren't always out of reach for the general public. In the early days of the Internet, how many people had the bright idea of starting an online auction house? Quite a few, probably—and Cone was one of them. She and a girlfriend used to sit around and talk about creating an Internet marketplace that resembled today's eBay. But while they were talking, Pierre Omidyar and his collaborators were out doing: raising money, getting licenses, hiring people, and building a business model.

Faley has witnessed the same distinction between café chatterers and down-in-the-trenches doers. "I think of entrepreneurs as gladiators," he remarks. "They don't want to talk about the theory of sword wielding. They want to do battle. They want to be down in the arena and making the mistakes and getting dirty."

Before he came to the Zell Lurie Institute, Faley started the University of Michigan's technology-transfer office in engineering. Over the course of three years, this office produced ten companies, including an Internet-security company called Arbor Networks that was launched "right at the tail end of the dot-com revolution but before anybody really cared much about security."

The founder, Farnam Jahanian, was a researcher in computer networking "who could not quit worrying about the issue once he had written his paper," Faley recalls. "He was like, 'I can't walk away from this. I know what the answer is. I have to move it forward.'" He persevered, and the company is flourishing today.

William D. Bygrave, the Frederic C. Hamilton Professor of Free Enterprise at Babson College, outside Boston, argues that older people, like older companies, are less likely to spot and seize opportunities than younger people or start-ups. "If you know too much, the liability of sameness, the liability of staleness, the liability of knowing too much can blind you," he says. "Someone with the optimism of youth knows enough to know what can be done, but not enough to know that it can't be done.

"I did raise venture capital in the late sixties," he says. "The innocence of youth! The optimism of youth! Had I known then what I know now about venture capital, I would never ever have tried to get it. Finding VC funding is rarer than becoming a professional athlete. Lucky I didn't know that."

Bottom line: Let your imagination run a little wild. Entertain nutty ideas. Look for business angles wherever you go. Frank Landsberger, a onetime business owner, venture capitalist, and university professor whose latest gig is investment banking (as managing director at CRT Capital, the largest privately held investment bank in the United States), considers entrepreneurs asocial, in the sense that they reject conventional wisdom. For example, conventional wisdom said the U.S. Postal Service worked just fine, but the founders of FedEx undercut that notion and built a huge business on doing something the post office never thought of trying: guaranteeing next-day delivery.

The wonderful thing is that entrepreneurs don't have to come up with a brand-new technology, Landsberger says, just a different approach. "Look at the iPod," he comments. "Apple just packaged existing technology in a clever way. The MP3 player—here was something the younger generation could really get into, and it was packaged in a way that made it a status symbol."

People can have a breakthrough vision in low-technology areas, too. If you start a bridal shop, Landsberger says, you are buying yourself a job. If you plan to launch a nationwide chain of bridal shops, you are buying yourself a vision. (Funny he should say that—two of the people featured in this book are sisters who plan to launch the first nationwide chain of bridal shops.)

"Or look at Toys 'R' Us," Landsberger adds. "Same old toys, but it was a breakout idea to sell only toys and almost every toy you can think of at a discount and at high volume."

• • •

But let's face it—high-tech is usually better. At least it was for Peter Amico, who spotted an opportunity to introduce sophisticated naval technology to the commercial market.

Amico is the founder of Airtrax, a company in Blackwood, New Jersey, that makes one of the weirdest, most innovative contraptions you've probably never heard of: omnidirectional vehicles. These machines roll along on four independently operated wheels, controlled by a joystick. By controlling wheel speed and rotation, either forward or reverse, the operator can move the vehicle laterally or diagonally, instead of swinging it around the way you would with a car. The vehicle simply stops going forward and moves sideways. You can even make them rotate full circle without leaving their spot. Amico loves showing off his first progeny, a forklift called the Sidewinder, to hot-shot executives at giant corporations, then watching them behave like boys in an amusement park. When he showed it to the vice president of Timken Company, a $4.4 billion maker of bearings and specialty steels in Canton, Ohio, the executive whizzed around the factory floor before pronouncing the vehicle a "disruptive technology" because it was so innovative it was going to redefine the market. "About forty other executives were lined up to take their turn," Amico recalls. "I joked I was going to charge them 25 cents a ride."

Amico didn't invent the technology; it was just hanging out there, waiting to be plucked by the first risk-taking opportunist who happened along. The U.S. Navy had bought it from a Swedish inventor and experimented with it for fifteen years, using five direct-current servo motors that cost $4,500 apiece, or $22,500 per vehicle. Not worth the price, the Navy concluded.

Since the technology was declassified, the Navy opened it to commercial exploitation. Several companies took a look but gave it a pass, for the same reason: too expensive. If only much cheaper alternating-current motors did the trick.

It was that "if only" that Amico bet his future on. The Navy sold the technology to Airtrax for $2,500 as part of a so-called Cooperative Research and Development Agreement. (Just knowing how to dip into the federal government's CRADA pie is in itself a manifestation of the knack for spotting and seizing opportunity.)

That could have been money down the tube, of course. Amico was aware the DC motors were too costly for a commercial vehicle and knew he'd have to find a less-expensive solution.

"I got into a big fight with one of my electrical engineers over this, who said it couldn't be done," he says. "But we had no other choice. You can buy an AC motor for $294. It was a major decision to get into the commercial market that I had to make."

Sure enough, as computers became more powerful and sophisticated, Amico was able to use AC motors to run his vehicles. It took longer than he thought—nearly four years instead of just one or two. But it happened, and in March 2005, Airtrax produced its first ten commercial Sidewinders, the first of hundreds on order, with its Cobra omnidirectional scissors lifts not far behind.

To enable Airtrax stock to trade publicly, Amico spotted yet another opportunity that nobody had noticed, this one veiled in U.S. securities law. In 1999, he did a reverse merger into a shell company, MAS Acquisitions, sidestepping the cumbersome and high-priced initial-public-offering route. It's an old trick, but he did it with a new twist: He had MAS merge into Airtrax, rather than the other way around. It was so unusual, he says, that the Securities and Exchange Commission signed off on the deal without asking any questions.

Well, entrepreneurs do unusual things. The element of surprise is part of their secret. Omnidirectional vehicles—who would've thought? Or diamonds from corpses—how can you top that?

If anybody can, it is probably Mark Hughes, founder of Buzzmarketing, a consulting firm that teaches how to use word of mouth as a marketing tool. In itself, that is not all that novel a business concept. It is how he got there that makes Hughes stand out.

Hughes kicked around in corporate America for a while with marketing stints at places such as Pepsico and America Mobile Satellite. An early hint of his creative potential was a commercial he made for Pep Boys Auto that showed a car screeching to a halt to avoid hitting a moose. The moose looked up and asked, "Did you buy those brakes at Pep Boys?" The driver said yes, to which the moose replied, "I appreciate it." Hughes made up buttons for employees at the company's 600 stores that pictured a moose and the words "Ask me about the brakes."

Then came the Internet explosion. Wanting a piece of the action, he surfed for unheralded ventures to which he could offer his services. He soon located a live wire named Josh Kopelman who was planning to launch a company called Half.com that would sell used books, CDs, and DVDs for half or less of their list prices. Not knowing how to contact Kopelman, Hughes sent e-mails to scores of possible addresses, until two finally got through.

Hughes talked himself into a partnership with five other co-founders and was given the official title of "marketing guru"—the equivalent of vice president of marketing. "One day Josh told me, 'I hired you for your persistence and your résumé but now you might as well throw them out the window,'" Hughes recalls. "He said, 'We need a huge idea to break through the clutter. We gotta launch our brand and prove to the venture capitalists that we are out-of-the-box guys.'"

Hughes scoured the Internet. He pored over lists of famous monuments. He thought up and rejected endless gimmicks, such as using the image of the Boulder Dam for an advertising campaign to "damn the high prices." Then, inspiration: Somewhere in the United States, there must exist a town called Half or some derivation thereof. Why not pay the residents to change the name to Half.com?

MapQuest showed forty towns with names that contained the word *half,* and he selected Halfway, Oregon, population 350. He got an appointment with the mayor to discuss what he called "joint marketing opportunities," flew to Boise, Idaho, and rented a rig to make the four-hour drive through two feet of snow.

Hughes sat down with the mayor for two hours and had a great conversation, but with one serious gap. Half.com was in a "quiet period" mandated by securities laws for companies that plan initial public offerings of stock, so he couldn't say what Half.com did unless the mayor signed a confidentiality agreement. And Hughes had forgotten to bring one along.

Even so, he pitched the idea to a town meeting that night. Even without knowing what the company did, the people who showed up seemed interested.

"I felt like the moon and stars were about to align," Hughes says. But then, "a headline came out prematurely announcing the town was going to change its name. It was triage control. Factions were developing that came out against it. There were public hearings."

Finally, the town voted to rename itself Half.com for one year in return for $100,000. Even then, most of the residents had no clue what the company they were renaming themselves after did. But the national publicity was instantaneous and massive. Half.com decided not to bother with a press release. And the idea was planted for a future company with the word *buzz* in the name.

Largely as a result of all the fanfare, eBay called to inquire about Half.com's plans and ask about its financial numbers. In 2000, five months after the IPO, eBay bought the company for $300 million. "And this was after the Nasdaq crash," Hughes says. "I did well."

He stayed at Half.com for another couple of years. In that period, Half.com put ads in 21 million fortune cookies a month. It made rubberized urinal screens with the message "Don't piss away half of your money. Head to Half.com." When nightclubs said he couldn't put the screens in their rest rooms, Hughes says, "We learned a good lesson: Don't ask. We sent interns into the ninety hottest nightclubs in Manhattan to do it anyway. We got tons of publicity—*Fortune, 60 Minutes,* the *Wall Street Journal.* It was all buzz. And it worked."

While still at Half.com, Hughes bought the Buzzmarketing Internet domain name for $600. He figured he would soon tire of the corporate life, and he was right. In 2002, he started Buzzmarketing, a consulting firm that specializes in consumer marketing. Then he wrote the book *Buzzmarketing: Get People to Talk About Your Stuff,* which was published in 2005.

• • •

A common reaction to stories of those who have stumbled on treasure chests such as these is "How come nobody thought of this before?" Sig Anderman, who co-founded and today is the chief executive of Ellie Mae, a provider of online connectivity to the mortgage industry in Pleasanton, California, was a young lawyer in New York in the early 1970s when he read a newspaper article about a group of firefighters and cops on Long Island, New York. They had started a business that offered discounted handyman services to home owners. Because they often had stretches of time off during the week, this was a good way for them to moonlight for extra money.

"I thought the idea was intriguing," Anderman says. "I thought about it, talked about it with one of my clients. It was a James Joycean process. Very detailed, very meandering."

Eventually, the two came up with the idea of offering home-maintenance contracts to home owners. Customers would pay a flat annual fee, and the company would handle all repairs, from plumbing to roofing to furnaces. They invested a few thousand dollars of their savings and created American Home Shield.

"All you had to do was pay $250 a year and somebody would take care of your house," Anderman says. "You wouldn't have to go chasing after a plumber at 3 A.M. on a Sunday anymore. It all seemed obvious. Yet nobody else was doing it. Or rather, they were doing it in pieces. Sears offered a contract to repair your refrigerator, General Electric to repair your stove, and so on. But nobody was doing the whole house."

Maybe there was a reason. It took years for AHS to break even, and growth was lackluster. What to do? Anderman toyed with the idea of asking real estate agents to sell contracts to home buyers, but decided against it. Then, inspiration: Why not persuade real estate agents to *require sellers* to buy one-year contracts for buyers?

This was in California. "In California, there are a lot of tract homes," Anderman notes. "They all look the same. If buyers were looking at two similar $200,000 houses and one carried a one-year warranty and the other didn't, they'd buy the one with the warranty.

"We didn't want to be stuck with just fixer-uppers, so the deal had to be for *all* the houses the Realtor sold. But that was okay because the buyers would often pay 5 percent more, and the houses would sell faster.

"To make the seller happy, we told them we would cover the house for free for as long as it was on the market."

The scheme worked. Revenue and profit soared. In 1982, with AHS owning 60 percent of a burgeoning market that was being invaded by upstart rivals, Anderman sold his 5 percent stake to a group of investors for $18 million.

He spotted his next opportunity in high interest rates.

It was the early eighties, and mortgage rates were reaching record levels of 18 and 19 percent. One day, Anderman had lunch with a real estate agent, who told him that these newfangled devices banks were using to ease the pain—something called adjustable-rate loans—were driving his agents crazy.

It used to be so simple, the Realtor said: a fixed mortgage over a fixed period, typically 8 percent over 40 years. But now lenders were coming up with all sorts of novel structures. One loan might be 7 percent for six months and then tied to some index, being set at 2.2 points over that cost, and adjusted every three months. Another would be 6 percent for one month, tied to one-year Treasuries, but 2.75 percent over the index and adjusted every six months. Plus there were various caps on rates.

"It was confusing," Anderman says. "And I suddenly thought, 'If I could figure out a way to compare all those mortgage structures, the Realtors would love it.'"

Thus, Compufund was born, with Anderman as sole owner. In essence, it was a computer program that allowed borrowers to comparison-shop among all the dozens of deals being offered. A real estate agent could dial into Compufund's computer, type in financial information, and within a few seconds receive a printout showing all the mortgage options for that customer. Within a year and a half, more than 1,000 real estate offices had signed up to pay $75 a month for the service. "It was nicely profitable," Anderman says.

His next venture was loan processing, and by 1987, he was handling 200 transactions worth $150,000 in revenue each month. After that, in partnership with a large savings and loan institution, he got into funding and servicing mortgages. By the late 1980s, he was originating about 25,000 mortgages a year. That company was a casualty of the S&L crisis, but Anderman nonetheless emerged from the fiasco a rich man.

Next, he saw opportunity in home inspection. The home inspectors whom he had observed were a ragtag group. Some typed up five pages of well-organized comments, while others dashed off handwritten observations or killed deals with offhand remarks about the plumbing.

"I thought: 'Let's give these inspectors a computerized grid pad that has a house design and you press the room in question, say the kitchen, and up pops all seventeen things you have to inspect: the faucets, the door hinges, the ceiling tiles,'" Anderman says. "At the end of the inspection, instead of going home and spending one or two hours to type out the reports, why not plug all the information into the grid pad as you go along and let it produce a nice narrative description and checklist?"

Inspectors liked the idea. Real estate agents liked the idea. So Anderman built the software and launched Inspectech. Within a year, 100 inspectors in the San Francisco Bay area—one-fourth the total number—had paid $20,000 each to join the program and were shelling out $50 per inspection report. Inspectech expanded into New Jersey. Eventually, Anderman sold his stake in the company for half a million dollars.

In 1997, Anderman retired to his ranch in Sonoma County. But driving a tractor around and raising chickens held only so much appeal. One day, while surfing the Internet, he made an observation. By typing *Beethoven* into a search engine, he was able to look up the composer's life and musical works in about six seconds. But type in *mortgages* and all you got was a jumble of unrelated sites and documents. It occurred to him that somebody ought to figure out how to let computers talk to each other so that you could gain instant access to the mountains of

credit reports, title reports, flood risk reports, appraisals, and other documents that go into a closing. Somebody ought to bring the Internet to
these brokers.

He talked up the idea to a venture capitalist he had fortuitously met
on a High Sierra hike a few years before. "We'll be the arms dealer to
mortgage brokers," he said. The friend offered to invest $500,000 in a
start-up for a 20 percent stake. Forget retirement. Anderman was back
in business, this time with a company called Ellie Mae.

By mid-2000, more than 2,500 mortgage brokers were paying $50 to
$100 a month to use Ellie Mae's Web site. In 2004, it made *Inc.*'s list of
America's 500 fastest-growing private companies after registering 1,012
percent sales growth over four years. And yet, Anderman kept poking
into new corners, stealing thousands of mortgage brokers from the competition by adding a new operating desktop software, introducing a
Web-based loan-processing software that was an instant hit with mortgage companies, and adding a document-scanning feature to Ellie Mae's
arsenal, all in the space of a year. He values the company at $400 million,
which would make his 6 percent ownership stake worth $24 million.

As Anderman's example shows, entrepreneurs are improvisers. But
in their rush to go after new opportunities, they sometimes let things
slide. Gary Doan saw a prospect in their oversights.

Doan discovered that the vast majority of small businesses had
either nonexistent or inadequate archiving systems for their e-mail traffic and computer data. This left them at risk of losing information that
was crucial to their day-to-day functioning (and to their legal protection if they ever got caught up in litigation). He calculated that 3 million
companies were leaving themselves vulnerable to this, and that tens of
thousands imploded every year because of lost information.

Why weren't small businesses backing up their files? Because, they
told him, the products they had looked at were too expensive, too time-
consuming, and too complicated. So Doan came up with the Rocket
Vault, a low-maintenance device that bundles both hardware and software and is so simple to use all you have to do is plug it in and administer it for fifteen minutes until it begins to archive data. His company,

Intradyn, based in Eagan, Minnesota, began selling the Rocket Vault in June 2003. With storage sizes that range from 240 gigabytes to 4 terabytes, prices start at $1,495 and go up to $14,000.

In essence, he was tapping into small-business owners' and managers' frustrations with the growing complexity of the technological demands made upon them—and into their belated recognition that in their failure to keep up with these demands, they were courting disaster.

"I could write a book just about the horror stories," he says. "One guy told us that he had thirty-six blank tapes as backup. A friend's accounting firm's server crashed, and they had to reenter hundreds of tax returns over a weekend." (Both have Rocket Vaults now.)

Doan subsequently realized that small brokerage firms, fund managers, and investment advisers had an even more pressing need to store their data in backup systems but were even more negligent about doing so. Aside from all the other risks, they were violating new Securities and Exchange Commission regulations that required them to keep all e-mail messages on nonerasable, nonalterable tape.

Why? Again, the stuff out there was too complicated and expensive. So in June 2004, Doan launched the Compliance Vault for a price ranging from $7,000 to $14,000.

Sales were slow at first but grew to a projected $2.5 million in 2005. And Doan devised a plan for jump-starting them using an unusual ally: government bureaucrats. The news about the new SEC rules hadn't filtered down to the little guys yet, but he figured just one hefty and well-publicized fine for noncompliance would be a wake-up call to the small businesses that they had better start backing up their files. "I'd almost like to find one who would take the hit for us," he says. "It would open up a monster opportunity" as they scrambled to buy data storage systems and took a look at his products.

• • •

Entrepreneurship has a peculiarly American stamp to it. "The fabric of the American character is entrepreneurial," says Carl Schramm, chief executive of the Ewing Marion Kauffman Foundation in Kansas City, a national center for the study of entrepreneurship. "It is as common to start a business in this country as it is to get married or have a baby."

As a teenager in his native India, where the politics were then imbued with an anticapitalist bias, Umang Gupta had no entrepreneurial ambitions. Like much of polite society, his "Marxist-type" mother and civil servant father shunned business as corrupt and money-grubbing. Gupta, who today is the chief executive of Keynote Systems Inc., a San Mateo, California, company that tests and evaluates corporate Web and wireless systems, was trying to decide between a career in the army and a government job. But that didn't mean he wasn't displaying the creative potential that would one day serve him well in Silicon Valley. "I had an inventive zeal as a boy," Gupta says. "I was always making things from kits or from scratch," such as a slide projector from just a shoe box, a lens, and a lightbulb with no guide except his obsessive curiosity.

After attending graduate school in the United States and doing management stints at a steel company and at IBM, Gupta returned to India to decide whether to resume his life there. He considered going into politics but rejected the idea, then explored business ventures from making computers to producing natural gas from cow dung ("a reasonable proposition at the time," he comments) before concluding that his future lay in America.

He tried to start his own computer company but couldn't raise enough capital, so he joined a start-up called Relational Software Inc., later to become the Oracle Corporation, and wrote its first formal business plan. He ran its fledgling PC business, and while there, he spotted a business opportunity in what he believed Oracle was doing wrong: trying to sell poorly conceived software to the burgeoning personal computer market. The company's specialty was software for mainframes and big minicomputers, Gupta concluded, and its heart just wasn't in scaling back its products for use in PCs.

He joined forces with a former Oracle programmer named Bruce Scott who had built a database for PCs that was smaller, lighter, and faster than Oracle's. The two men launched Gupta Technologies, the world's first client/server database software, which allowed companies to downsize from IBM mainframes to corporate networks at a fraction of the cost. "We were a pretty hot company," Gupta says. It went public in 1993 and for a time had a market value of $400 million, a pretty big market cap for an IPO in those days.

He thought he had it made, but when Microsoft and Oracle revved up their fight for his market, the company faltered and he sold out his stake. In mid-1997, he decided to invest some money in a company called Keynote Systems Inc., which measures the performance of companies' Web and wireless systems, and to join the board. By the end of the year, there was a management coup against the founder, and he was asked to take over as chief executive. Two years later, he took it public.

In the high-tech world, one trick for getting ahead is recognizing opportunities for jumping on a bandwagon early. Back in 1995, the big new wave of the future was the Internet. Timothy Mahoney, co-founder of a boutique venture capital firm called Union Atlantic, grasped the marketing potential of getting the firm's name on the information highway ahead of his rivals.

He identified the premier venture capital Web site as www.vFinance.com and tried to get listed on it. When the owner, who had never heard of his company, said no, he decided to buy it.

When the owner named his price—$100,000—he hesitated. The Internet was still a mystery to most people. Nobody really knew what it was going to develop into. "My partner and I looked at each other dubiously," Mahoney recalls. But they ultimately agreed to go for it, betting that the site's small-business audience might be worth something someday.

They were right—www.vFinance.com was one of the first 10,000 commercial dot-coms and, unlike many others, it had information its target users needed.

As the dot-com craze took off, Mahoney kept upgrading the site, adding content such as a business plan template that people could download. And he never charged anybody a dime.

He steadily enlarged his pool of users and persuaded them to volunteer content that he could add to the site. Today, he has built his company, vFinance Inc., into a financial supermarket for entrepreneurs and investors. In addition to the Web site that connects the two groups, vFinance offers products from venture capital, brokerage, and investment banking services to asset management.

He makes money by saving entrepreneurs time they can't afford to waste searching through a data bank of more than 2,000 venture capital firms and 23,000 angel investors. "We know that the average person who is looking through either list clicks on 4.7 links; he quickly realizes he'll be there for three years if he wants to click through all the names and try to figure out who would be interested in him," Mahoney says. For a fee, vFinance uses information on the business's industry, revenues, number of employees, expansion plans, and the like, and figures it out for them.

For Mahoney, the proceeds are a minor source of revenue. The real payoff is what he calls "owning the audience" of entrepreneurs, VC firms, and angel investors.

"To run your business, you have to have investment banking," he says. "To raise money, you have to have relationships with institutions. You need research, trading platforms. You need retail brokers because you have to do I.P.O.'s and the like. Everything we do is designed to service the needs of an entrepreneur. We help them grow, gain value. We manage their finances. They often come back as investors."

(Postscript: In 2005, Mahoney announced he was running for Congress as a Democrat in one of Florida's few swing districts. He came out swinging, vowing to "put an end to the failed and reckless leadership in Washington, D.C.," and playing up his entrepreneurial credentials.)

• • •

Judith Cone of the Kauffman Foundation talks about various entrepreneurial thresholds, like getting fired from a comfortable corporate job at the age of fifty-five and concluding that starting your own company is your best bet. But that raises the question: If desperation pushes them into the game, are they true-blue entrepreneurs?

Many experts have their doubts. But John Heagney, founder of John

Heagney Public Relations in Holiday, Florida, makes a strong case that they are.

Heagney had always displayed a restless energy and a flair for writing, but his early career in journalism took an unhappy course. He thought landing a job at an outlying bureau of the *St. Petersburg Times* was his big break until he walked into its cramped office between a real estate agency and a barbershop in a shopping plaza and was greeted by a woman flossing her teeth at her desk. His disillusionment turned to despair after he was put on a beat of mostly school menus and chicken dinners. His boss put him out of his misery by firing him after he forgot to cover an assigned story.

Jolted out of his lethargy, he took stock of his talents—a strong work ethic, a way with words, a vivid imagination, a persuasive personality—and pitched himself as a freelance writer of advertising copy. "I had a friend take a photo of me wearing a vest and tie and sitting at a Smith Corona typewriter with smoke pouring out from a petri dish with smoldering 3-in-One oil that we had placed inside it," he recalls. "I made a flyer with that photo and the headline 'Hot Copy,' and a description of myself as a 'copy righter,' not just a copy writer. I sent it out in a mass mailing to all the advertising agencies in the area. I guess at that point I became an entrepreneur."

He started picking up assignments from small advertising agencies. Then he received an assignment from a local community's clueless publicist who wanted him to stage a photo shoot of buxom girls in bathing suits posing on an earthmover. Perplexed by this ham-handed ploy, he decided to open his own PR firm, certain he could do "much, much better."

That was more than two decades ago. In 1982, he started John Heagney Public Relations, which today employs five people and has more than 40 active clients, including piano maker Steinway & Sons.

Heagney sees plenty of opportunity in other people's ineptitude. "I know I could make a ton of money with a janitorial service, because nobody does it well," he says. He also thinks his gift for gab and eye for color and design would make him a natural real estate agent or home decorator. He's even spotted an opportunity in the slovenliness of today's youth, figuring he could teach a pro bono course on how to dress and behave in the business world.

Helping people get their act together is one of the drivers of the small-business world. Heagney would like to teach twenty-something louts to mind their manners. Doan is making it easier for harried small-business owners to do their electronic filing. A friend of mine reorganizes people's homes, from rearranging the furniture to cleaning out the closets, and can't keep up with demand for her services.

Charlie Horn is mining a similar vein. While doing consulting work for insurance companies in 1994, he got to wondering if there might be some way to exploit a flaw in the health care system—that people without prescription drug insurance pay higher prices for medicine than people who have insurance.

Why not organize the losers, he asked himself, even if they didn't know they were being organized?

First, he persuaded a couple of small pharmacy-benefit managers, the people who administer prescription drug programs for corporations and health plans, to let him use their services for uninsured people.

Then he talked insurance companies such as Blue Cross/Blue Shield of Florida into taking the prescription drug discount cards he provided and distributing them to those among their customers who lacked prescription drug coverage. "It didn't cost them a thing, and they got the goodwill of their members and thus a higher retention rate," he says.

Horn made a percentage on the deals, and for two years, his little home-based venture thrived. When business fell off he switched gears, setting up his own discount network for people without drug coverage. He recruited pharmacies to join it by arguing that while they would have to offer discounts to cash customers, they would attract a higher volume of them.

Next, he signed up corporations and other sponsoring organizations that didn't provide prescription drug coverage. "We'd tell them, 'We negotiated these discounts for your benefit. You don't have to do a thing,'" Horn says.

Today, he has built that concept into a Tucson company called the Promirus Group with 150 employees, 10 million card holders, annual revenues of more than $30 million, and a profit margin greater than 15 percent.

In the course of launching nine health care companies over the years, Horn has always plowed one of the most fertile fields he knows of for business ideas—his colleagues' brains.

For example, a lawyer and a pharmacist who worked for him came up with a concept for a smart card that would allow pharmaceutical companies not eligible for lower co-payments in drug plans to issue electronic coupons to close the price gap with the ones that were. Not only would the card lower consumers' prescription bills, it would end the hassle for doctors and pharmacists of switching prescriptions to cheaper brands all day long. Horn liked the idea and financed a start-up called Affordable Medicine Solutions to test it out.

His latest project—still in the pondering stage—is to buy or build a national chain of compound pharmacies, or apothecary shops that mix ingredients on a custom basis for drugs such as prescription skin creams and hormone replacement therapies. "I feel there is a tremendous untapped market for this," he says.

•   •   •

Crown Zellerbach didn't see the trees for the forest. And therein lay an opportunity for Michael Huddy.

Before running his own company, Huddy worked for Crown Zellerbach, a now-defunct forestry products conglomerate, and later defected to Weyerhaeuser, the world's biggest lumber producer. But even as a salaried employee at those corporate giants, he was an entrepreneur in the making, showing an independent streak and a knack for finding new ways of doing things.

Crown wanted to start him off in an office, but he talked his way into a forest job, roaming the woods for a year and a half. Then he went into research and became fascinated by the success of an experimental farm Crown ran in Louisiana that used a system called short rotation to grow hardwood trees quickly. "The question I asked was whether we could do this out West," Huddy says. "Nobody had tried it."

He decided he would.

In 1980, he persuaded Crown to let him start a pilot plant on 2,000 acres it owned along the Columbia River in Oregon. The company gave him free rein to run the project but no working capital; raise it yourself, his boss told him. There is no greater test of the entrepreneur's mettle.

Huddy went straight to a pulp mill near the Crown property and told the managers he could end their worries about a looming shortage of hardwood pulp. "They were skeptical at first," he said. "But we had done research on their technical needs, and I showed them numbers." The mill pledged $2 million a year and ultimately increased the amount to nearly $4 million.

The experiment was so successful that Huddy expanded it to 13,000 acres, with plans to go to 20,000. Crown started putting money into it, and Huddy was all set to make a pitch for $30 million over ten years when the company became embroiled in a hostile takeover by a British financier. This put an end to his pet project.

But Huddy wasn't giving up. In 1985, he moved to Weyerhaeuser, and a few years later he joined a group that was searching for new products. A Canadian company called Barrier Technology soon recruited him to talk Weyerhaeuser into collaborating on developing a fire-retardant technology. This led to his creation of a company in 1993 called Barrier U.S.A. "I'm a corporation-created entrepreneur, but it is as if I owned my own business," he says.

In the construction industry, there are opportunities for finding new ways to alleviate workers' discomfort, he says. For example, it's hard to assemble a firewall in tight spaces like attics. "My idea would be pre-fabricated trusses that are fire-rated and that could be swung up by a crane and put in place," he says.

Herbert Jian knows all about discomfort. As a desperately poor student in Communist China in the late 1970s, he was chronically malnourished and felt suffocated by the regimentation of every corner of his existence. "The feeling grew in me, 'You can't live like this for the rest of your life.' It became an obsession," he says.

The first opportunity he seized was the Cultural Revolution, a youth movement launched by Mao Zedong in 1966 to thwart his perceived enemies. At age fourteen, Jian joined Mao's Red Guards and marched across the country, not out of revolutionary zeal but for the free food and transportation and for release from his closed world. He quickly became the leader of a ragtag group of children even younger than he was, and they began invading people's homes in searches for "antirevolutionary material."

Over time, the Red Guards became divided into two warring camps that fought first with posters, then fists, then knives and homemade swords, then guns, then automatic weapons. "I can show you today the corner of a park where a couple of hundred children are buried," Jian says. "Other kids who were killed were just thrown into the river."

One day he was in a building engaged in a firefight with rival students when a classmate fell against him, his neck soaked in blood. With bullets flying, Jian carried his wounded comrade out a back door. The boy died in his arms.

He dropped out of the Red Guards that day. But the nightmare wasn't over. Mao ordered the nation's students to the countryside, to be "educated" by the peasants. From 1968 to 1974, millions of youngsters were escorted to primitive villages that didn't want them, with little to live on and no means of escape.

Racked by hunger, he and his friends hunted snakes in the mountains. "Over eight years, I must have caught more than 200," he said. "I'd grab them and tear off their skins. Then we'd make soup."

Another time, Jian jumped after a dog that had fallen into a well and killed it with a knife. The owners would have beaten him or worse if they had caught him, but it was a risk worth taking: He and his friends feasted on the meat for five days.

Maybe it was that survival instinct that propelled him to become an entrepreneur. Throughout his "eight years of total drudgery" in the countryside, Jian says, he never ceased plotting his flight to freedom. "I understood I had to create opportunity for myself through exercise, reading, and learning," he reports. "I had to be ready when the time came."

Sure enough, when he finally got back into the mainstream of Chinese society in 1978, he enrolled in West China University of Medical Sciences with the stated goal of teaching English to medical students. The school was located in Chengdu, the capital of Sichuan province, which had a single hotel for high-ranking government officials and tourists. He zeroed in on the tourists.

"I had no money, no connections, no way to fulfill my dreams on my own," Jian says. "I had to think about doing something different, something risky, something nobody else would do. I began walking up to the tourists and offering my help—to show them around the town, to chat, to interpret. My plan was to build up a group of foreigners who were willing to help me get out. I'd always ask for their addresses, and then write them when they got back home. About one in ten would write back.

"For four years, I went out every day, almost without fail. My name for what I did was 'going hunting.' I'd tell myself every day, 'It's time to go hunting.' It was the only way I would ever get out of China."

Over the months, the group took shape. At the core were six Americans—two college professors, a journalist, an engineer, the owner of a Pittsburgh insurance company, and an Idaho farmer—and a German psychiatrist. Jian served as a tour guide, acting as an interpreter for the journalist at great risk to himself, for example, and arranging a forbidden visit into the university campus for the insurance executive and his wife.

"It took a lot of time and patience to make people help me," Jian says. "I did it in a delicate way, never pushing, so they would do it on their own initiative." And they did. The German sent him books and eventually a money order for $5,000, a fortune by Chinese standards. The farmer bought him a year's subscription to *National Geographic* and sent him books on American history and works of American literature. The insurance executive pulled strings to get him enrolled in the University of Pittsburgh.

This was his ticket to America, where in time Jian would become a Yankee-style entrepreneur, with his own furniture business in suburban Los Angeles, and go on to launch an export-import business in Cambodia with two partners. But the real test of his entrepreneurial mettle had begun years before, in a society that had no place for free-market capitalism. As a near-starving child, he didn't have the slightest clue what an entrepreneur was. But even then, he was on his way to becoming one.

• • •

Cameron Johnson had launched a string of successful dot-coms and become a wealthy man—make that wealthy boy—long before he earned the right to walk into a bar and order a beer.

From his grade-school days, Johnson (who turned twenty-one in November 2005) seemed to know instinctively what so many people have had to learn through trial and error: If there is a seemingly obvious opportunity that nobody has grabbed, don't sit around wondering why—fill it.

He started his first Internet venture at age nine, a company called Cheers and Tears that made greeting cards for relatives. He had to open a checking account to stash his earnings of $200. At eleven, after buying his sister's Beanie Baby collection for $100 and reselling it on eBay for $1,000, he became an early disciple of the moneymaking potential of Web auctions and began buying secondhand Beanie Babies as well as several other brands of dolls on the Internet and selling them on eBay. Over the following year or so, he made $50,000 in a frenzy of activity until his father made him "retire."

His first really big kill came two years later, when he was fourteen. He and a fellow child genius in a faraway town (whom he had met only once) formed a pay-to-surf Web company called SurfingPrizes.com. Their company did right, he said, what he grasped a deep-pocketed Internet start-up called Alladvantage was doing wrong.

"They were going to pay Internet users 50 cents an hour to let them rotate ads at the top of their screens," he says. "But Alladvantage attracted too many members, millions, and couldn't pay out that much. The formula was three ads a minute, 180 ads an hour. But with millions of users, they couldn't sell all their ad inventory. They got killed. It was one of the biggest Internet flops ever." Johnson still marvels at Alladvantage's free-spending ways, burning through $150 million in venture capital and loans when he started his company on almost nothing.

"I had read everything about the subject you could find. I thought, 'All we gotta do is pay them less and keep ads sold.'"

He and his partner launched the site on March 1, 2000, and three months later, they were doing 15 million ads and $15,000 in sales each day. "Checks would come in the mail for $10,000, $20,000, $60,000. We hired a company to cut checks to our users." In the end, he says, they couldn't keep it going—he was, after all, a freshman in high school—and so they closed it and sold the assets.

At last report, Johnson was between companies and not doing much except single-handedly running his father's giant Ford dealership in Roanoke, Virginia. But he says he is constantly on the alert for new opportunities, "the next TiVo or next anything."

How do entrepreneurs come up with the ideas that they do for new products? Part of it has to do with knowledge: They do their homework. And, of course, they are smart. But there is something else that is hard to define but that seems to be a universal experience among them—the eureka moment, a sudden insight that marks a turning point in their thinking.

Alex Lidow is Exhibit A in the power of epiphany.

Lidow's father was a Lithuanian Jew who fled Hitler for America in 1937 and ended up starting a business in California that made rectifiers for converting the alternating current transmitted by power lines into the direct current used to run appliances and electric motors. The company, International Rectifier, went public in 1958. Lidow, the youngest of three sons in the business, would one day be its leader.

His first revelation came when he was a graduate student in physics at Stanford University in the mid-1970s. "A professor explained to me something that had enormous implications," he remembers. "He took off his glasses and handed them to me. He said, 'Why do you suppose these are so expensive?' I came up with some answer but he said no, the price represented the total buildup of energy it took to bring them to this state—everything from melting the glass to plating the frame to refining the metal to refining the gasoline for the truck that delivered them to heating the store in which they sat until they got onto his nose."

Every dollar spent on distributing, storing, converting, and consuming the energy that goes into any product is one dollar less spent on the basics of life, the professor said. In time, the competition for diminishing supplies of energy would lead to a cataclysmic decline in the world's standard of living, he said.

That grim scenario inspired Lidow on the spot to do all he could to harness technology to conserve energy. He made it his mission to develop a more efficient way of converting alternating current to direct current, and in the late 1970s he and a collaborator, Tom Herman, developed a power MOSFET (a metal-oxide semiconductor) called the HEXFET that did just that.

"There were two fifteen-minute bursts, the first in July 1978, the second in November 1978," Lidow recalls. "That's the way things occur, don't they? When you realize how something works, it only takes a minute. I can point to the days when Tom Herman and I 'aha!'d on that."

The HEXFET spawned a revolution in power conversion. Its applications ranged from fluorescent lightbulbs to motor drivers to stereo amplifiers to welders. And yet, more than a quarter century after the technology was invented, barely 20 percent of all electricity used in the United States flows through it.

The stubborn resistance of Americans to convert to energy-efficient appliances and lightbulbs inspired Lidow's second epiphany in 1995: Nobody pays for energy efficiency, so you have to give it away for free.

"This is where it gets fun," he says. "You can't make the technology for free. So you have to sell it in a way that it adds value outside of the energy savings."

For example, he says, the latest washing machines have variable-speed drives that control the water's slosh patterns. But people don't buy them for the savings in energy costs. They buy them because they are silent, are more efficient, wash clothes more gently and so produce laundry that's cleaner and softer, and have a faster spin to wring the clothes out faster. People pay extra for those features and end up with machines that use half the energy of the old ones.

Then came insight number three: International Rectifier had to reconfigure itself as a "technology-pull" company, that is, shift from the traditional model of a company pushing and shoving its technology into every corner of the universe to that of a company that combines other technologies with its own to drive down the cost of production. Pull hard enough, he reasoned, and the push will follow of its own accord.

To reduce the cost of a variable-speed drive for a washing machine from $200 to a consumer-friendly $20, International Rectifier drew on a whole range of technologies, including high-performance analog integrated circuits, mixed-signal integrated circuits, new control algorithms, and new digital architectures, about twelve in all, each of which had an importance that evolved over time.

"We were co-designing technologies to work together," he says. "This is what I call the technology-pull strategy, and we believe it is unique."

He must be doing something right: International Rectifier had $1.2 billion in revenue and $137 million in profit in fiscal 2005 and had $941 million in cash on its balance sheet.

Alex Lidow, meet James Poss. He has the same mission as yours: making the world more energy-efficient. And, like you, a eureka moment helped him along.

Back when he was a sophomore at Duke University, Poss came up with the idea for making an energy-efficient clothes dryer by closing the chamber to create a near vacuum, in which water evaporates at a much lower temperature than in an ordinary environment. Unfortunately, a quick search found ten patents on vacuum chambers for dryers.

Ten patents, not one. Aha! "I suddenly realized that you can't patent a concept, you can only patent a method," Poss says. "And then I realized that there are ways around a patent, that a patent held by somebody else doesn't necessarily take away opportunities."

Even though his vacuum chamber never materialized, he continued jumping into gaps he saw in the marketplace. He built a prototype of a beveling shoe sole with lateral slats that would relieve the pressure on your ankle when you turn sharply in competitive sports. Then he constructed a releasable snowboard binding that is superior, he believes, to a similar product that was introduced shortly thereafter (though unlike his, he sniffs, its "front foot doesn't rotate").

In fact, he often detects flaws in the way the biggest of the big corporate giants do things. "General Electric is doing it wrong when it goes and puts its wind turbines offshore," he said. "It's the wrong way to go about it. I'll fight to the end on arguing on that one."

Poss, who eventually became a geological engineer, says his life's goal was always to make one of his renewable-energy ideas into a company. Originally, he wanted to start a floating windmill farm, but realized that would require too much capital. So he turned his attention to the sun.

Using solar energy to benefit humanity is such a grandiose concept that it seems almost undignified to apply it to garbage. But for Poss, all the numbers added up. The United States produces about five pounds of waste per person per day, and hauling it is a $40 billion-a-year industry. Even a sliver of that market could be bounteous, especially if he could play a small role in cleaning up the environment at the same time.

So, in 2003, he founded the Seahorse Power Company, a maker of trash containers with the brand name Big Belly that use solar power to compact the contents when they are full, sharply reducing the number of collections needed.

"Garbage trucks get 2.8 miles per gallon, with all their starts and stops," Poss points out. "They have the worst performance of any vehicle on the road. They burn 1 billion gallons of diesel fuel a year, spewing contaminants. I want to do something about that."

His latest ambition is to link up with a company that makes material-separation machines and combine their technologies to develop solar-powered recycling units that could be "scattered around in front of stores, on street corners, in parks," he says. He has also been contacted by an executive at a media company about providing solar power to illuminate ads on phone booths that can't be connected to electrical outlets. "If the ads were lit up at night, he could make 30 percent more because he would get that many more 'eyeballs,'" Poss says.

• • •

Like many entrepreneurs, Karl Eller has done time at the top in corporate America, running Columbia Pictures and Circle K, the convenience store chain. He was more at home doing his own thing, though, such as building a tiny billboard property into a media conglomerate called Combined Communications, or creating a billboard giant called Eller Media.

It started when he saw a chance to capitalize on the rivalry of two players in the billboard industry. Ousted from Circle K and deep in personal debt, he was driving the streets of Phoenix at the suggestion of a business colleague to check out Gannett's billboards and noticed that many were dilapidated. He soon learned that Gannett's Phoenix billboard business had been losing ground for several years, and while a local billboard company named Outdoor Systems coveted it, Gannett would never sell out to an upstart competitor.

Time to play middleman.

Eller talked Gannett into selling him the Phoenix billboards for $20 million. Then he made a take-it-or-leave-it offer to sell what he didn't own to Outdoor Systems for $30 million. Since he had no money and no credit rating, he added, Outdoor Systems would have to finance the deal. Eller would walk away with $10 million in cash.

It didn't quite work out that way. Legal glitches surfaced. But in the end, in a complicated transaction, Eller acquired 350 billboards on somebody else's credit, and Eller Media was born.

Eller also detected riches in government regulation. The Highway Beautification Act of 1965 imposed strict constraints on billboards, so people were hesitant to invest in them. Eller dived in, figuring that whatever billboards remained would be more valuable than ever. He was right and made a nice pile on that decision.

"Entrepreneurs see things other people don't," Eller comments. "I don't know why. They are aware of the world, aware of what is going on around them."

Today, well into his seventies, he still runs the Eller Company, a small consulting firm, and he keeps on spotting opportunities. "Right now, I'm

involved in a deal to build digital signage that will change the whole outdoor advertising world," he says. "Those signs you see in Times Square
weigh $6\frac{1}{2}$ tons and cost a small fortune to build. What I see is a flexible
back plane made of vinyl or plastic that contains no mirrors and all the
other stuff that goes into the LCD and that can be rolled up and
stretched across a billboard. Transistors would be embedded in the back
plane. It might cost $25,000 or $30,000 for a 12' × 24' sign, and you could
change the copy any time by wireless computer. A car could be blue in
the morning, red in the afternoon, and yellow at night. This business has
been the same for 100 years. What I see is a whole new world."

If Eller found opportunity in government regulations, Dr. Paul
Brown found it in the *lack* of government regulations.

While doing his residency at Columbia Presbyterian Hospital in
Manhattan in 1967, Brown got a close look at the laboratory testing
business and didn't like what he saw. "I realized it was huge, fragmented,
of poor quality, and filled with abuse," he says. "There were no regulations. As a result, there was a tremendous amount of fraud." In one
scam called the "sink test," he said, unscrupulous operators would take
blood samples, pour them down the sink, and make up the results.
Knowing about the irregularities, the insurance industry refused to
reimburse the costs.

In a flash of intuition, Brown realized the industry was fertile
ground for an honest business pioneer such as himself. If he could gain
a reputation for producing timely, accurate results, he mused, business
would boom and insurance companies could be swayed to change their
minds.

So lax were the rules in those days that he got a license to conduct
blood tests in an empty New York City apartment with no questions
asked. "The inspector came and stamped the license and wished me
luck," he recalls. Thus Metropolitan Pathology Laboratory Inc., later
MetPath, got off the ground with a borrowed $500. Brown took a course
counter to the instincts of most businesspeople: He lobbied hard for
stricter government regulation of medical testing, forcing his corrupt
and negligent competitors out of business.

By 1982, MetPath had grown into the largest clinical laboratory in the world, and Brown sold it to Corning for $140 million. Today, the company is known as Quest Diagnostics and racks up more than $4 billion in sales annually.

And Brown is at it again. While he has gotten involved in a half dozen or so other companies since he left MetPath, the one he is now throwing his heart and soul into is HearUSA, a chain of hearing care centers, which he started in 1986.

As with blood testing back in the 1960s, the inadequacies of hearing was his gateway to success. Insurance companies viewed the industry as "a cross between aluminum siding and used cars," Brown says.

After a slow start, HearUSA has grown into the third-largest hearing care provider in the country, with 150 hearing care centers and a network of 1,400 affiliated audiologists. In 2005, with sales closing in on $80 million, the company finally went into the black. "We've moved from the survival stage to the growth stage," he remarks.

*   *   *

Business, large and small, is about selling. That's obvious.

An entrepreneur has to know what he is selling. That is not always so obvious.

Joe Macchia, who started the Macchia General Agency Inc. in 2005, just weeks shy of his seventieth birthday (after losing control of another insurance company he had founded a few years earlier), recalls a twist on that theme that he developed in his first job as a commercial line salesman with Liberty Mutual.

"My technique was not to sell insurance," Macchia says. "I sold an $8\frac{1}{2}$" × 11" policy organizer. Most people's insurance policies are a mess. They're lying in the bottom of a drawer and haven't been looked at for years. I'd walk in with my organizer and say, 'All I want to do is look at your policies, put them in the organizer, and comment on them.'"

The actual sale of a policy was usually not far behind.

"Entrepreneurs take advantage of opportunities," Macchia notes. "They never believe in problems. Problems are just opportunities waiting to be unlocked."

Kevin Plank discovered that. When playing football during his senior year at the University of Maryland, Plank came up with the idea for moisture-absorbing athletic underwear. "I was short and slow and I sweated a lot," he says. "My cotton garments would get drenched and the extra weight would slow me down. During warm-ups, I'd have to keep changing them. I wondered why nobody had ever made an alternative fabric that wouldn't absorb water."

He launched Under Armour Performance Apparel at age twenty-three to do just that. Focusing on football in the early years, he knew he needed to latch on to a big commercial name to get the word out to the masses, and what better partner than the National Football League? The NFL wasn't interested, but he stepped through a side door, coaxing the NFL Europe into making him an official supplier and leveraging the connection to make it seem as though the domestic league was on board, too.

"You can't really read the word *Europe* in the NFL Europe shield when it is shrunken small enough on the page, so you just have the bottom of every tag," Plank says. "And every advertisement we had said, 'NFL official supplier.'"

Now a $240 million company with 450 employees, Under Armour makes a huge variety of products—from jockstraps and sports bras to gym bags and jackets—for every imaginable sport, for men and for women, for warm weather, cold weather, and temperatures in between. Redefining his business as "moisture management" not just for athletes but for any consumer who might be frustrated with sweaty clothes, Plank is now targeting markets such as ordinary T-shirts and clothing for soldiers stationed in hot climates. He is even thinking about starting a line of infant attire called Baby Armour. "Everything is relevant," he says. "What better product than one that prevents moisture and doesn't stink?"

·   ·   ·

Promoting racial understanding is a worthy endeavor, but is there money in it? Luke Visconti found out that there was.

When he was in the Navy stationed in Guam, his squadron's commanding officer complained he needed more storage space but couldn't get authorization. Bridging the cultural divide, Visconti chatted up the Guam civilian who was running the Navy's disposal plant and cajoled him into letting him use two beat-up truck trailers that were officially marked for demolition. Visconti was the only one who saw that crossing the cultural barrier would lead to a resolution of his officer's problem.

One day, riding with a black friend on home leave, he had his epiphany. They were chatting about music when the friend, a helicopter pilot, mentioned his way of dealing with stress: listening to tapes of Martin Luther King Jr.'s speeches.

"I realized, 'Here's this guy that I think the world of, the same rank, the same rhythms, the same wings as me. Yet here's something of fundamental importance to him that I'm not in touch with.' It really got me thinking."

He thought about how diverse the Navy was and how important it was to manage that diversity the right way. Later, he got a job recruiting minority officers, bringing people with a wealth of valuable new skills and talents into the ranks.

Once out of the Navy, Visconti and a partner started a company to sell space in special advertising sections for magazines. They discovered that many of the corporations they sold to were woefully unprepared to manage workplace diversity.

They identified this as a business opportunity and in 1999 created a Web site called Diversity.com. Three years later, this evolved into *DiversityInc* magazine. Both are dedicated to the proposition that creating diversity in the workplace is a management discipline that can give corporations a competitive edge. Both are profitable, with combined revenues of $7 million in 2004.

"Nobody else was in that space," Visconti says. "There was no competition. We couldn't believe it."

Happens all the time. Liz Ryan was a late bloomer. She joined a punk rock band after high school and went on to spend nine years as an office worker at a Chicago greeting card company. Hardly a promising start to a business career.

But a lightbulb went off. In her time at the company, revenues had grown from $2 million to $100 million. "The owners were probably pulling down a million and a half a year each," she says. "They had found a sweet spot, just under the radar of the giants. They were just chillin'. I said, 'Whoa. I could start a greeting card company.'"

She didn't do that, but after she landed a job in 1988 as head of human resources at a maker of computer modems, she started a consulting business in her Evanston, Illinois, home. Soon she was traveling around Chicago, networking. "It wasn't mechanical, me-first, let's-make-a-deal networking," she says, alluding to the way men operate. "Most of the people I talked to were women. You'd talk a lot about yourselves and your interests and maybe just touch on business stuff."

One day in 1999, gazing at a stack of business cards she had collected from business and professional women, Ryan thought, "I've got to do something." As she recalls, "Somebody told me she wanted to buy a Welsh corgi puppy and asked me if I knew anybody who knew about Welsh corgis. I said yes, I had met a woman who knew all about them, but I couldn't remember her name. And that gave me the idea: Start an Internet discussion group for women in technology. So I did. I called it ChicWIT." (WIT stands for "women in technology.")

"People started joining," Ryan says. "It was a small community. They'd ask questions like, 'Hey, what's the difference between qualified and nonqualified stock options again?' And 'Can anyone recommend a good ballet teacher for my six-year-old daughter?' The group seemed to have experts on just about any topic."

Since then, ChicWIT has grown into WorldWIT, the world's largest e-mail discussion group, with a projected 100,000 members by the end of 2005. The network expanded to scores of local groups, including NYCWIT, SilWIT (Silicon Valley), RussWIT (Russia), and Wildwest-WIT (Montana, Idaho, and Wyoming), as well as affiliated private chapters for such groups as college alumni associations.

Though WorldWIT has just seven full-time employees and projected revenues of $1 million in 2005, Ryan thinks she has stumbled on a new opportunity that had been lying in plain sight: creating internal discussion groups for corporations modeled on WorldWIT.

When an airline worried about defections of female employees expressed interest in the concept, she says, her reaction was: "Aieee! It was so obvious, I wanted to whack myself on the side of the head." Within a year she had deals in the works with a computer manufacturer, a consumer products distributor, and several other companies. She thinks such e-mail networks at big corporations, which will be connected to WorldWIT, will be her company's financial salvation.

●　　●　　●

For the longest time, Richard Wellman was an entrepreneur and didn't know it. He thought of himself as a soldier of fortune with a pilot's license and an eye for making a quick buck. After serving in the U.S. Air Force, he got a job as a mechanic at an air cargo firm in Ogden, Utah, home of Hill Air Force Base. On his days off, he roamed the big surplus yards in the countryside, looking for castaways that he could fix up. One day, he bought a stack of 200 landing lights for $100, cleaned them up, and sold them to regional airlines for $8 each. "That opened my eyes," he says.

As the years unfolded, he kept doing deals, and they got more and more lucrative. He remembers paying $5,000 for fifteen rust-free DC-7 engines that had been in a yard for nine years, steam-cleaning and oiling them and reselling them for $5,000 each.

"I haunted Air Force surplus yards all over the country," he recounts. "Sometimes I'd pick up stuff literally for nickels and dimes. When I had nothing else to do, I'd hang around the airplane. People always come up to talk to you, often as not to ask if you could get them this or that part. I'd always say yes. Then I'd find it and tell them how much it would cost them."

He also acquired a DC-7 for himself and took on unusual jobs, from hauling 18,000 sheep from India to Oman to ferrying 8,000 cattle from a ranch in Brazil to the Peruvian jungle. When he had had enough of flying, he decided to make fixing up old airplane parts a full-time endeavor and founded the International Airline Support Group in 1980. He built it into a $33 million company by 1993, but overexpansion and financing gone wrong ultimately did it in.

He went on to start a cargo transport firm in Ft. Lauderdale, Florida, and a jet charter venture in Las Vegas. "I'm still in the game," Wellman, now in his late sixties, says.

All kinds of opportunities abound. It is not always so much spotting an opening nobody else has noticed as it is knowing whether to seize it. For some, the eureka moment takes the form of a summoning from above—as an offer, so to speak, that you can't refuse.

Myke Templeton, pastor of the 3,000-member Owensboro Christian Church in Owensboro, Kentucky, got the call on a church retreat after his senior year in high school. He had planned to go to Marshall University in his native West Virginia to study politics and history, but a pastor asked the youths to think about joining the ministry. "Something in me said yes. Maybe it was the Holy Spirit. But the invitation struck a chord," he says.

A preacher who sets out to create or build a church is, by my definition, an entrepreneur. He or she has to be driven yet patient, know how to roll with the punches, be adept at raising money and managing people, relish the challenge of making things happen, harbor a grandiose vision yet temper individual ambition with a healthy dose of pragmatism, and above all be prepared to grab any opportunity to prod an often recalcitrant flock into doing the work of the Lord.

At his first (and very tiny) church, Templeton was having trouble persuading the three dozen or so worshipers to cough up enough money to kick off a much-needed building program. Then one day, a mouse bit a little girl in Sunday-school class.

"I used that as an opportunity to go on a holy tear, telling the church that the condition of the building had fallen into such a state of disrepair that rodents were attacking our children," he recalls. "That very afternoon, the elders met and made the decision to build. I guess the lesson is you have to exploit a bad situation to God's purposes."

Years later, with the affluent neighborhood around his fast-growing Owensboro church resisting his efforts to buy property for expansion, he had another brainstorm. He talked the congregation into buying a 180,000-square-foot mall on a twenty-four-acre site for $1.2 million and converting it, store by store, into a huge church complex. The businessman in him couldn't help giving a nod to Mammon. "Not long afterwards, somebody in town offered us $2 million for it," he says. "We figured we had made a good move."

What's next? "We're talking about buying 100 acres and starting to build again," Templeton replies. "I may not live long enough to see it. I've found that once a dream is hatched, it takes seven to ten years to make the transition. But I feel I've got to lay the seeds for the next guy."

CHAPTER 2

Running Your Own Show

Entrepreneurs want to be in charge.

Let's rephrase that.

Entrepreneurs have a fierce aversion to the very thought of reporting to a boss. (Perhaps because most once did.)

They aren't necessarily control freaks. Nor do they have any particular desire to lord it over underlings. They just can't imagine taking marching orders from another human being, especially when they know they could do the job better.

This rejection of authority is perhaps the only dogma that entrepreneurs, otherwise known for their freethinking, pragmatic ways, hold sacred. "I would never, never work for somebody else, not under any circumstances," asserts Luke Visconti, founder of *DiversityInc,* the diversity management magazine. The only ambition he will consider besides running his own company, he says, is running his own philanthropic organization someday.

Of course, nobody likes to kowtow to authority, but most of us will if it means we can pay our bills and take several weeks of paid vacation a year. Such considerations aren't even glimmers at the edge of the entrepreneur's mental universe.

Kevin Plank got early training doing his own thing, shoveling snow and mowing lawns from the age of eight, selling concert T-shirts in high school, and setting up a flower business in college. He was pretty much on his own even in the paying jobs he took, such as parking cars and tending bar. The one exception, the summers he spent working $9-an-hour construction jobs, only fortified his conviction that he was cut out to start a business someday.

"I realized I didn't want to haul trusses up stairwells for the rest of my life," says Plank, who instead founded Under Armour Performance Apparel, a highly successful sportswear maker in Baltimore. "The idea of working for somebody else never did anything for me. I always knew I could make money, and what better time to take risks than when you're young?"

But the operative idea behind this impulse is freedom, not power (though it is power over your environment that permits the freedom). When asked about the need to call the shots, Liz Ryan, founder of WorldWIT, the e-mail community for professional women, shakes her head.

"I don't see myself as having ever felt like I needed to be 'in charge' of WorldWIT," she says. "We have so many women entrepreneurs in our group, and very rarely do they talk about needing to be in charge of subordinates."

But when the definition is rephrased from being in charge of people to being in charge of their own lives, Ryan nods. "I think that's so right," she says. "We have so many women who out of desperation at the corporate schedule and the set of expectations they faced felt they had no choice."

Entrepreneurs wax lyrical about the joys of calling their own shots. Timothy Mahoney, the founder of vFinance Inc., the financial supermarket for small businesses, recalls the distress he felt in his days as a corporate executive trying to sell ideas to his boss. He proposed his ideas. His boss sometimes shot them down.

Worse, the higher he rose, the more his career was at the mercy of somebody else. "I was at General Electric when I realized I had no control," he says. When Jack Welch came in to run the company, he adds, "all of a sudden he was lopping off heads."

Today, Mahoney rhapsodizes about breaking loose from that prison of uncertainty.

"You have no idea of the freedom I walk around with every day. I don't have to do anything I don't want to. That freedom is the greatest gift. It's not a power thing. It's the fact that I follow *my* vision. I'll let you play with the paint, but I decide what you'll paint. We're not doing Cubist renditions of a guitar. We're doing *my* landscape."

For him, and for a surprising number of people like him, the freedom he cherishes is a gateway to having fun. Fun can be hard to come by in an office cubicle, with a supervisor roaming the aisles more intent on ferreting out laggards than listening to ideas.

But if you're in charge, by definition, you get to do what you want. Like hanging out with interesting people. Just the other day, Mahoney says, a doctor who is using a new technology to perform surgery on fibroid tumors dropped by. "What could be more fun than talking to people like that?" he asks.

His advice to would-be entrepreneurs? "Don't be afraid to start a company. Just do it."

* * *

The professionals who ponder the workings of the entrepreneurial mind say running your own show is the key component. "It's the desire to control one's own destiny," says Judith Cone, vice president for entrepreneurship at the $1.7 billion Ewing Marion Kauffman Foundation in Kansas City. "When we've taken surveys and ask, 'Why are you an entrepreneur? Why are you doing this?' the answer is almost always, 'To be in control of my own destiny.'"

Jeff and Rich Sloan, brothers who founded StartupNation, a radio show and multimedia company to help budding business owners, say that the compulsion to take command is without question a defining characteristic of the breed.

"There is no doubt that entrepreneurs want to do things on their own," Rich Sloan confirms. "They would rather fail on their own than succeed for somebody else."

He adds, "There are some people who function better working on a team, pursuing somebody else's dream, and checking out at 5 P.M. They want to go home with nothing to worry about."

Frank Landsberger, who founded a project at Britain's University of Cambridge in cooperation with the Massachusetts Institute of Technology to teach entrepreneurial skills to biotechnology researchers, believes entrepreneurial personalities will be smothered in any sort of controlled environment, no matter how long a leash they are given.

"I don't think you can really be an entrepreneur in a big business, even though corporations try desperately to attract entrepreneurial people and promote an entrepreneurial culture," he says. "Entrepreneurs have a need to work outside a specific structure, to create their own structure, to start from scratch."

Landsberger, himself the founder of a company that developed cancer-fighting vaccines and a former member of a prominent venture capital firm, recalls a vignette in the book *The Monk and the Riddle*, by Randy Komisar, in which "a guy wants to start a funeral business, not because he has any passion for it, but just to make money. The author asks: Do you want to lead an actual life or live the deferred life plan? If the latter, go work at the post office, where you'll clock in for forty years and then have a nice retirement package.

"But in the *actual* life plan—there, the outcome is less of an issue than the moment," Landsberger says. "Entrepreneurs want to run their own show. They are maniacally focused on what they want to do; they could never work for somebody else."

•   •   •

Allow for a little poetic license in that last assertion. Many entrepreneurs do work for somebody else early in their careers, before they discover their true calling. Even after they've taken a shot at going it alone, some return to the corporate fold for one reason or another, usually viewing it as a staging ground for their next project and making sure they have wide leeway to do things their way.

Pete Newman's passion was municipal finance. Now, some people might find it difficult to work themselves up into a fever of excitement over municipal bonds, but Newman wasn't one of them.

"I understood the link between what investment bankers do and how they benefit the community," he explains. "Very few people sit back and notice that. Schools, city halls, museums, water projects, hospitals—without municipal financing we wouldn't have the America we have. If you're underwriting a bond for the city, you're making a direct contribution to the welfare of people. That's why I spent so much time on my company. The cause was just."

Before exploring the nonprofit world, Newman did stints in the officeplace—as a paralegal at a law firm, as an intern at a public relations agency, as a stockbroker—but found the work frustrating and sometimes boring. Then he landed a part-time job as a marketing consultant to handle special events for a nonprofit that ranked companies on their social responsibility. The firm gathered data on criteria such as minority hiring and commitment to a clean environment, with the goal of selling the research to "green" mutual funds and consumers.

He became quickly disillusioned. "The people there mismanaged employees, had no strategy, and were broke most of the time," he says. "They had lost their chance to make a difference, and that made me angry. I was starting to regret turning down a job as a corporate bond analyst of timber and paper companies that went against my sensibilities but at least had a future in it."

Then it struck him: He could launch a for-profit business that would allow him to chase his dream. In his Brooklyn home, he started Gotham Software Inc., a maker of software to help investment banks structure municipal bonds more efficiently, thereby lowering the cost for towns and cities.

"When I incorporated, then I knew: I was an entrepreneur," Newman says. "The more I thought about it, the more I realized my life had been leading up to that point. In the end, I wouldn't have been happy as an employee of a nonprofit. It's a control issue. I wanted to maintain control over my idea. The power of an idea was all I had."

Had another and much deeper-pocketed company not come along

before he had a chance to get Gotham going, Newman might be a municipal-software mogul today. Instead, seeing the writing on the wall, he sold out to his bigger rival, i-Deal LLC, and now is working there on contract, supervising the software he developed.

He is also mulling over his next venture. Maybe he will devise a new board game, he says, or write a screenplay, or start a restaurant. It might seem odd to jump from the high-technology world to such old-fashioned pursuits, but not to him.

"Entrepreneurship is ultimately about having freedom and being self-reliant, and doing things that matter to me and that can help other people," he says. "Some of my great-great-uncles opened a store, a tavern, and a livery stable in a town the family founded in central Washington. They were entrepreneurs of the West. That streak runs in me."

Dr. Kerry Sulkowicz, a psychiatrist and psychoanalyst who founded the Boswell Group LLC in New York to advise senior corporate executives on leadership skills, says this I-gotta-be-in-charge individualistic streak is almost universal among entrepreneurs—including himself. After he started Boswell, he agreed to sell it to a management-consulting firm but continue running it as a partner. It was a bad move. "I just didn't like reporting to other people, even though they gave me the widest slack," he reports. "I just didn't like having to fit my identity into a larger corporate identity. I would bridle at perfectly reasonable demands. I lasted ten months." He worked out an amicable settlement with the firm, and now he does pretty much what he did before, but on retainer.

• • •

Some future entrepreneurs clunked around from job to job, appalled at the incompetence all around them but not knowing quite what to do about it. John Heagney of John Heagney Public Relations, for example, realizes that the seeds were planted in his psyche. "I always knew the way things should be done," he explains. "This notion has been with me forever. And I was always frustrated by ways of doing things that were imposed on me."

After graduating from college, he had a string of mundane jobs. He worked for a discount store called Clover, selling tires and garden equipment, where the only requirements were to stand there and wait to assist customers. But there was a lot of downtime, and Heagney surrendered to a compulsion to rearrange the shelves. "It bothered me that there were two car polishes here and one over there; I put them all together," he recalls. "I worked like a demon. Once, I completely reorganized several hundred fifty-pound bags of peat moss by various categories. The department manager came out and watched me without saying a word, then took full credit with the store manager for what I had done. My initiative got me nowhere. After all, this wasn't my job."

Similarly, as a reporter at a backwater bureau of the *St. Petersburg Times,* he was distressed by the shambles in the "morgue," a newspaper's library of old articles. "It was a nightmare, an archaic, disorganized nonsystem," Heagney says, a hint of indignation creeping into his voice after all these years. "On my own time, I devised a way to reorganize it. I came in on weekends. But the bureau chief put a stop to my efforts. He said, 'It's worked well enough so far. It's good enough for me.'"

It was dawning on him that, yes, he wanted to be his own boss. And the *Times* ultimately helped him realize that dream by firing him, he says, with good cause.

Today, he is his own boss, and he revels in the fact. Now in his mid-fifties and making a small bundle, it is unlikely he will ever find himself ruined because of some monumental miscalculation. But the notion doesn't bother him, he claims. If his company folded tomorrow, he would start another one.

"I would never take a salaried job with another company, not in a million years," he says. "I just like working on my own."

For Peter Amico, the founder of Airtrax, the company that makes omnidirectional vehicles, it wasn't so much his bosses' indifference to his workplace initiatives as their capriciousness. It riled him that they could make him do things that had no productive purpose except to inflate their egos.

"I did not like other people telling me what to do when they were so wrong," Amico says.

When he was eighteen, he worked for a shipyard. It lasted one day. His boss asked him to get him a soda. That wasn't part of the job description, but he did it. "Then he asked me to go get him another one, and walk quickly so people would think I was working," Amico recalls. "I guess he had nothing for me to do. I told him, 'I'm not playing games,' and asked him to give me something meaningful to do. He said, 'You'll have to wait.' I quit on the spot. Life is too short to play games like that."

· · ·

Carl Schramm, chief executive of the Ewing Marion Kauffman Foundation, says an emerging body of evidence indicates that entrepreneurs' almost neurotic need to take charge is in some cases biologically determined. Dyslexics, for example, "who can't master huge amounts of recorded wisdom, who can't play by other people's rules," have to create environments where they operate on their own, Schramm says.

"Something like 4 percent of the British population is dyslexic," he says. "Something like 8 percent of the CEOs of big corporations are dyslexic. And 28 percent of founders of start-ups are dyslexic. And this is really just a subset of a much broader phenomenon of people who are temperamentally unable to fit into somebody else's system."

Judith Cone, the Kauffman vice president, takes the argument a step further. Dyslexics and other learning-disabled people might have no choice—but just about anyone can be driven into business ownership out of necessity, she says.

"There can be different thresholds," she points out. "Let's say you're happy as a corporate manager, but you lose your job and can't find another that pays anywhere near as much. So you start your own company." Similarly, she says, immigrants, who most likely had to fend for themselves back home and who displayed their risk-taking mentality by setting out for unfamiliar territory, often have no choice but to take the plunge.

"So the threshold is different for different people," she concludes. "And of course there are some people who would never, ever become an entrepreneur. Not everyone can handle living with all the stress of starting a company, raising the money, dealing with lawsuits and setbacks, resolving workplace conflicts, and all the rest of it. Some people simply can't tolerate anxiety. Or they lack energy. Or they are disorganized. They'd rather go on food stamps."

Manfred F. R. Kets de Vries, a professor of leadership development at INSEAD in Fontainebleau, France, and a practicing psychoanalyst who is an authority on leadership, talked about this in a 2004 interview in *Management* magazine. Asked if there was a single characteristic that he had observed in virtually all entrepreneurs, he said it was probably their difficulty in "working in a structured situation" and dealing with authority.

"You have things like genetic predisposition, birth order, parents, the history of child successes and failures, family status, even serendipity— pure chance," de Vries said. "All these play a role. But at the heart of the inner theater of the entrepreneur is the issue of control."

By contrast, he said, corporate CEOs "like structure. They have different life anchors. The life anchor for entrepreneurs is to create and build something, whereas for most professional executives it's more a matter of power, status, and money."

* * *

Walk into the Lara Helene Bridal Atelier on East Sixty-ninth Street in Manhattan between Fifth and Madison Avenues and you'll know that the founders, sisters Lara Meiland and Lisa Helene Meiland, are in charge of every square inch. Tiffany lamps illuminate puffy tulle strapless dresses and hand-embroidered lace columns draped on seven-foot-high brass bars. Minimalist blue handmade rugs scatter across brown hardwood floors, and surrealist Nitin Vadukul photos of Lara Helene gowns hang on stark white walls. There's even a fireplace in the changing area and a luxuriant garden out back where, the sisters joke, the father of the bride can seek spiritual solace after he sees the bill.

Lara and Lisa always knew they wanted to run their own business. That is why they joined Columbia University's MBA program in entrepreneurial studies, where as part of the curriculum they bought a Hickey Freeman men's clothing store franchise in their second year and made a profit of $60,000 on record sales of $300,000.

After graduating from college, they joined big corporations to get a little management experience under their belts. Lisa started off in private wealth management at Morgan Stanley but soon got bored. J. P. Morgan then offered her a job in its banking mergers-and-acquisitions unit, but she balked at the rigid structure she saw there. "I told them I needed something entrepreneurial, where the business was developing, where I would have a certain amount of authority," she recalls. "The guy trying to recruit me searched high and low." Finally, he got her a spot doing research on a trading procedure known as credit default swaps for a forty-person group that had the feel of a start-up. "I had freedom of movement," she says. "I was given a lot of responsibility for an analyst, writing reports and distributing them internationally."

Lara got a position at Saks Fifth Avenue as an assistant buyer of women's evening wear by designers such as Vera Wang and Pamela Dennis. "I was in charge of that for all the stores," she says. She expanded her specialties to numerous other lines, including the beaded gowns and bridal gowns of two big-name male designers.

She liked the job but hated the inefficiencies she saw all around her—inefficiencies she would have addressed if *she* ran the show. "When a firm grows to a certain size, that's what happens," Lara says.

Today, Lara says, she and her sister revel in being in charge of "everything in the store." And she does mean everything. "I made the furniture," she says, referring to the green suede chairs and couches. "And once, we spent an entire day looking for just the right doorknob."

People who launch start-ups or run small firms tend to be in charge of everything, from ordering new computers to tipping the pizza delivery boy. Martin G. Klein, the chief executive of Electro Energy Inc., a maker of bipolar nickel metal hydride and other rechargeable batteries in Danbury, Connecticut, is a chemical engineer and one of the country's top experts on batteries. "Today, I had rate negotiations with the garbage collector," he says with a chuckle.

*   *   *

To be in control of a company means fending off those who would wrest control of it from you. Except that it isn't always so clear that that is what they are up to.

Venture capitalists—also known as vulture capitalists—are pretty deft at masking their intentions. These investment groups are very discerning about where they put their money, but when they spot hot prospects, they can be generous. Their munificence, however, comes with strings attached. And a lot of small-business owners have learned to keep their distance.

Take Paul Brown, founder of HearUSA, the hearing care provider. Back when he was getting his medical testing company, Metropolitan Pathology Laboratory, off the ground, he sought financing from a group of venture capitalists. At the time, MetPath had high promise but skimpy revenue. To his surprise, they offered him $1.5 million for a 49 percent stake in the company. He was elated and shook on the deal.

At their next meeting to review the contract, one of them said, "Oh, by the way, we'd like to form a committee to approve all purchases of over $5,000." Brown would be a member, of course. Again, he agreed.

The next "suggestion" was to form a compensation committee to set employees' salaries. He'd be a member, naturally. Sure, he said.

Another meeting was held. This time the venture capitalists wanted to set up a committee to set the fees that MetPath would charge customers. Brown hesitated. "My lawyer asked me to step outside with him," he recalls. " 'Do you see what's going on?' he asked. 'If you agree to this, it won't be your company anymore. They'll be making the decisions.' We walked away from that deal."

Cameron Johnson, the boy wonder who launched numerous dot-coms in his teens, walked away from a lot more than $1.5 million, for pretty much the same reason. He and a partner had each invested five figures in a start-up called CertificateSwap.com and had big plans to build it into a $100 million company. A venture capital firm offered to put $10 million into it for a 70 percent stake, on the conditions that Johnson not go back to school for four years (he had dropped out to run CertificateSwap.com) and that he move to Washington, D.C., where the VC firm was located.

"Our hands would be tied," Johnson recalls. "We'd have to move to D.C. I wouldn't be able to go back to school. I'd be making less money than I did in the ninth grade. The venture capital firm would run the company. We'd have no control over what they did. They could use my name and run it into the ground, destroy my reputation." The two partners turned down the offer and sold their company for a price in the six figures.

Gary Doan, the founder of Intradyn, the Minnesota maker of backup data systems for small businesses, is even blunter in his distaste for VC firms. "The number-one challenge small companies face is funding," he says. "We're still struggling, doing private placements. We chose not to use venture capitalists, though that is where the money is. They want to own you. They want control. I've turned down several offers from them, and I still get an average of two calls a week from them. It's not friendly money."

James Poss, whose company makes solar-powered garbage compactors, seconds that. "What they do is they kind of force you to up your burn rate so they can just keep sinking their teeth in deeper and deeper," he says. "I've seen it happen. If a VC is ever in on our financing, it will be in for a very small part of the round."

None of this is to say venture capitalists are bad people. To the contrary, they are smart investors who want to negotiate the most profitable deals possible. And they tend to think they are smarter than the people who run the companies they have their eyes on.

Just as it is possible for them to manipulate business owners, however, it is possible for business owners to manipulate them. When Umang Gupta was revving up his first successful company, Gupta Technologies, he avoided venture capitalists for four years. When he finally realized he needed their money, he was determined not to cede control to them. He says he set up a "little bit of a horse race among multiple venture capitalists" and got several commitments, leaving him and his partner, Bruce Scott, by far the biggest shareholders.

Wanting to take charge was hardwired into Gupta's personality. At the India Institute of Technology, for example, he ran for president of his class and used every legitimate trick in the book to snag the office. "Why was it important to win?" he muses. "I like being the leader. The act of winning was fun in itself, but I liked the idea of setting the agenda for the next year, of being in charge."

Years later, when he made the decision to go into business rather than politics or the military, the careers favored by his parents, he says, "I had gotten used to the idea that I just did my own thing."

* * *

Greg Herro, the co-founder of LifeGem, says he never thought of himself as an entrepreneur until somebody called him one. He now realizes he has been one since he started his paper route at the age of twelve.

Like Gupta and many other small-business leaders, Herro was elected president of his class (in his junior year in high school). Not long after that, he and some buddies started a band, and when he and one of the other members went off to Illinois State, they formed another band. After two years of kicking around academia, he told his parents he was dropping out and heading West.

They said OK, but first he would have to make some money. He got a job on the assembly line of a factory that made metal toy trucks. The building was hot, the walls were gray, and his task was to make 24,000 spot-welds a day.

"Two weeks into it, I asked a woman how long she had been on the assembly line," Herro recalls. " 'Seventeen years,' she told me. I took off my gloves and walked out of the plant. I'm not a quitter, but that was the bitter end."

After college, he got a low-level office job and watched his co-workers drag themselves through the day. He churned through the tasks assigned to him and asked for more responsibility but was refused. "So after lunch I'd read a book," he remembers. "There was an exact moment when it dawned on me, 'I'm not cut out to be a nine-to-fiver.' I quit and went to Colorado."

It eventually occurred to him that the only way to accommodate his aversion to the humdrum and his love of the "weird and funny and strange" in life was to start his own company. LifeGem has certainly delivered the goods on both counts.

Luke Visconti, the magazine owner quoted earlier in this chapter saying he would "never, never" work for anybody else, says his parents wanted him to enter a safe profession, such as accounting. "I think I'd have killed myself," he says. He studied biology but didn't want to be a biologist either, especially after watching researchers in action at a pharmaceutical company that made antiparasite drugs for cows. "These guys have Ph.D.'s and they're searching cow poop for worms?" he remembers thinking.

Even when he did report to a boss, he found ways to stay in control. As a car salesman, for example, he negotiated his own deals with customers, free from the scrutiny of a supervisor. "You have to maintain that autonomy when you are selling something," he notes. "It is the mark of a good salesman." Later, he flew planes for the U.S. Navy, one of the most dangerous but exhilarating jobs there is.

So determined is he today to maintain his editorial independence that he limits the space he gives to any single advertiser. "I could tell anybody to jump off a cliff," he says.

That same refusal to bend to outside pressure marked Laura Gasparis Vonfrolio's tenure at a magazine she once started called *Revolution: The Journal of Nurse Empowerment*. The magazine took aim at doctors and hospital executives and their condescending attitude toward nurses.

"I recruited some hot-shot advertisers, like Hewlett-Packard. But they demanded to see the editorial content," says Vonfrolio, the president of Education Enterprises. "They were afraid of being associated with something that might offend the hospital industry. So I sent them back their money. By the third issue, the only advertisers I had were small, nurse-owned businesses."

•   •   •

Ross Levin was always getting elected president of this or that organization.

At the University of Minnesota, he was president of his college fraternity and president of the interfraternity council as well as an orientation leader for freshmen and one of three student advocates. At age thirty-four, he became president of the International Association for Financial Planning, as it was then known.

"Always, I wanted to be in charge," says Levin, the founder and, yes, president of Accredited Investors Inc. in Medina, Minnesota. "If I believe strongly in an organization, I don't want to be on its board unless I can be president someday." That includes the $600 million Minneapolis Foundation, of which he is board member and executive committee member.

He got into financial planning in 1982 at the age of twenty-three, in the early days of the industry, as an employee of an insurance organization. In 1986, he started his own firm, but a year later he was lured away to run another one. Almost immediately, he regretted his decision. "I was the president but I had to pacify the owner and deal with financial planners instead of clients," he recalls. "I took the job to satisfy my ego without looking at my job set."

He started the Ross Levin Financial Group in 1985 (renaming it Accredited Investors two years later) and never looked back. But he warns disgruntled or ambitious corporate managers that going it alone is not for everyone. He advises them to take a simple test. "You have to crave the freedom," he says. "I'd have been strangled in a company. I struggle taking orders from anyone."

Levin, too, gets lots of feelers from venture capitalists and other potential investors, including one from a national financial planning company that wanted to put together a group of ten large fee-only firms including his and go public within a few years. He was tempted. "What intrigued me about the offer was the synergy of combining with nine other firms," he acknowledges. "I would have had formal access to them all. But in the end I wanted to stay independent."

Peter Gyenes, the former chairman and chief executive of the Ascential Software Corporation in Westborough, Massachusetts, is one of those entrepreneurs-within-a-corporation who technically answered to a higher authority (his corporate board) but always maintained an independent mind-set.

At first, his career had the markings of an ordinary office drone. While studying at Columbia University, he got a night job as a computer programmer at IBM. Later, he joined a Xerox unit as a technical support person for salespeople and then became a salesman himself. After about three years, he became a sales manager in New York.

One year later, in 1977, he was recruited by a Massachusetts company, Prime Computer, then doing about $20 million in sales, to be a district manager in New York. It was a new ballgame. "I was the new boss of a territory, I had half a dozen sales guys plus technical support people who reported to me, I had a franchise, I was thirty-two, and my company isn't going to manage me," Gyenes recalls. "It's going to support me, ship products to me, familiarize me with its goals. I was in charge. I was on my own. It wasn't like Xerox, where you needed seven signatures for a $100 expense account."

There were boundaries. One of the company's prospects, Citibank, wanted the loan of a $1 million minicomputer (the size of four huge filing cabinets in those days). The margins were high, but Prime Computer would have to build it, ship it, install it, and maintain it. If Citibank sent it back, Gyenes would be in trouble.

He approved the transaction, and his boss signed off on the deal. "I was shocked; this was almost too easy," he says. "Then he said, 'If it ever comes back, I'll kill you.'"

After two big promotions, he decided to go out on his own and "not be beholden to anybody." He and his older brother, an executive at Warner Communications and, like him, fluent in French and Hungarian, set themselves up as an "investment team" and went looking for opportunities in Europe. But they mostly "dilettante-ed around" for a couple of years before ending their experiment and returning to the United States.

He joined a computer start-up and then another one, both times as the partner in charge of sales marketing, before joining Data General in 1990 for a four-year stint as chief of international operations.

But he still had a boss. Once, the CEO gave him special permission to take the Concorde from London to New York and back to attend a funeral, then called him on the carpet the next day for his poor judgment in flying the high-priced supersonic jet. It was at that point that it struck him: He needed to be president of a company.

"I just felt that I would spend a lot of time going back to management meetings that somebody else was running," Gyenes says. "I felt I had to explain myself a lot beyond what I wanted to do, really. I think it was sort of a personal realization that I wanted to be in charge."

And he was, too. First, he was asked to spruce up a company and put it on the market. Then, in 1996, he was asked to be the CEO of Ascential. (In 2005, he engineered the sale of Ascential to IBM.)

.   .   .

Michael Huddy, the chief executive of Barrier Technology Inc., went through a similar metamorphosis. He grew up in a working-class family in Michigan where everybody worked for General Motors and "put in their forty and got two weeks off." But he aspired to something higher than shift supervisor. "In other words, I wanted to be the boss," he says.

Crown Zellerbach, the forestry products company where he started his career, gave him ample opportunity to tap into his latent innovative zeal, letting him take over smaller companies and create new products. While big companies are inefficient incubators of new products and new ideas, they are still incubators, he points out.

"If you look hard enough, you can find that stuff, and that is what I did," he says.

After he joined Weyerhaeuser, his urge to be in charge kept propelling him to assignments—such as shaping up the company's troubled Eastern hardwood operations—that gave him free rein to do whatever had to be done. "It was just as you do if you're running a small business," he says. "I made quick decisions and I took risks."

He became part of a Weyerhaeuser team that looked at new products, and soon he was running a "company within a company," he says. He fell in love with a fire-resistant material called Blazeguard, made by a Canadian firm called Barrier, and begged Weyerhaeuser to buy the technology. "We argued we had a great trademark, a great product, an identifiable market, distribution capacity, and a pilot plant," he recalled. But Weyerhaeuser refused to pay the asking price.

Then Barrier asked him to start a company in the United States to be called Barrier International, and he jumped at the chance. He had had enough of "the whims of the politics of the big organization," he said, where you can never tell whether the higher-ups will "stick with a company or spin it off, throw money at it or take the money off the table."

Today, he says, "I'm a corporation-created entrepreneur, but it is as if I owned my own business."

A little more than a decade later, Barrier is profitable and "on the move," Huddy announces, with revenue projected to more than double in fiscal 2006 to $10 million from $4.4 million in 2005 and with a new $2.8 million plant in the works that eventually will increase its capacity to 50 million square feet from 8 million in 2005. He owns 1.45 million shares in Barrier, more than 5 percent of the 28 million outstanding, and has almost complete freedom to call the shots. "I guess I ended up here because I have always had a compulsion to be in charge," he muses. "I've always rejected authority."

Huddy warns that being in charge of a fledgling firm can be full of booby traps. If the market turns, the price points don't add up, or a major customer disappears, your life's dream can evaporate. But would he do it all over? "Yeah," he says. "I would rather be bankrupt than work for a big company."

Even so, he has learned to relinquish authority. Once, he thought he had to be in charge of everything. But then it occurred to him that being in control of his *life* is what mattered. His real love is developing new products—it is a bit like starting a business, he says—so he plunges into that and gives others a bigger say over how the company is run.

In a similar vein, Mark Hughes, founder of Buzzmarketing, a consulting firm in Swarthmore, Pennsylvania, says he turns away a lot of business because he doesn't see the point in killing himself. "My publisher was like, 'Dude, you could grow this into a 100-person consulting firm,'" he remarks. "But I don't want to create a huge conglomerate. If a start-up grows into something big, the founder becomes less an entrepreneur and more a manager. They start using terms like *deliverables*. I want to keep it simple, have complete control, do just what I want to do." That includes spending a lot of time with his three kids, ages twelve, three, and one and a half.

Joan Schweighardt started her book publishing business, GreyCore Press, out of her home in Pine Bush, New York, in 1999 and has been struggling ever since. But she is having fun. "I work with creative, interesting writers, and I have the freedom to do exactly as I please," she says, relaxing in her study in a frayed sweater and worn slippers.

"It's like hanging out with a bunch of friends. I'm indulging myself. It's like an addiction. Each time I work on a book, I say to myself, 'If this doesn't work, I'm not doing this anymore.' But I do. I can't say no."

·   ·   ·

Perhaps the most reluctant entrepreneur I interviewed was Kirtland Poss, a kind of a counterexample to so many of the others. (He is also probably the most methodical—and that is saying something.)

Kirt, the older brother of James Poss, whose company makes solar-powered trash compactors, enjoys running the show. It's just that he doesn't view it as the main point.

The main point, he says, is to succeed—to develop the best product, to make the company grow, to leave the competition in the dust. As a rule of thumb, he says, aspiring entrepreneurs should first spend several years gaining experience in managing people and honing their expertise in their chosen field, perhaps at a big company.

That is what he did. In college, he worked summers at a medical device company. He was more interested in studying the design and efficacy of its products than in taking charge of a project. Later, while thinking about going to medical school, he got a job doing research at the Center for Molecular Imaging Research at Massachusetts General Hospital. He continued working in the lab and simultaneously taking science courses for two or three years to build his understanding of medicine, technology, and health care.

After a stint at Kendall Strategies as a consultant for health care companies, he enrolled in the F. W. Olin Graduate School of Business at Babson College in 1999. "With a combined background in health care, business, and consulting, I figured that after business school I would have the background to work at a big health care company," Poss says. "I think I had the right attributes to start a company, but was thinking I might do that fifteen years down the road. I thought then, and I think now, that starting a company is a brutally hard endeavor and you might as well have as many odds stacked in your favor as possible. I was willing to wait a long time for the right circumstances to develop that would increase my chance of success."

Call it the making of an entrepreneur in slow motion. It might be a smarter path than rushing in, though following it requires a patience with organizational hierarchy that most start-up junkies lack.

The same is not true of his brother, James Poss, who says that by his late twenties, "I absolutely knew I would never go looking for a job, I would never interview for a job, I would never take a job."

Kirt urged his younger sibling to spend ten to fifteen years in a big corporation to learn how the industry works. James refused. "My brother and I don't really talk much about business," Kirt says. "It gets too emotional."

But Kirt, too, succumbed to the entrepreneurial itch before putting in that many years in the corporate trenches. The head of the Massachusetts General lab where he had worked talked him into joining him in launching a company, VisEn Medical, to develop technologies for molecular imaging of the body that could lead to early detection of disease.

Even so, Kirt still pooh-poohs the notion that he must always be the boss. He believes he is doing a good job of running his company but says he will lead the search for a chief executive more seasoned than he is to take over from him. He shows none of the aversion so many others in his shoes do toward venture capitalists, saying that if a group of them ever made a big investment in VisEn, they would no doubt keep him if he measured up and squeeze him out if he didn't, a proposition that is fine by him. "I'd do the same," he said.

After all, if VisEn ever fails or he is pushed out, he can always get a job in strategic planning at a big corporation. "Still . . . ," Kirt says. He pauses for several seconds. "You can say that, but the more time you get used to running the show and used to the excitement and pace of running a company, the more you wonder how true that is.

"I'm having a ball," he adds. "I'm running a company."

Nadine Thompson is having a ball, too. As a black woman in a white man's world, she is struggling to take charge of the company that she has built from scratch. At the moment, however, her wealthy business partner holds the financial strings and has the final say on strategy, and that grates on her.

Born in Trinidad and raised in Toronto from the age of nine, Thompson earned her master's degree in social work from Smith College. She became a counselor for troubled children and their families in Manchester, New Hampshire, and, in 1993, dean of multicultural affairs at Phillips Exeter Academy. Then a chance meeting propelled her into the small-business world.

At a class reunion she attended with her husband, a Phillips Exeter graduate, a "sweet-looking guy" named Daniel Wolf invited them to stay at his Manhattan penthouse apartment. They took him up on the offer and, while staying, noticed little bottles of creams and lotions with exotic names on the labels that he kept in the refrigerator.

She asked about them, and he told her they had been created by an herbalist and healer in Arizona from all-natural ingredients found in the desert. He was so taken with the unguents, Wolf said, that he had bought the rights to them for something like $350,000. Realizing it would cost millions to produce and market them, he stashed them in his fridge and was trying to decide what to do next.

"We're sitting at dinner and he's telling us this story and I'm like,

'Daniel, only rich white dudes buy companies that they don't know what they're going to do with. You're crazy. You just bought this company and stuck this stuff in a refrigerator?' He's like, 'Well, what do smart black women do with stuff like that?' I said, 'You start a damn company and you start selling stuff.'

"He says to me, 'Great idea.'"

Despite her lack of business experience, she agreed to a partnership. Her up-from-the-bootstraps background and the work ethic and ambitious spirit instilled in her by her mother gave her the confidence to think she could pull it off, especially with the help of a deep-pocketed benefactor.

But from the beginning, the imbalance in the relationship—she did most of the work, he held all of the power—bothered her. He granted her the title of chief executive, but he owned the company that they had created, Warm Spirit Inc.

She quickly discovered that she wasn't alone in wanting to take control of her life. So did the independent contractors she recruited to sell Warm Spirit's moisturizers from their homes. She had hoped to enlist low-income women eager to make a few extra bucks, but instead attracted mostly college-educated professionals, many of them refugees from the corporate world.

A few of these marketers are already making more money than Thompson's $125,000 salary, a sticking point between her and her partner.

Another bone of contention has been his habit of hiring overpriced outside talent to nose around and make suggestions that she ignores. Another is the vagueness of a handshake deal the two made about her eventual ownership stake, she says. She is hoping for 20 percent, but he is playing his cards close to his chest.

Thompson says she is grateful to him for giving her her big chance and for investing about $10 million in the company thus far.

"But on the other hand, I made it happen," she points out. "I've put in the sweat equity. Ninety-nine percent of the consultants are African American women who do this business because of the leadership I've provided. I couldn't do this without Daniel's money, but Daniel's money couldn't do this without me." (Postscript: In October 2005, the two worked out an "amicable deal that we both feel good about" for sharing profits and giving her an ownership stake, she says.)

LEADERSHIP

It isn't enough for entrepreneurs to have an urge *to be* in charge. They also must display a knack for *taking* charge.

They have to be leaders. That means they have to know how to motivate people to follow them. And that is more a gift than a skill. Either you've got it or you don't.

It is difficult, after all, to train yourself to like people, to be curious about them, to treat them with respect. You can't take a course on inspiring loyalty in others or being down-to-earth. You can't put integrity on a to-do list. You can't practice having zest for life.

You either have those attributes or you don't. And if you don't, you won't be able to fool your employees into thinking you do.

It's not about selling yourself, though, so much as selling your *vision.* "All the business literature now is talking about leadership instead of management," says William J. Dennis, senior research fellow at the National Federation of Independent Business's Research Foundation (NFIB). "About getting people to see your vision."

Judith Cone of the Kauffman Foundation elaborates on the point: "You have to be a leader, and a leader is able to explain a vision in a compelling way that motivates people to follow or to become a part of that vision." Charisma has nothing to do with it, she says. Rather, leaders "are solid, smart, they have integrity, people respect them, and people want to follow them because of the kind of quality person they are."

Charisma doesn't hurt, though. John D. Gartner, a psychiatry professor at the Johns Hopkins Medical School and author of *The Hypomanic Edge: The Link Between (a Little) Craziness and (a Lot of) Success in America,* compiled a list of traits of the "hypomanic" personality, which he believes dominates the entrepreneurial world. Among them, he said in a 2005 article in *American Enterprise* magazine, the hypomanic is fast-talking, is witty and gregarious, and has a natural self-confidence that can make him charismatic and persuasive.

Similarly, in a 2004 interview in the *Harvard Business Review,* Manfred de Vries of INSEAD in France said the first thing he looked for in successful leaders was their "emotional intelligence."

"Basically, how self-reflective is the person?" he asked. "Of course, emotional intelligence involves a lot more than just being introspective. It also involves what I call the teddy bear factor: Do people feel comfortable with you?"

Mark Rice, the Murata Dean of the F. W. Olin Graduate School of Business at Babson College in Babson Park, Massachusetts, says that "building relationships" is crucial to success.

"That came naturally to me; being in a big family, you can't be a prima donna," Rice says. "You have to figure out how to cooperate, collaborate, and survive."

In workplace lore, the most reviled figure is the career opportunist who "kisses up and kicks down," in the crude but instructive popular phrase. By contrast, a good boss comes across as a regular Joe (or Jill) to people in both high places and low. As an executive at a steel company in the Middle West, Umang Gupta put on a hard hat and roamed the shop floor, shooting the breeze with the workers. "It just worked for me, even though they were Americans and I was Indian," he says. "That didn't matter somehow."

The trick, says Peter Gyenes, the former Ascential Software boss, is to *listen* to employees. Listen so hard they can see you are taking them seriously. Listen so hard they aren't afraid to speak their minds.

"I took a lot of time to get to know them and to have them know me," he comments. "If you spend a lot of time with somebody, you'll learn a lot about him. I have to know how to motivate you and at the same time allow you to be comfortable about arguing with me."

To pull that off, you have to actually like people. Ross Levin, the Accredited Investors founder, found classes boring in college but relished his job of selling shoes because he enjoyed the give-and-take with customers. "I was having fun," he says. That is a theme that ran through all the interviews for this book. Whatever these hard-core capitalists do, they always seem to be having fun.

It is a contagious frame of mind. "People think I'm funny," Levin remarks. "I have a lust for life. I'm not afraid to stick my head out and get shot at. People get a sense I like them. I'm inclusive and find something about most people that they can like about themselves."

Paul Brown, founder of HearUSA Inc., says successful executives and business owners have a magnetism that is hard to resist. His advice for dealing with standoffish types: Avoid them.

"We went to Boston once to buy a company, and the chairman took us on a tour and didn't say hello to anybody, and nobody said hello to him," he recalls. "We decided against buying the company on that basis alone. Only he had an office; everybody else sat in a cubicle. Our policy is, whoever gets to the parking lot first gets the choicest spot. There is no executive dining room."

Here are some other basic rules Brown recommends: Let employees know in no uncertain terms what is expected of them. Reward the producers, not the talkers, among them. Don't penalize them for honest mistakes. Trust them and don't second-guess them. Have an open-door policy and meet with them in small groups frequently. If you have to let a loyal employee go, take care of her financially. And last but not least, fire problem employees immediately.

Kevin Plank, the founder of Under Armour, likens motivating his team to driving a bus. "A sports car, you turn the wheel to the left and your car goes left," he says. "But a bus, you've got to turn the wheel and it's got that little knob on it so that you turn the thing three or four times just to make a left turn. You need to make sure everybody is on board."

• • •

Liking people is really just another manifestation of the irrepressible curiosity that drives some people to take radios and lawn mowers apart as kids and explore neglected corners of the marketplace as adults. They can't wait to find out what makes their fellow human beings tick—and who can resist that kind of attention?

Their employees return the favor in the form of loyalty, a competitive edge that money can't buy (though it helps).

This same inquisitiveness about the world makes many entrepreneurs voracious readers, a habit that can give them insight into the workplace personalities they interact with. Luke Visconti of DiversityInc plows through more than 100 books a year, often two or three at a time, with a penchant for both fiction and nonfiction with military or leadership themes. "What I am always looking for, especially in books of history and military history, is how people make decisions under a high degree of stress," he says. "I'm fascinated by that."

His reading has helped him form an important lesson about managing people: Keep your mouth in the off position. "Take advice without giving feedback," he offers. "Listen quietly. Just allow them to talk. Let them go on. You get more insight that way than if you are constantly inserting your views." The payback is twofold: They will like you. (Ever notice how popular good listeners are and how annoying nonstop blabbers are?) And you will learn a lot.

Lara Meiland claims women have an edge on that score. "They are active listeners," she says. "They process what people say. Men just barrel ahead." It was a similar observation that gave Liz Ryan the inspiration for her company, an e-mail discussion community for women.

Of course, it takes more than just a friendly face to win over the troops. Brown of HearUSA says his employees know he created a lot of millionaires at his first company, MetPath, and will take care of them, too. He likes to cater to their whims. After one executive expressed unhappiness with the view from her window, he gave her an office overlooking a pond. "That's the one thing that would get her to work at 6 A.M.," he says.

Brown also gives his employees medical advice, recommends doctors to them, and visits them in the hospital. Martin Klein, the battery guru, says it is a "reflex action" for him to give people paid time off to deal with personal ordeals such as divorce or rebellious kids. "I want to make allowances," he says. "And I think that creates a lot of loyalty. When it comes time to work hard, to do something extraordinary, there is no question that everybody is in it together."

In the summer, Levin gives employees two paid Fridays off a month. He also closes the office twice a year to allow them to paint homes for Habitat for Humanity. He pays the airfare for an employee to fly home to Texas once a month for a four-day weekend with his family and doesn't count the extra days off as a part of his vacation.

Sig Anderman, the founder of Ellie Mae, tracked down a computer guru he had known years earlier and offered him one-third of his 80 percent stake in his start-up to build a Web site for it. Klein gives stock options to twenty out of seventy employees. Insurance maven Joe Macchia personally guaranteed everybody's bank loan to buy preferred stock in a private placement at one of his previous companies. Visconti matches 50 percent of his employees' 401(k) contributions, with no limit. Once, "scared to death" that his receptionist, a divorced mother of five, wouldn't be able to afford her 50 percent share of a new family health care plan, he raised her pay to cover the extra cost. "It is morally unacceptable to me that any one of my employees goes without health insurance," he says. He also pays tuition for any employee who is studying for a degree relevant to his business and gets a B average or better.

In negotiating the sale of Ascential to IBM in 2005, Gyenes says he made a point of asking, "What are you going to do for my employees? How are you going to motivate them? What will you do to keep them? What is the mission going to be? All that kind of stuff." And he signed off on the deal only when he was satisfied that IBM would take care of them.

It would be hard to beat the generosity that Laura Gasparis Vonfrolio has shown over the years. After she started Education Enterprises, she realized she was a staff nurse, a college professor, an organizer of cardiopulmonary resuscitation classes (for teaching people to revive victims of heart attacks and car accidents and the like), and an organizer of seminars, all at once, and was feeling overburdened. "So I gave my CPR company away," she says. "I'm sure I could have sold it for a good price, but I just gave it away to a fellow nurse. I said, 'I'm getting out. Here are my accounts, take them.' I also gave him my mannequins."

Later, she gave away her nursing magazine to the California Nurses Association. She says she gives away $30,000 a month to families in need. In her peak earning years, when she was making $3 million and up at Education Enterprises, she bought houses for several employees as well as for people down on their luck whom she read about in newspapers.

If nothing beats money (or free houses) for winning employees' affection, respect probably places a close second. Levin once told a client to take a hike because he was rude to the staff. The client got a reprieve by apologizing and promising to change his ways—and he did. Such a gesture speaks volumes about a boss's regard for his subordinates.

Bob Hillier, the architect and real estate investor, says his secret for holding the attrition rate at his firm to 2 percent from the industry average of 15 percent is telling people how wonderful they are, even when he is telling them that they aren't so wonderful.

"Hire good people, treat them with respect, never embarrass them, pat them on the back, and above all else make them feel important, make them feel they play a critical role," he advises. "They'll stick with you because they'll be afraid they won't be considered important if they go somewhere else."

So gracious is his delivery even of bad news, he says, that when he is criticizing their performance, they think he is mentoring them.

According to Klein, it is actually quite easy to motivate people. You need to make them feel they are part of the decision making and give them breathing room in carrying out their duties. "Most people want to do a good job, and if you give them opportunity and respect, at whatever level in the organization, they will come through for you," he says. "Giving them that basic respect is more important than money to them."

VisEn's Kirt Poss agrees. "I don't think it's the money, it's the being involved and succeeding in something exciting," he says. "As much as possible you have to let people run things."

By delegating authority, entrepreneurs unleash the same force in their subordinates that makes them so productive: the thrill of being in charge. At International Rectifier, one of Alex Lidow's deputies, Robert Grant, says it happened to him. "I came to Alex with an idea to create a business unit in the company driving e-commerce sales. This was an area the company hadn't thought of before. Not only did he allow me to do this, he funded it as a start-up."

Of course, not all entrepreneurs buy into the touchy-feely formula. The best motivator is your paycheck, they say; either deserve it or depart. It is a philosophy that rids them of the deadwood that plagues so many businesses, large and small. "Employees have to be self-motivated," says John Heagney of John Heagney Public Relations. "And the greatest motivator is the specter of unemployment because they didn't do their job. I know that from experience." In his job ads, he tells potential applicants that if they want to work eight to five, McDonald's is hiring. "I'm not looking for people to coast," he asserts. "I've fired any number of people because they thought that good enough was good enough. It never is. The firings aren't personal. All I care about is the product."

His hard line doesn't really put him all that much out of the mainstream. Just about every business owner admits to canning poor performers. Even so, Heagney recognizes that the free spirit he once was would not be at home in the work environment he has now created. After he was fired from his newspaper job years ago, he recalls, "I had lunch with a colleague and I was calling this editor a jerk and that editor an asshole and this other editor an idiot. He just smiled at me and said, 'When you have a business of your own someday, you're going to be the asshole.'"

INTEGRITY

It doesn't stop at treating your employees fairly. You have to be a man or woman of high character. "You inspire loyalty by always, always being ethical and honest," Kirt Poss says. "You have to lead by example; set a standard. People see that. They know."

Amico once pulled advertisements depicting a prototype omnidirectional truck after the images of the vehicle in action drove his company's stock price to $9 from $1.50 in 30 days, making him realize the ads had conveyed the false impression it was already on the market. Another time he resigned from a YMCA board because he couldn't get adequate information about its budget and refused to sign any documents until he did, throwing its operations into turmoil. Macchia quit a high-paying job at an insurance company rather than sign off on what he believed was a flawed evaluation of it by the new owners.

Plank says Under Armour's core value is "first and foremost integrity" and says he has never missed a bill or bounced a business check. "People know they can count on me," he says. Eller of the Eller Company wrote a book titled *Integrity Is All You've Got*, in which he argues that honest people generally succeed and dishonest people usually fail. Integrity, Eller says, is the oil that keeps all the other entrepreneurial traits working harmoniously together. It also gives any business a huge competitive advantage, he contends, and should be at the heart of any company's culture. After he was forced out of Circle K with $100 million in personal debt, he offered to pay back his creditors at 10 cents on the dollar—or in full if they would give him enough time. About half agreed to wait, and all of them got back every penny.

Openness is an element of honesty, and entrepreneurs pride themselves on not beating around the bush. Gyenes, the ex-boss at Ascential Software, recalls a moment of truth many years ago when Prime Computer sent him to London to take charge of its fledgling European operations. He was young, enthusiastic—and in near panic. He was "100 percent certain" that he was in over his head, he says, and to make matters worse, he knew the French managing director had coveted his job and was resentful.

"I arrived on the Sunday of Labor Day weekend and spent the afternoon and evening walking the streets of London wondering, 'What am I going to do? How am I going to survive? They're going to think I'm a kid, an amateur,'" he recalls.

Some people's natural temptation is to fake it till they make it. While that can be a short-term route to success in dating and poker, as a business strategy it is probably ill-advised. "I decided I was going to tell the managing directors everything: why I was picked, what I didn't know how to do, how much I needed their help," Gyenes remembers. "I'd tell them, 'I need you to help me. I can help you, too, to get better connected with the U.S. people and get them off your back. I'm your boss, but I'm going to help you.'"

He focused on the heavyweights, the managers in charge of Britain, France, and Germany, and won them all over almost immediately. More than a quarter century later, he says, all four remain good friends.

Another quality that entrepreneurs invariably display is a sense of humor. It is both a survival mechanism and a crowd pleaser in the office. Doan, blaming the initially lackluster sales of his Compliance Vault data storage system on the failure of regulators to enforce new document retention requirements, jokes that "there's a big market opportunity for us in fines right now."

Dot Smith, founder of Pepper Patch, a maker of gourmet jellies and chocolates, describes how she and her partner divided duties when they were getting started. "She did the kitchen, I handled the books and sales—and I'm dyslexic," she says. "An accountant taught me that you need a zero at the bottom of the page. That was a revelation to me. He didn't have much hair, but what hair he had he pulled."

Brown, the HearUSA chairman, says that he deserves a place in the *Guinness Book of World Records* for running a public company for seventeen years and never making a profit. Gyenes laughs about his parents' sensitivity in sending him, as a nine-year-old newcomer to America who was fluent in French and Hungarian but spoke no English, to a yeshiva to learn Hebrew. He claims an overnight shift he worked in college at an IBM office in Manhattan gave him some of the best perks he has ever had—a view of Bunnies going in and out of a Playboy Club across the street and easy access to bars that stayed open until 4 A.M.

Probably the biggest wisecracker in the pool of people I interviewed was, of all things, a Christian minister. But when you think about it, it makes sense. Get a bunch of ornery folks together under one roof, and how on earth are you going to bind them together if you can't make them laugh together?

. . .

Virtually any entrepreneur you talk to will tell you he has always felt in his bones that he was meant to be a leader. If you lack that sense of a calling, don't quit your day job. "I always aspired to be in a leadership role," Gyenes notes. "Why? I'm not sure I ever thought about it. What I have thought about is, 'How do I get myself to be effective in the leadership role I'm in, in a way that makes me ready for more leadership?'"

As Levin says, "I've always been in leadership positions. Most business success has been from wanting to be a leader." (This is the guy who has been president of every organization you can think of except the kitchen sink committee. He once asked a local chapter of the International Association for Financial Planning, "Is there anything I can do nobody else is willing to do?")

David Weinstein, president of the Chicagoland Entrepreneurial Center, says he has been a leader in any job he has ever held. "I assemble people," he says. "If I'm in a room with ten people, I'm always the guy that gets a debate going. I've probably had ten jobs and at every one I've been the boss. I'm very passionate and very ambitious." Weinstein is so eager to take the reins that he says his first mentor "has been with me ever since I met him."

Umang Gupta saw leadership as his path to success, almost as his destiny. At the ultra-prestigious Indian Institute of Technology, he discovered that he was no longer the smartest kid on the block. Of 100,000 applicants, 1,500 had been selected, and in such elite company, he was ranked 500-something. "Suddenly, I wasn't the smartest kid in school," he recalls. "There was no way I would be number one. I had to find my niche, a way to exercise my leadership."

Earlier, in military school, he was appointed a prefect of his house, the number-two spot, in his junior year. In his final year, he was promoted to house captain. He relishes the memory. "My responsibility was to promote law and order," he says, grinning. "The students were all required by school rules to march to their classes, and then from their classes to the dining hall, and everywhere else. Wherever we went, we marched. And I'm standing there, commanding them, 'Left, right, left, right,' the whole thing. I loved it. I learned so much about various styles of leadership. Especially about getting people to do stuff without forcing them to do it. Getting people to respect you for who you were rather than for your rank."

But he also learned that the carrot needs the stick. Once, in a quiet study period he was overseeing, one of the students started making whistling noises.

"Who whistled?" he asked sharply. No answer. Then somebody else whistled. "Who's whistling?" Again, silence. And then a third time, and a fourth time. "This was an interesting problem for me," he remembers. "How can I find out who the culprits are without appearing confused or not in charge?" He hit on a solution. Of course they couldn't snitch on their buddies, he told the class. How much more honorable a course it would be for them to run for one hour around the playing field after their sports period. "Nobody ever whistled again," he concludes. "I remember thinking, 'Hmmm. That worked.'"

CHAPTER 3

Nurture vs. Nature

Is there such a thing as an entrepreneurial gene? Scientists generally scoff at the concept. Yet some entrepreneurs swear by it.

No one has located this gene, but a case could be made that people who display such personality traits as curiosity, enthusiasm, and tenacity are born into the breed. John D. Gartner, a psychiatry professor at the Johns Hopkins Medical School, makes a spirited argument for a genetic role in *The Hypomanic Edge: The Link Between (a Little) Craziness and (a Lot of) Success in America.* Gartner interviewed ten entrepreneurs and concluded that they all had hypomania, a psychological state of high energy and boundless self-confidence that falls just short of the self-destructive frenzy of manic-depression (also known as bipolar disorder) and never collapses into suicidal despair the way that manic-depression does. He speculates that Americans' work ethic is some sort of "internal biological compulsion passed from parent to child through their hypomanic genes."

Cone of the Kauffman Foundation says that in the debate over whether entrepreneurs are born or made, high energy is probably the trait that comes closest to being embedded in their DNA. "Your energy level is largely a question of physiology," she comments. "It's hard for me to imagine an entrepreneur who is lethargic."

Landsberger, the former MIT professor, says he suspects a large number of the breed are borderline bipolar. He cited a student of his who is sacrificing her career to start a company. She has trouble forming close relationships with people, he says, because "she can't deal with anybody who isn't as driven as she is."

Other researchers say a migratory gene—a DNA-encoded predisposition to explore the unknown—goaded the most restless thrill seekers of our prehistoric ancestors in Africa to spread out across the globe, with those who traveled the farthest (e.g., to India and China) displaying the greatest drive. That same dynamic is at work in the world today, this theory goes, with homebody societies such as Japan displaying little risk-taking get-up-and-go, and wanderlust populations such as Americans bubbling over with it.

Still other experts contend that entrepreneurship is a cultural phenomenon that defines entire civilizations (notably the Anglo-Saxon, Chinese, Indian, and Jewish peoples), as well as smaller tribal groups including the Ibo in Nigeria. In this camp, Max Weber, the German sociologist who wrote *The Protestant Ethic and the Spirit of Capitalism* a century ago, stands tall. Weber argued that the Calvinist doctrine of predestination spurred hell-fearing Protestants to embrace the work ethic and engage in commerce to show their elect status, thereby revving up capitalism throughout anti-papist Christendom.

Whatever the origins of people's bent for business, entrepreneurs themselves generally say it is "in their blood," whether inherited or learned. And the stories they tell suggest it is a bit of both, a seed that is usually planted by their parents and nurtured early in life.

The Meiland sisters' father started several businesses over the years and now runs an international executive search firm. Plank's dad was a land developer who played a lot of tennis and didn't go to the office that much. Vonfrolio's father was a bar owner. Anderman's father had a dry cleaning business. Klein's father delivered seltzer water to people's homes. Ryan's father was a magazine publisher. Levin's was a traveling salesman. Lidow's father started the semiconductor company that the son now runs. Amico's father was a poultry dealer who built one of the first automated plants for slaughtering and packaging chickens.

Gyenes's father owned a textile business in his native Hungary and started two more textile ventures in the United States. Mahoney's father was one of the first computer programmers at AT&T. Doan's dad spent his entire career at Northwest Airlines but worked his way up from mechanic to assistant director of flying operations. Newman's father is a college professor. Not all of those occupations fit the precise mold of the swashbuckling risk taker, but they do require initiative and hard work.

Whatever their vocations, the fathers generally pushed their sons and daughters to think hard and work hard and fired them up with ambition. "Dad wasn't an entrepreneur, but he instilled in us the risk-taking mentality," says Timothy Mahoney, founder of vFinance. Daniel H. Jara, a consultant and insurance agent in Hackensack, New Jersey, traces his drive to his father's example in his native Peru of running a distributorship for General Motors parts and three stores that sold bikes imported from England.

It wasn't just their dads who set the example. Karl Eller's mother ran a boardinghouse. Hillier's mom not only started a flower shop in Princeton, New Jersey, she also bought the two other flower shops in town, retaining their names to hide her ownership from people she had offended over the years. When the family moved to Washington, D.C., she started another flower shop.

Liz Ryan's mother, the daughter of an Irish cop, was one of the first women to graduate (in 1951) from the Georgetown School of Foreign Service. "She was an overachiever," says Ryan, the founder of WorldWIT. "Throughout the fifties and early sixties, she was doing her own things and working on the governor's commission for this and that. She wrote historical travel articles for the big dailies. She was a fanatical Catholic. She would make us get up at 6 A.M. on Sundays to watch her on some obscure Sunday morning talk show." She played in a recorder society and sang in a women's barbershop quartet. She was into decorating, history, historic preservation, and cooking. She spent years creating an elaborate Victorian dollhouse with decorative wallpaper, finely wrought rugs, and miniature people. She became director of admissions and director of publications for Montclair State College. After she and her husband retired, at her instigation, they started a bed-and-breakfast in a 1775 North Carolina plantation house. They sold it a few years ago, but the mother still plays tennis, does aerobics three times a week, runs church committees, stays active in the North Carolina Bed & Breakfasts and Inns Association, and writes a column for a home-and-garden magazine.

The Sloan brothers' mother would read to them from the Patents column in the *New York Times,* describing all the latest inventions and telling them repeatedly, "You boys should get a patent someday," as Rich Sloan recalls. "She was stirring up that idea constantly." Hughes's mother set an example of just-do-it as the author of a dozen biographies aimed at teenagers as well as a playwright who, now in her mid-seventies, "is still shooting for a Broadway production," her son says.

Kevin Plank's mother, a high-level official in the Reagan and first Bush administrations, took her son on business trips in the summers and introduced him to politicians and industry executives. "I would meet and greet all those important people and got the feel for that sort of thing," remembers Plank, the founder of sportswear maker Under Armour. He also had the example of his grandmother, a self-described "tough old broad" who outlived three husbands, got a real estate license to make ends meet, and accumulated more than a dozen properties in the posh Georgetown section of Washington by the time she died at age ninety-two.

Gyenes's grandfather on his mother's side was a Hungarian wine merchant and real estate investor. One of Paul Brown's grandfathers was a vest maker—the last one in America, he says; the other owned a hardware store. (Mark Brown, son of Paul of HearUSA, is a chip off the old block, an ocular plastic surgeon who has created a Web site called eyeplastics.com for the nation's 300 other ocular plastic surgeons. Mark helped create his five-man practice and hopes eventually to start a business to show doctors how to create practices.)

Pete Newman's grandfather on his mother's side sold refrigeration systems in Hawaii and had the brilliant idea of transporting Christmas trees to Hawaii from the mainland in refrigerated cargo containers.

Unfortunately, when the ships got there, a longshoremen's strike prevented the trees from being unloaded, and all the needles fell out. The grandfather became at that moment a lifelong, die-hard Republican, Newman says, hastening to add that he himself casts his lot with the Democrats.

David Weinstein of the Chicagoland Entrepreneurial Center, the only child of two psychologists, felt closest to his grandmother, who took over her husband's furniture business when he died and kept it thriving. "I used to sit and watch her deal with truckers," he says. "She'd pick up the phone and scream and swear at the Teamsters for not delivering a shipment on time. She taught me about customer service. I learned it is better to have repeat clients than to make a ton of money on one big deal."

Even parents or grandparents who pursued traditional careers made a habit of instilling creative thinking in their offspring. Newman's father, a history professor at Kent State University, spent ten years writing a controversial book about the rise of English nationalism that debunked a lot of prevailing theories. "From him I learned the value of debate and the power of an idea and the importance of talking about and fighting for ideas," he says.

Nadine Thompson's mother held a low-level job as a keypunch operator in a Canadian bank, but she drilled the notion into her kids' heads that economic salvation lay in starting their own businesses someday. "She told my brother and me over and over, 'You cannot be dependent on other people for a paycheck. You can't be dependent on white people,'" Thompson says. "She still talks about it every day. She says, 'I should have never worked for those white people at the Royal Bank, they just robbed me of all my time, this pension is nothing. Don't make the same mistakes I made, get your own business, get money in the bank. You should own two or three homes.' She says the same thing every day, every time she calls, all the time."

•   •   •

Many business pioneers speak of an extremely close relationship with one or both of their parents. A smaller number describe an aloof but exacting parent (usually a father) whom they are still trying to please even if he is in the grave. Yet others allude to ineffectual parenting that forced them to grapple with the hardscrabble world on their own.

Laura Gasparis Vonfrolio, who organizes seminars for nurses, idolized her father, a rough-hewn but bighearted Staten Island, New York, tavern owner. "He was my best friend," she says. "He was the best guy in the world, and I'm like him. I'd never last in anybody else's business. I'm too stubborn. I refuse to suck up." He was also "a real ball buster," she says. One day, around 1968, somebody robbed his bar and beat him up. The cops couldn't solve the case and told him to forget about it, but he became obsessed with tracking the guy down. And he did. He broke into the other man's house and found the money inside a toilet tank. He forced the miscreant to strip naked, tied him to the back of his Volkswagen, and made him run behind the car twelve miles to the police station.

Another time, an automobile mechanic forgot to reconnect the fuel hose in a routine checkup, and the car caught fire. The garage refused to pay for the damage, so her father had the wreck towed to the garage entrance to block vehicles from entering or leaving, placed a huge plywood lemon he had made next to it, and stood vigil over the scene all day.

Vonfrolio's generosity came from her father, she says. If he won at the races, he'd take his kids on walks through poor neighborhoods and hand out $50 bills to street people. "They'd cry and hug him," she recalls. "He got the biggest kick out of that." His name was Jimmy Vonfrolio, but his nickname was Jimmy Shorts, because he gave so much money away he was often short on cash. Only recently, Vonfrolio's sister met a woman at a party who recounted an incident thirty years earlier in which a stranger rushed up to her after she had crashed her car into a lamppost. He escorted her to a nearby bar, bought her a drink and comforted her, and then drove her home. A few days later, the man pulled up in front of her house in a new car and handed her the keys. She had never found out who the stranger was, the woman said, but he gave his name as Jimmy Shorts.

Lisa Helene Meiland says she and her sister, Lara, are "unbelievably close" to their parents. Their father, A. Daniel Meiland, today is the chairman of Egon Zehnder, a global headhunting firm. At age fourteen, he made $200,000 importing antiques from England to Denmark. In the army, he sold transistor radios to his fellow soldiers. On a trip to the United States with his new wife, he talked his way into the Harvard Business School even though he didn't have a B.A. After graduating, he started a soda bottling plant in England that failed, did stints at the McKinsey consulting group and the old Kidder Peabody securities firm, and joined Egon Zehnder in Brussels in 1977, rising quickly through the ranks. Over the years, he started a tool bit company in China with his brother that prospered until the government shut it down.

Lisa Helene Meiland calls her mother, an obstetrician-gynecologist who puts in seven days a week at her practice, the girls' inspiration. "To see my mother with patients, how her face lights up!" she says. "I've never seen anybody more tired or more happy."

Alex Lidow of International Rectifier says his aging father is his best friend. "We share everything about our lives," he says. "It's an unusual and extraordinary relationship and I'm very fortunate to have it." Peter Amico of Airtrax says his father was his "guiding principle" and the two were "extraordinarily close." Gupta, too, was "very close to my parents." Cameron Johnson, the Internet start-up meister, says of his father, "We're really close. I think that kind of closeness plays a big part in being an entrepreneur."

Mahoney of vFinance says he learned to be aggressive and focused from his mother. When he was a teenager, she kept her exercise bicycle in his bedroom closet, and every morning at 6:30 he would wake up to the *shumm, shumm, shumm* of the wheels as she pedaled and recited the rosary. He and his brothers sat around the dinner table in their underwear because she would make them wash their clothes at the sight of the slightest fleck. "Mom ran the finances of the family," Mahoney says. "I still think she was a loan shark, trying to collect money I didn't owe her."

. . .

Not everyone's reminiscences of parents are so warm and fuzzy. Newman says he is close to his parents (you have to be if you hit them up for seed money for your start-up, he quips), but he confesses he had a troubled relationship with them as a child. He was five when they got divorced, and fourteen when he moved out of his mother's house to stay with his dad, because he knew he needed tough love. "I learned that making the right decision for myself was more important than pleasing my mother," he concludes. "But that still ranks today as the hardest decision of my life."

For Thompson, just being on the phone with her mother today can be an ordeal. The older woman's admonitions for her to succeed have taken on a more hectoring tone as Thompson has moved up the small-business ladder. Her daughter is running a $16 million body care products company; why doesn't she have three homes? Why doesn't she have a written contract with her rich white partner spelling out her ownership stake? Over a Christmas dinner, the older woman asked her, "How can you be so smart and so stupid at the same time?" Thompson recalls. "That was really hurtful. I felt like I was three."

Bob Hillier of Hillier Architecture also still has a strained relationship with his father, a standoffish product of a British household. A physicist and a perfectionist, he was "never, never" satisfied with his son's accomplishments, no matter how hard the boy tried to please him. When he and a classmate were awarded the eighth-grade mathematics cup, the father told him it was a shame he had to share it.

Today, Hillier puts a positive spin on his dad's aloofness. "I'm afraid of failure," he says. "I think that comes from my father. But I think fear of failure is a positive force. You don't want to let anyone down. Not your clients, not yourself. You want to make your clients proud of you. In a way, your clients become your dad."

Some experts say the combination of a distant father and a nurturing mother is especially potent in awakening the leadership potential of their sons. "There is evidence that many successful male leaders had strong, supportive mothers and rather remote, absent fathers," Manfred F. R. Kets de Vries, a professor of leadership at France's INSEAD business school, told the *Harvard Business Review* in a 2004 interview. He cited Jack Welch, General Electric's former CEO; Richard Branson, chairman of Virgin Atlantic Airlines; and former president Bill Clinton. And Andrew Davidson, a writer for *Management Today* who spent ten years interviewing entrepreneurs, said in a 2001 article that he had "lost count of the times I have sat in a room with a successful man telling me how close he was to his mother."

In a few cases, miserable childhoods became the breeding grounds for entrepreneurs. Heagney's father browbeat him to work harder, calling him stupid and lazy. Rather than motiving his son, though, his admonitions had the opposite effect. Heagney wallowed in low self-esteem and recoiled from challenging the status quo until a college professor finally steered him in a new direction and he bloomed.

Ross Levin, president of Accredited Investors Inc., says his father was an alcoholic whose behavior has made him guarded toward other people to this day. But it taught him to fend for himself and adapt quickly to changing circumstances. He theorizes that alcoholism or some other disruptive illness in one's family background can be a harsh teacher of self-reliance.

Most small-business innovators, however, report that their fathers (and sometimes mothers) gave them a long leash to explore the limits of their capabilities. Levin says that whatever his father's addictions, he tried to send his son the message he could do anything he wanted to do.

"If you know your father supports you in everything you do, you're more likely to be a risk taker," Johnson says.

Newman's parents, both teachers, encouraged him and his sister to joust with them in the world of ideas. "I'd get a lecture from my father on the French Revolution while he was driving me to a girl's house for a Saturday night date," he recalls. "We debated intellectual issues for the fun of it. He'd take absurd positions just to force us to hone our arguing and logical skills."

The closer parents are to their children, the more likely the parents' go-get-'em impulses are to rub off on the kids. In Chapter 2, several entrepreneurs discussed how important integrity and compassion are to business success. Lidow says his father taught him those virtues by example. "He would literally drive 100 miles to return money to somebody because they gave him the wrong amount of change. Absolutely honest and honorable in everything he did."

Many entrepreneurs talk about how their parents drilled a work ethic into them. Amico says his father worked so hard he didn't know how to relax. Anderman of Ellie Mae says the hours his father put in at his dry cleaning business amounted to legal slavery. "He drummed it into you that you just have to work harder than anybody else, and study harder, and be more honest, and all of those hang-ups," Anderman recalls.

Heagney absorbed the work ethic of his father, who came to the New World at age fifteen. "He rode the rails; he was a semiprofessional boxer; he played semipro hockey; he worked on farms, in gold mines, in uranium mines," Heagney says. He told his son the best defense against poverty was always to hold down two jobs.

Hillier learned from his mother to work hard, take risks, and above all else keep the customer happy. "She always wanted to make a sale," he remembers. "If she were closing her shop at 6 and a customer came by and said he just remembered it was his wedding anniversary and he needed a dozen roses, she'd open the shop back up."

• • •

What about the personalities of entrepreneurs themselves? How did Johnson, for example, concoct sophisticated moneymaking schemes while still in grade school? Certainly, the Johnson clan's business history set the stage for him to act out his impulses. When she was fourteen, after her father died, his mother helped run the family's food distribution business. At eighteen, she bought her mother out. For more than a decade, she managed the company, increasing its annual revenues to $200 million, before selling it to U.S. Food Service.

His father, meantime, inherited a Ford dealership in Roanoke, Virginia, which was started by his great-grandfather during the Depression, and built it into the biggest in his part of the state.

Young Cameron absorbed his parents' business smarts almost by osmosis. "Dad raised me in the car business," he says. "He and my mother would travel for business meetings when I was five or six and take me with them." He was around adults so much, he says, he began to talk like them.

But while he acknowledges his parents' influence, he doesn't think it explains his risk-taking, seize-the-day personality. "It wasn't a plan I devised when I was five," he explains. "It wasn't something my parents pushed me into." Rather, it was an inclination that bubbled within him from his earliest memory. Nature or nurture? Probably both, in Johnson's case. Nurture was the soil that allowed nature to bloom.

Like most of his innovative confreres, Johnson had a gift for salesmanship. At age seven, he peddled tomatoes grown on his family's farm door-to-door, charging $1 per tomato and refusing to budge when housewives complained the price was too high. In the fourth grade, closing a deal became a compulsion. Selling raffle tickets for a school fund-raiser, he roamed his father's dealership and the travel agency where his mother worked, hitting up everybody in sight. He pestered relatives, neighbors, friends, strangers on the street. "I became obsessive," he recalls. "I ended up selling more tickets than anyone in the entire school, which went through the twelfth grade."

Still just seven, he started a lemonade stand and drove his neighborhood rivals out of business by adding cookies, brownies, and muffins to the menu. As the weather turned cold, he opened a store called Rainy Day Sales in his basement, charging friends a commission to unload their old toys and knickknacks.

Oddly, since most of his ventures were ultimately spawned on the Internet, he got a slow start in computers because his private elementary school lacked them. But when he got a desktop computer for Christmas at age nine, he made up for lost time. Showing the tenacity that is a hallmark of successful entrepreneurs, he went to his room and clicked away for ten hours straight, until his mother ordered him to bed.

Within weeks, he launched his first Internet start-up, Cheers and Tears. Using a software program, he designed birthday cards, business cards, wedding invitations, and the like and sold them to relatives and family friends.

"All my friends got allowances, but not me," he says. "My folks said there was no need, I was making so much money on my own."

Networking, a talent helpful in any occupation but crucial for survival in the small-business world, came naturally to him. Barely had he gotten Cheers and Tears up and running than he finagled a red-carpet welcome to New York City from real estate mogul Donald Trump.

His parents had been planning a trip to Manhattan and told Cameron they would be staying at the Plaza, then owned by Trump. The boy immediately scoured business publications to find out more about the developer. "I said, 'Wow. Someday I want to be like him,'" he recalls. "I wrote him a letter, saying I was nine, I had my own business, and I wanted to meet him." Trump was out of town when the Johnsons arrived, but he had instructed his staff to put them in the suite where the sequel to *Home Alone* had been filmed. He also had a letter waiting for Cameron congratulating him on his exploits, and arranged a private tour of FAO Schwarz, the famous toy store on the other side of Fifth Avenue.

Fast-forward three years. Johnson is twelve. It is the early days of eBay, and he spots an anomaly: Some items are selling on the Internet at huge markups from the retail price. It is the height of the Beanie Baby craze, and collectors are bidding hundreds of dollars for some of the dolls, which cost maybe $5 in stores. It happens that Johnson's five-year-old sister has a collection of twenty Beanie Babies. He pays her $100 for them and resells them for $1,000 on eBay.

"She couldn't have been happier, and neither could I," he says.

Johnson's young mind churned. He could try to buy up the Beanie Baby hoards of his sister's friends, but supply would be limited and word might get out of what he was up to. Lightbulb: Go to the source. He bought and sold secondhand Beanie Babies on the Internet. He also became an Internet retailer for the makers of three other plush bean-filled dolls. They didn't ask about his age. He filled out the applications, giving his name, address, credit card number (the credit card came with his checking account), and an explanation of how he planned to market the product.

He ordered thousands of Beanie Babies at $2.50 each and sold them at $5 through beaniebabywholesale.com and cheersandtears.com, as well as to neighbors and friends. He became the number-two Beanie Baby retailer on the Internet, he says, with 5,000 dolls in stock at any given time. He would box forty or more orders a day, a couple hundred Beanie Babies, often with his mother's help.

"In the morning, I'd have everything laid out," he explains. "I'd have boxes everywhere, the Priority Mail boxes I got from the post office, with the invoices and Beanie Babies to be put in them. Once I got home, I'd package them, address them, put them in two or three big black garbage bags, and take them to the post office to mail them. Mom had to drive me."

The checks poured in. The first year he made a profit of $50,000; the next year it was a bit more. His parents joked that he should start thinking about his retirement. He incorporated the company.

He was now thirteen.

Next came MyEZMail.com, a free e-mail forwarding service for kids that concealed their real e-mail address from the sender. That was followed by SurfingPrizes.com, described in Chapter 1, which paid Internet users willing to put up with endless banner advertisements to surf the Web. At its peak, it attracted $15,000 in ad revenue per day, but Johnson and his two teenage partners shut it down because it required more work than they had anticipated and they had a lot of homework.

He became famous. He gave speeches to high school students, and he flew to Japan to join the advisory board of a Japanese learning center called Future Kids.

At sixteen, he took over the Web site of his dad's Ford dealership. Sales boomed. He started Zablo.com to maintain the Web sites of other dealerships across the country and give them advice on how to sell cars over the Internet. The company was bringing in more than $15,000 a month before he sold it in 2005.

That same year, he had another brainstorm: Gift certificates are a pain in the neck. They are showered on people who don't want them, all $40 billion a year worth of them, by one estimate. They languish in drawers while their unredeemed value nestles comfortably on the bottom line of the issuers. So Johnson started CertificateSwap.com to let people stuck with gift certificates they didn't want sell them at a discount to people who did, with a small commission going to him. Venture capitalists liked the concept so much they invested $10 million in it.

• • •

Few entrepreneurs can claim such illustrious childhood careers. But most did show flashes of originality and independent-mindedness that presaged big things.

At age eleven, Paul Brown, chairman of HearUSA, made birdhouses from scrap lumber, sold them for $4, and then supplied his customers with birdseed. He also peddled stretch socks, then a novelty, door to door. (His son Mark, as a freshman in high school, started a local car-washing business called the Gleam Team that was so successful he printed up business cards and hired other kids to do much of the work.)

Herbert Jian and his brother ran a clandestine rabbit business to help with the family finances, even though any form of capitalist enterprise was strictly forbidden in Maoist China. "We didn't put a sign out in front of our house, Rabbits for Sale," he says. "It was all by word of mouth."

Hillier sold Siamese fighting fish, known as bettas, which he bred in an alcove of his mother's flower shop, to Princeton University students, who would bet on which of two males would win a battle to the death. The fish fights swept the campus, and to fill the surge in orders, Hillier took the train to New York City with containers of water to stock up on bettas. He paid $1 each for them and resold them for $4. "A fair markup for a perishable product," he judges. In all, he made $3,500, enough to cover half the tuition his father insisted he pay at the Lawrenceville School, where his mother wanted him to go.

Herro showed the same sort of ingenuity in one venture after another. At a doughnut shop where he worked, he helped himself to the doughnuts that were thrown out each night and sold them at school the next day for a quarter apiece. At another job as cashier at a local pharmacy, he started a side business right at the counter, selling trinkets that he bought in bulk and keeping the profits, which dwarfed his wages. His boss caught him and threatened to fire him, thinking Herro had been dipping into the till, but when he learned what was really going on, he relented—on one condition. "I learned a lesson on distribution channels," Herro says. "The store wanted its cut."

Like many boys, he had a paper route, but he showed unusual doggedness by sticking with it for six years so that he could buy a car when he turned sixteen. And not just any car, but a mint-condition 1966 Mustang to which he added sixteen-inch rims and air shocks. "My buddies were driving around these $300 beaters and I roll up in this $4,000 classic," he says with satisfaction.

He also organized a high school band called Wicked Romance that gained a reputation as the coolest group around without ever playing a gig. With their long, bleached hair, the members developed a cult following among the freshmen and sophomores, and when word got out they would be holding a concert on a farm on the edge of town, charging $2 for admission and beer, 600 kids showed up.

So did thirty squads of cops. The kids headed for the hills before a note was played, and in the ensuing melee, Herro and his buddies, dressed in spandex and leg warmers, quietly drove away from the scene in his mother's staid Honda, with $1,200 tucked safely in a box and their two kegs of beer intact.

"Our legendary status went through the roof after that," he says. "Everybody now considered us absolutely the best band of all. But we had never played a lick. And on top of that, we were really terrible."

He and a buddy formed another band in college called Simon Barnsinister after the *Underdog* cartoon character who wanted to destroy the world. They wore long spiked hair and skin-tight jeans and looked like "freaks of nature," Herro says. By their junior year, they were packing the house wherever they played, doing several performances a week at $600 a shot. Showing a flair for marketing, they recruited student bodyguards to add glamour and edginess to their act even though their audiences were quite tame. "The bodyguards got in free and thought it was cool to be up there with us," he recalls.

Mark Hughes, founder of Buzzmarketing, traces his business roots to the time he earned four sandwiches for cleaning up the trash at a dog show at the age of eight. When he was eleven, he started investing in stocks, making a small bundle in Chrysler and A. H. Robins. But the endless hours he put in at his father's chain of weekly newspapers on Cape Cod from the age of ten onward almost turned him off to the idea of running his own small business.

"I'd get dragged off at 5 A.M. to stuff papers and load them," he recalls. "On weekends, I'd work in the office, dropping the ceiling, laying down carpet, painting the walls. I was an assistant pressman. I took photographs. I did marketing. It was all-consuming. I remember sitting at the dinner table and thinking, 'All we ever do, all we talk about, is newspapers, newspapers, newspapers. I want a life. I want to be able to practice soccer like a normal kid.'"

But the DNA was too strong to allow for normality. In college, where he held down simultaneous jobs as a dishwasher, convenience store clerk, and security guard, Hughes says, "The entrepreneurial synapses and roots started to take shape." In his second year, he took charge of his fraternity's recruiting "rush" with stunts that ranged from putting out a tabloid newspaper with photos "showing us drinking beer and surrounded by gorgeous chicks at a barbecue" to renting planes with promotional banners to fly over football games.

Myke Templeton, the Kentucky pastor, bought calves at the veal market when he was in fifth grade, fattening them up and selling them for a profit of $80 or more. When a bull calf caught distemper and died, he jokes, "It took me a day to get over the fact I had lost my cattle empire."

When the Meiland sisters were just four, their father gave them written tests to "make our minds more creative," Lisa Helene says. As little girls, they set up "shops" in their Bronxville, New York, home to sell used belongings to their friends. At ten, they started a babysitting business, plastering flyers all over the neighborhood. At thirteen, they cleaned their mother's Manhattan office twice a week for $15. And, still in their twenties, they started their bridal shop.

Gupta didn't start any moneymaking ventures as a boy—that sort of thing was frowned on by his highbrow parents—but he was always poking around to see how things worked.

"I was very creative; I had an inventive zeal," he says. "I was always making things from kits or from scratch." One of his grade-school buddies told him it was possible to build a "magic lantern" slide projector from a shoe box, a lens, and a lightbulb. He had no manual to figure out how to do that; all he had was a photograph of a slide projector in a magazine advertisement. Nevertheless, he got a shoe box and put a lens in the front, a slide in the middle, and a bulb at the back. But the image came out not much bigger than the slide itself.

He was too young to have any notion of optics or lighting, but he became obsessed with figuring out the solution. He spent hours each day adjusting the size of the hole, the placement of the magnifying glass, and the position of the box.

Finally, he noticed that the photo of the projector showed a funnel sticking out. "I said to myself, 'What is that?'" Gupta recalls. "Suddenly, I realized you have to have a funnel outside the box to manually move the magnifying glass back and forth, like a zoom lens. So I created one and experimented. When it finally worked, it was so amazing."

He also made a paddlewheel boat, using primitive tools and following instructions in an English manual to cobble together wood, copper tubing, a rubber band, and a candle for creating steam. "I didn't even know what copper tubing was," he notes. "I was all on my own, hammering away with a hammer." Later, when he was twelve, he made a telegraph set, learned Morse code, and sent messages to his friends.

•   •   •

That impulse to tinker, almost as much as the talent for spotting opportunity and the gift for salesmanship, is a common theme running throughout the childhoods of successful businesspeople. Lidow helped build an electric car in high school. "We had to take a car and basically weld in an electric motor and build a motor drive and install it," he recalls. He drove it for several years and, even though it smelled of battery acid and had a lot of other quirks, took girls out on dates in it.

James Poss might be considered the princeling of tinkerers. "From the age of eight, I was constantly in our basement workshop making and breaking things, taking things apart: toys, appliances, anything I could get my hands on," he remembers. He collected batteries and motors of every stripe. He built crossbows, battery-powered fans, model planes, and rockets from kits. He would mix and match the rocket parts and try experiments. He sent a rocket up with a load of rocks and rigged another so that it would take a photo of the ground at the highest point in its trajectory.

When he was a junior in high school, he invented something he called Shark's Teeth, a multilayered sanding pad. Once you wore one layer of sandpaper down, you'd tear it off and there would be a sharp new sheet underneath. He went to the patent section of the Boston Public Library to see if anyone else had claimed the concept. Eventually, he discovered 3M had. "It was for floor sanding, but it was an all-inclusive patent," he says. "So I let it drop."

In high school, he got into renewable energy. In physics, instead of taking the final exam, he built a three-foot-long car that ran off a rotating flywheel. Halfway through his freshman year at Duke, he came up with an idea for making an energy generator from the tides. "There would be two dams, like two locks, and you would control the flow of water through turbines that would supply an energy grid," he explains.

He tried to get Duke's technology office to help him file for a patent but gave up after realizing that a prototype would cost millions of dollars and the design might be covered by other patents anyway.

Martin Klein, the CEO of Electro Energy Inc., fixed bikes and autos, monkeyed around with Erector sets and electric trains, and read popular science magazines. Like so many aspiring capitalists, he also had a newspaper route, but like Herro's, his had a twist. His subscribers were all teachers and administrators at his elementary school, and instead of plodding through snow and rain on a bike he was able to deliver the papers in a few quick minutes.

Luke Visconti, the founder of DiversityInc, did him one better on his newspaper route—he actually fired his worst customers. "I would cut off people who didn't tip well, just stop delivering the paper," he says. Visconti also figured out a way to ski for free—by organizing ski trips for a guy who chartered them.

As social chairman of his fraternity, he scouted out all the other parties on campus and took note of what worked and what didn't. "I did disco parties," he recounts. "I didn't like disco, but the girls sure did. Our parties were a huge hit." In contrast, his successor as social director was a Grateful Dead enthusiast whose parties ended up as five stoned guys sitting around staring into space.

Another time, realizing he was being overcharged by a beer distributor, Visconti enlisted ten other fraternities to buy the brew in bulk. The distributor caved. "Somebody called me on the phone, all hush-hush, and said he wanted to make me happy," he recalls. "He said they would cut prices for me and gave me a number to call any time of day or night. He said they'd make sure a keg was delivered at 2 A.M. if necessary if we ran out of beer."

Visconti's background makes a good argument for the existence of an entrepreneurial gene. His parents had grown up in poverty. His mother told how her Greek parents had fled their home with a chicken still in the oven when Turks attacked their village. "There was an atmosphere in our house that whatever you had could be taken away from you at a moment's notice," he says.

His parents pleaded with him to enter a "safe" profession such as teaching or accounting, but the thought put him in a suicidal mood. They had a horror of risk, Visconti says, while "I lived for it."

Like Gupta, Gary Doan, the founder of Intradyn, was always a fiddler as a child, experimenting with his chemistry set, undertaking endless electronic and science projects, and developing film in his own darkroom. He and a friend made muskets with real gunpowder and built a bomb with fertilizer that they ignited with a cherry bomb attached to a very long fuse, the same basic design as the explosives used in Oklahoma City. They blew a six-foot hole into the ground in the woods across the street from where he lived and took off like bandits.

Later, in high school, he got a job at a depository inside a Sears store that sold damaged or returned merchandise to employees. He kept a sharp eye out for bargains. Whenever he saw an item that was grossly underpriced, he would buy it and resell it at a profit.

At age ten, Eller started a paper route (yes, that again) and built it to 500 customers, more than any other kid in Tucson. When he moved to Miami in the seventh grade, he made the front page of the *Miami Herald* not only for having the biggest paper route in the city, but also for being its youngest paperboy.

It wasn't until Eller went to college that he blossomed into a full-fledged entrepreneur, however. A kitchen worker at a sorority house, he led a successful campaign for higher wages for the kitchen help and later charged sororities to send replacements for no-shows. He made a bundle at football games, selling ads for the program that he hired students to sell and even leasing homeowners' driveways to rent out as parking space to fans.

Peter Gyenes's main push in high school was helping his father maintain his textile concern, which in truth was more of a hope than a reality. The elder Gyenes's wife was his only employee, and most of the business activity took place in their Queens home. Gyenes acted as his translator, listening to him dictate letters in Hungarian and typing them out in English.

With money tight, the teenager found a profitable outlet for his creative energy: pool. By the time he was sixteen, the game had become a huge part of his life. He played nine-ball for $2 a game, a lot of money in those days, and won enough to pay for cigarettes, gas, and Saturday night dates. ("Of course I smoked," he says. "How could you hustle pool and not smoke?") In 1966, he and an equally broke friend drove across the country, sleeping in their car and shooting pool at truck stops to subsidize breakfasts of eggs and waffles.

His father's struggle to stay solvent had a happy ending. His initial effort to import fabric for women's sportswear from Europe flopped. Then he tried his hand at Japanese metallic yarn just as the market for it was turning white-hot. In a three-month period, he made several hundred thousand dollars. Today, two decades after his death, Gyenes's older brother keeps the venture going so that his mother will have a place to spend her days. At the age of ninety, she still shows up four days a week, answering the phone, talking with truckers and distributors, and writing letters on her Selectric typewriter.

From the time he was twelve, Charlie Horn, the founder of the Promirus Group, a Tucson provider of prescription drug discount programs, sold replacement filters for furnaces at the onset of winter. He would buy them for $2 at the hardware store, go around the neighborhood knocking on doors, and install them for $5. The wives were thrilled because their husbands had usually not gotten around to the task.

He also sold Christmas cards door-to-door in the fall and seeds in the spring. He did some mowing but not a lot—there was too much labor involved for the money he made. It was an important lesson about the virtues of salesmanship that would serve him well in his adult years.

SALESMANSHIP

If you can't grasp the magic of marking up prices as high as the consumer will tolerate, you're probably not an entrepreneur by nature. Maybe Horn should have charged $8 for the furnace filters; after all, Hillier bumped up the price of the bettas he sold fourfold. Lidow tells the story of how his father, an aspiring engineer educated in Berlin in the 1930s, blew up a small piece of equipment during an electronics experiment in a laboratory. The rule, just as in pottery stores today, was: You break it, you pay for it. The device cost more than a month's rent. "My father told himself, 'That's the kind of business I want to be in, to be able to make something cheaply and sell it for a lot of money,'" Lidow says.

The passion for salesmanship (a compulsion of the successful entrepreneur that is treated in greater depth elsewhere in this book) and the related joy of marking up prices beyond all reason first captivated Under Armour's Kevin Plank when he was thirteen. His brother Scott had just returned from a summer of studying Spanish in Guatemala and brought back 2,000 woven bracelets for which he had paid $50, or 2½ cents each. He recruited Kevin and another brother to accompany him to a Grateful Dead concert with a plan to sell the bracelets for $3 each, or two for $5, a markup of 10,000 percent. The threesome took a subway to the show and split up at 10 A.M., agreeing to meet at 1 P.M.

When they reassembled, one brother confessed he had sold just two bracelets and given the others away because he felt guilty about the price. The other had sold a handful and pocketed $80. "It was then I knew I was a born salesman," Plank says. "I had been sold out for the past hour and a half and had $680 on me. And I said, 'I'm not about to split it with you, either.' I loved hustling those bracelets."

The success of that excursion propelled him into a career of peddling T-shirts at concerts in his high school and early college days. He would have them emblazoned with crazy designs or the name of the band that was playing for $2.50 each and resell them for $15. The exercise taught him several business lessons:

- You can make a lot of money selling to people who are having a good time.
- Limit your inventory and unload it as quickly as possible, because competitors will move in to fill a supply gap and undersell you, with a snowballing effect that in short order will wipe out your profit margin.
- Pay attention to quality. Twice he misspelled the names of bands and was left with mounds of unwanted T-shirts.

But such missteps were few. Plank estimates he made $1,000 to $2,000 per show and cleared $50,000 by the time he abandoned the scene—for the rose business. In his freshman year in college, he noticed that florists were charging $80 for a dozen roses as Valentine's Day neared. A wholesaler he found in the Yellow Pages quoted him a price of $3 a dozen. It was time to undercut the competition.

Plank bought a small truckload of roses and a stack of boxes for a quarter each. He commissioned an artist to sketch cartoons of Calvin and Hobbes on a roses theme and to plaster flyers all over campus advertising roses for $25 a dozen (cheap). As the orders came in, his girlfriend (now his wife) helped package the flowers. He paid students to deliver them. He sold out within three days. His take was $2,400.

His sophomore year he sold 250 dozen roses and leased a credit card processing machine for cash-strapped students. His junior year he sold 600 dozen in a single day. His senior year, he put ads in the *Washington Post* and the *Baltimore Sun* and sold 1,176 dozen roses in one day, for a profit of almost $24,000. By then, he had seven phone lines, five customer service representatives, a dozen people assembling the flowers, and forty-six drivers.

Thompson, too, was always selling something, starting in grade school with homemade cupcakes (using her own special recipe), West Indian fudge, and sugar cakes, graduating in high school to Avon beauty products and Regal Ware household items.

Heagney didn't show much business sparkle as a kid, although he got his first job at 11 by lying about his age to obtain a paper route with the *Evening Bulletin* in Philadelphia. But one galactic burst of energy hinted at things to come. Just as Johnson, the guy who notched up a dozen dot-coms before his twenty-first birthday, went on a frenzy of selling raffle tickets for a school fund-raiser, leaving all the other students in the dust, and Plank, who sold out the Guatemalan bracelets at a rock concert, Heagney blew the competition away. When it came to collecting clothes for a Boy Scout clothing drive, the other troopers hit up their parents and next-door neighbors. But Heagney banged on doors for blocks around, unable to stop himself, until he had filled 250 large brown paper bags.

His passion for selling awakened him to possibilities he hadn't thought existed. "That probably gave me my first inkling that I was an entrepreneur," he said. "I just loved going out and selling something."

Vonfrolio gave the first glimmers of her business acumen as a girl of nine, loading up beer and soft drinks from her bar owner father's stash onto her little red wagon and selling them to a crew of city workers repaving her street. At twelve, she held a carnival in her backyard that made her $2,000. In high school, as captain of the cheerleaders, she figured out a surefire way to raise money to replace their ratty uniforms:

selling sandwiches they made at home to students starving for something besides cafeteria fare.

As a teenager, Weinstein became de facto manager of a hot dog stand, working six hours after school and eight hours on Saturdays and Sundays. Chicago's annual gay parade went right past the stand one year, and he came up with the idea of selling pink lemonade to the marchers. The gambit netted $2,000; his boss was so delighted he gave him a $500 bonus.

Some entrepreneurs insist they showed no special spark as kids. But they tell stories that suggest otherwise. Anderman peddled Christmas cards door-to-door as a Boy Scout. "I sold hundreds of boxes," he says. "Hundreds. So many more than anybody else it was crazy." The magnetism of his personality got him elected head of his grade-school class, and he won more votes than there were classmates in the race for crossing-guard captain at P.S. 41 in downtown Manhattan.

Similarly, though he shrugs at queries about his entrepreneurial boyhood, Michael Huddy of International Barrier Technology started a movement at Lake Superior State for students to have a greater say in campus affairs, got himself elected president, and persuaded the school to finance the organization. "I was always a leader," he says.

In Newman's academic family, ideas trumped salesmanship. So, instead of taking apart the toaster ("Dad knew I'd screw it up, and he didn't have much interest in that sort of thing, either," he says), he engaged in more cerebral pursuits, writing movie reviews and editorials for his high school newspaper and, after his senior year, a social history of the Ravenna, Ohio, weapons arsenal.

At Kent State, disturbed by all the soda cans he saw in trash cans, he started a recycling program for a cluster of three dorms. The local fire department provided the receptacles, and he lugged the bags to the pickup center.

When he was eleven, Levin rode through his neighborhood on a bike, knocking on doors to raise money for George McGovern, the Democratic presidential candidate. He collected $20 in a jar, rode to his town's McGovern headquarters, and plopped it on a table.

The sheer diversity of the jobs he held working his way through college hinted at his active imagination: sorting mail at an ad agency, selling cemetery plots by phone, filling out charts in a hospital, weighing garbage trucks, selling shoes at Dayton's. One summer, he and his wife started a business called Post Camp to watch kids between summer camp and the start of school. They made more money in two weeks than they had as camp counselors over the previous ten weeks.

Liz Ryan, too, never considered herself an entrepreneur in her younger years. The sixth of eight children, she had no interest in business but pegged herself as an actress and musician. She cut high school classes in Montclair, New Jersey, to go into New York City for off-Broadway auditions, an act of bravado that foreshadowed her future risk taking. "They'd ask my age and chase me away," she recalls. "Once, I sang and danced for a part in the chorus line, and the guy asked me, 'Don't you babysit for me?' The answer was yes, I did."

But from her elementary school days, the juices were bubbling. She organized carnivals and musicals in her backyard and created haunted houses in her garage. In the sixth grade, she and a friend started an art school for preschoolers. They repotted spider plants and sold them on their block from a red wagon. Ryan rang the bell at Christmas for the Salvation Army and got paid $25 by Planters Peanuts to cavort in a Mr. Peanut suit in front of the local A&P.

"Always some crazy scheme," she says. "We'd do everything, just do everything. Me and opportunity, you know: Jump in there. So there was no aversion to trying something silly or offbeat. But it was just, 'What the heck—let's do this and see if anything happens,' which is still of course exactly what we're doing."

Hard work is another thread woven into entrepreneurs' youth. Macchia says he has never been without work since his first job as a caddy at the Long Shore Country Club in Westport, Connecticut, when he was twelve. At fifteen, he sold ice cream at the state's first Dairy Queen and later unloaded boxes and sorted mail at a Sears & Roebuck store. In college, he worked weekends at Pepperidge Farm and held down construction jobs in the summers.

• • •

So which is it that makes for a successful entrepreneur? Genes or family? Nature or nurture?

Not surprisingly, the experts take a nuanced position on the matter. They remind me a bit of Franklin D. Roosevelt's comment about economists: He wished he could find one with only one arm, because all the others he had met were forever saying, "On the one hand this; on the other hand that."

If I were to summarize the ruminations of specialists on the matter, it would be that while there is no such thing as an entrepreneurial gene, there is such a thing as genetic predisposition to certain behaviors that might be considered entrepreneurial. Those who lack that predilection may never become true entrepreneurs. Those who have it might or might not, depending on their childhood environment. If they grow up around small-business role models and are encouraged to pursue creative activities, they are more likely to strike out on their own. If they grow up in households that value security and predictability, and attend schools that squelch creativity and encourage conformity, they probably won't. However, a few hardy souls overcome even those obstacles, so powerful are their take-charge inclinations.

"Entrepreneurship is intrinsic," says Frank Landsberger, the former University of Cambridge professor. "The person who wonders whether he is an entrepreneur isn't an entrepreneur."

Carl Schramm, chief executive of the Kauffman Foundation in Kansas City, agrees that either you've got what it takes or you don't. "Some people can see the opportunity just around the corner—that something that needs to be done—and others don't," he says.

You can't teach somebody who isn't an innovator to become one. What you can do is teach the right skills to those whose instincts have been stifled, they say. "An analogy to art schools is appropriate," Landsberger remarks. "They don't create artists; they teach natural artists, the Rembrandts of the world, about brushes and paint and style."

Schramm recalls a comment that Neal Patterson, the head of the

Cerner Corporation in Kansas City, once made to him about entrepreneurs: "We're all mutants. We were all born this way. We can't help ourselves."

Entrepreneurs tend to recognize their own kind almost instantly at cocktail parties and other gatherings, Schramm says. "They're like politicians that way. They gravitate towards one another, and they talk with one another in ways the rest of us don't understand."

Dr. Kerry Sulkowicz, the psychoanalyst and founder of the Boswell Group, comes down on the side of nurture as a predictor of entrepreneurial success but thinks the influence of entrepreneurial parents or other authority figures is only one factor. He sides with Levin of Accredited Investors in theorizing that the trauma of growing up in a dysfunctional household run by an alcoholic or otherwise mentally impaired parent is an even more potent force.

Guy Kawasaki, the venture capitalist, says it is a logical fallacy to assign a set of "traits" that set off entrepreneurs from everybody else because the traits lie dormant in all of us and flower in those who (a) take the plunge and (b) actually succeed.

"The reason people believe entrepreneurs are born is they look at people like Richard Branson, Steve Jobs, Bill Gates, and they say: 'They have all these entrepreneurial traits, they must have been born that way,'" he remarks. "I would argue that the fact that they got traction enabled these traits to be developed and perfected.

"Within reasonable bounds," Kawasaki says, "anybody can be an entrepreneur. All it takes is serendipity."

William J. Dennis, the National Federation of Independent Business's senior researcher, says the theory that entrepreneurship is genetic "has been largely discredited." And yet it is true, Dennis says, that some kids just seem to have a knack for it. He rattles off examples he has seen up close, including the twelve-year-old who patented a sprinkler in the shape of a horseshoe that you could put around a sapling, or the boy of sixteen who installed phones in people's homes and was so successful he formed a company and built up a staff of forty within two years.

What explains that? Nature? Nurture? "I do believe we may well find a combination of genes that makes people more outgoing, perhaps, or gives them more energy," says William D. Bygrave, the Babson College professor of entrepreneurial studies.

The problem, as Judith Cone, the Kauffman Foundation vice president, sees it, is that the creativity that most people are born with is stifled at an early age. But those impulses can be reawakened later in life, Cone believes, especially by desperation. "When there are mass layoffs, the number of entrepreneurial start-ups tends to increase," she says. "People just learn how to do it. Not long ago in Kansas City, Sprint laid off a lot of staff, many of them senior people. We put on a training program for them to learn how to be entrepreneurs, and some amazing companies have come out of that."

A world-renowned liver specialist at the Kansas University Medical Center decided to start a business around a patent that he had been awarded and took a crash course at Kauffman on how to do it, Cone noted. He later said that for all his scientific expertise, he had never felt so stupid in all his life as when he walked into the first class. "I never thought I could do it," she says he told her. "But I did, and I'm actually quite good at running a company."

However, Cone concedes, even though some people *can* master the entrepreneurial art, most can't. In fact, all the experts are pretty much in agreement on that. Bygrave recalls a student who took his course and thanked him afterward for making him realize he wasn't cut out for the risk-taking life. What he wanted for his family was what his schoolteacher parents had given him: a predictable life and long summer vacations.

In other words, you've got to have the right stuff.

Genes or family? Entrepreneurs themselves lean toward the DNA theory.

"Competitiveness is in my genes," Gupta says. For reasons of political ideology and tradition, his kin shunned business, but almost everybody in the family showed the fierce single-mindedness that is a trademark of entrepreneurs, rising to positions of prominence in academia, journalism, show business, photography, politics, and the military.

"I can't prove that great entrepreneurs are born, not made, but that is what my gut tells me," Eller says. "I'm not sure you can teach it. What you can do is give a set of tools to young people who think they are and unlock their entrepreneurial energy."

CHAPTER 4

Turning on a Dime

Entrepreneurs are nimble. They dodge and weave, backtrack and plunge ahead, make stupid moves and mount surprising recoveries. They are famous for turning on a well-known American coin.

But what really defines them is less their agility than the cast of mind that experts call a "tolerance for ambiguity"—a willingness to plunge into the marketplace and weave their way through its confusions, contradictions, and blurred boundaries.

"You can spot it every time," says William D. Bygrave, who teaches courses on entrepreneurship at Babson College in Massachusetts and who has a long small-business history of his own. "They see angles in every messy situation. They have untidy desks, whereas the accountant type has to have everything completely wrapped up. Tolerance for ambiguity is the one thing I look for in my students. They have that flexibility and opportunity, recognition that is going to save them and set them back upon their horse."

Dr. Bygrave recalls teaching a course a few years back to students with backgrounds in science and engineering and observing how they waited expectantly for him to provide the correct answers to the problems that cropped up in case studies.

"But in really great case teaching you deliberately leave them with what I call 'ambiguity space,'" Dr. Bygrave says. "You don't spell out everything for them. You let them wrestle with it. We want to see how far they can go wrestling with this ambiguity and develop their own models."

Dr. Bygrave began his professional life as a physicist in Britain and says he was discombobulated when his "Newtonian universe" of precise calculations gave way to quantum mechanics and its claim that the most physics can do is predict the probability of outcomes. Einstein himself found quantum theory so unsettling that he fought it for years.

"I think physics is great training for being an entrepreneur," Dr. Bygrave says, "because suddenly there is no absolutely right answer."

He tells the story of two students, Ross and Mario, who started a travel agency on the Babson campus. One Saturday night, Ross called him to announce in a voice quivering with anger that he was bailing out of the business. He just couldn't take it anymore, he said; here he was in his room, trying to catch up with all the paperwork, and Mario was out partying! "He wanted everything tied up and neatly packaged, and so he went off and got into production management with a big corporation," Dr. Bygrave notes.

Mario, by contrast, stuck with the business, saving it from disaster time and again by superhuman bursts of activity, then neglecting it for a while until a new crisis arose. On one occasion, government safety regulators grounded a charter airplane that Mario was using to ferry students south during the spring break, and the young man told his mentor he would never recover from the financial setback and bad publicity. "I said, 'Mario, you're going to bounce back like a rubber ball,'" Dr. Bygrave remembers. "'I've seen you do this over and over again.' And he did."

Finally, Mario cashed out, selling the agency to an Internet company for stock. Shortly thereafter, the dot-com crash wiped out his newfound wealth. He then repurchased his old firm for almost nothing and got it on a growth path. He recently sold it for $40 million.

The stories entrepreneurs themselves tell about hacking their way through the underbrush give an inkling of what it takes to succeed in a world without clear pathways and bristling with predators. One lesson is that if you want to take charge of your destiny, you had better be ready to switch directions at a moment's notice.

Consider an extreme case. Pete Newman, the founder of Gotham Software Inc., had been putting in sixty-hour weeks, first to raise money and then, on a shoestring budget, to develop software to help investment banks put together bond offerings more efficiently. So what if he was little more than a one-man show? "Nobody else was doing this," he says. By being the first to fill the gap, Gotham would grow quickly and carve out a nice niche in the financial-services industry. That was the plan.

In November 2001, unfortunately for Newman, an investment banker who was working for him came across the Web site of a new company called i-Deal LLC. It was doing what Gotham was doing but had a huge competitive advantage in that it was jointly owned by Thomson Financial, one of the biggest players in the municipal bond industry, Smith Barney, Merrill Lynch, and Microsoft. Newman knew he was beaten, but he didn't waste more than two seconds fretting about that.

"My first thought was, 'Oh, no. Our window of opportunity is gone,'" he says. "My second thought was, 'You can't turn back now. You have to figure out how to get them to buy you. Transfer the risk and get the payoff.'"

Starting on that day in the fall of 2001, Newman directed all his energies to making his software more attractive to i-Deal LLC. He monitored the company and its products closely and tailored his own to mesh with theirs. He got one of the members of its advisory board, the chief executive of Bond Hub, a respected online bond trading firm, to put in a good word for him.

He made formal contact one year later, holding two sales meetings, one organized by an investment bank in Dallas, the other by an investment bank in New York. "Both banks told i-Deal, 'You should buy these guys,'" Newman says. "Then, i-Deal took a hell of a long time to make a decision. I had to hammer them, bug them to get them to pay attention to what we were doing." He finally made the sale: a $225,000 interest-free loan to pay back investors and creditors at 10 percent a year, a revenue share of the profits of future sales of the software, and business support and resources from i-Deal to continue building the product. He and his business partner also got guaranteed employment with stock options. While not exactly fulfilling the dream he once had, he says, the deal "beat going bankrupt like nine out of ten small businesses do."

* * *

Newman's reinvention of Gotham Software Inc. was a classic entrepreneurial shuffle through the shoals of ambiguity, according to Judith Cone, vice president of research at the Ewing Marion Kauffman Foundation in Kansas City, which studies and promotes entrepreneurship.

"I think entrepreneurs are able to live comfortably with paradoxes," Cone notes. "You have to believe your dream, but you also have to listen to the skeptics. You have to show single-mindedness and openness at the same time. You have to have an almost religious faith in your product, but also be able to switch course in an instant."

In fact, she says, studies have shown that from the time someone gets an idea for a product to the time he (or, increasingly, she) launches a business, the concept has "morphed" several times.

Liz Ryan, the founder of WorldWIT, a professional women's networking Web site, sees that happen all the time. She once interviewed a woman on WorldWIT's radio show who had quit medical school to start a pet store. The woman came to realize that the only way to make serious money in pet stores was to own a chain of them, but she didn't have the resources to expand. So she decided to specialize in birds, the most lucrative part of her operation. Then she discovered that most of the birdcages on the market were dull and poorly designed boxes, so she started making her own. She also got into wholesale distribution of some products. "Now she's three different companies and they call her the bird lady," Ryan says.

Other small-business pioneers tell of making similar about-faces. James Poss scaled back his ambition to develop floating devices for gathering data on wind speeds and directions and other weather patterns at sites for offshore wind plants, and turned his attention to the more modest manufacture of solar-powered trash compactors.

Kerry Sulkowicz, the founder of the Boswell Group consulting firm, maintains that tolerance for ambiguity is an essential feature of the business innovator's mind. To describe the phenomenon, he uses a phrase coined by John Keats, the nineteenth-century British poet: "negative capability."

"It is a felicitous phrase," Sulkowicz comments. "Keats used it in a letter to his brother in which he was trying to explain Shakespeare's genius. I think it also applies to entrepreneurs and leaders in any sphere. He said that negative capability described someone who was capable of living in 'uncertainty, mystery and doubt.'"

Venture capitalist Guy Kawasaki's take on the tendency is more down-to-earth. "Near-death experiences are great motivators," he explains. "If an entrepreneur is running out of gas, he has to be nimble, he has to go for it. He can't commission a two-year study."

•   •   •

Charlie Horn, the chairman of the Promirus Group, a Tucson provider of prescription drugs savings programs, says he got a little bit too complacent in his first moneymaking venture. He had been making good money selling discount card plans to insurance companies for members who lacked prescription drug coverage, and figured he had hit upon such a good thing he could keep doing it forever.

In the capitalist marketplace, there is no forever. After two years, business shriveled, and Horn poked around for a new opening. He found it in the nation's 50,000 retail pharmacies, setting up discount programs for their cash customers. The big chains were skeptical at first, but he reeled them in by playing up the competitive advantage they would gain over rivals that he excluded from the network.

"I was forced into a new model," Horn says. "Innovation comes from necessity."

More recently, Horn has devised a novel system for forming corporate alliances—creating the partners himself. Rather than clutter up his company's corporate structure with divisions that deviate from its core business, he either spins off a company or starts one from scratch to develop ideas he comes up with for new health care services.

For example, he and two of his senior executives recently launched Affordable Medical Solutions, based on the same concept as Promirus's ScriptSave card but with a different technology, a different market, and a different way of dealing with drug manufacturers. "We expect it to become profitable within a year," he says. "I'm a part owner but a passive investor; they run the show."

Likewise, in 2000, he invested in a start-up called HealthTrans LLC to develop electronic claim-processing software for pharmacies that use the ScriptSave card. "We used to use a vendor, but we were paying out 50 percent more in fees than it would have cost us to acquire a system or create one," Horn remarks. "But we didn't want to become a technology company; we wanted to remain a marketing company. We said, 'We'll start a new company, with Promirus as its first customer.' The guys in charge run it way better than I could do. Some people think they have to be in control of everything, but I like to choose the most efficient path."

The question is: Who does and who does not fit the model of tolerance for ambiguity that is so crucial to success? One clue might lie in your childhood. You may recall how Ross Levin, the Minnesota financial adviser, speculated that the craving to be in charge could in many cases be traced back to the turmoil of living with an alcoholic or psychologically disturbed parent. Umang Gupta, the chairman of Keynote Systems Inc. in San Mateo, California, mulls that one over and wonders whether the principle could be broadened to include anyone growing up in an erratic or bewildering environment.

In his case, he struggled against information overload, a kaleidoscope of conflicting cues sent out by his parents and peers. "My mother and father came from different castes," he says. "One was a believer, the other was an atheist. One was quiet-spoken and controlled, the other was flamboyant."

Meantime, he was bouncing from one cultural milieu to another, mingling with rich kids and servants' kids, Indian kids and British kids,

Hindu kids and Muslim kids, and absorbing their often starkly distinctive patterns of thinking and behaving. At the age of seven, he was sent to a boarding school that counted 196 Christians, two Zoroastrians, one Muslim, and one Hindu—him. "So I was living in a foreign culture in my own country," he says. "And I quickly learned to adapt."

He even reinvented his personality—"building it and rebuilding it by trial and error," as he describes it—to allow him to fit in with his ever-shifting environment. Whatever else the exercise did, it allowed him to make friends with just about anybody he came into contact with, an advantage in any enterprise. The identity overhaul also made him more efficient, he believes. "Even today, I have this ability to wake up in the morning and say, 'This habit or way of doing things that I have followed for the past ten years or the past forty years is not the right approach. I've got to change,'" he says. "And I do."

If the discordance that kept him on his toes as a boy stimulated an independent spirit in him—the take-charge mentality that we explored in Chapter 2—it was also good training for negotiating the ambiguities of the world. "I saw shades of gray wherever I looked and concluded there was no absolutely right way or wrong way to live your life," he says. "I think most entrepreneurs are like that—they grow up early and learn to live with ambiguity."

If you had a ragged emotional life as a kid, according to this line of reasoning, you are a good candidate because you are prepared for unexpected outcomes and therefore quick to react to them. Gupta says he now sees how his boyhood response to all the mixed signals coming at him works in his favor today.

"Your ability to change tactics is crucial," he says. "When you're creating something from nothing there are so many unknowns: What is your product going to be? Who are your competitors going to be, who are your customers going to be, what are your prices going to be? Your method of thinking is a gestalt of all the possibilities. It's like playing a chess game. You realize you can't control 99 percent of the variables so you concentrate on controlling the 1 percent that you can."

• • •

Few entrepreneurs in the making set out to reconstruct their personalities, as Gupta did, but they do tend to remake their future in a restless search for their true calling. Did you drop out of college for a year? Switch majors and then regret it? Land your dream job as a graphic designer and then decide what you really wanted to do is go on an archaeological dig? Don't get me wrong; changes of heart are part of the human condition, and almost universal among people under thirty, but if you have a long history of them, perhaps your subconscious is telling you that you need to kick out on your own.

Certainly, if you have a paying job and your boss thinks you have high promise but you have no interest in making the steady march up the corporate ladder, preferring to poke around the company for interesting corners, you might want to try starting your own business.

Even if you don't, you'll likely end up in a profession that lets you call your own shots. Chances are good you will become one of those midlife career switchers—the lawyer who goes off to medical school, the corporate executive who takes up teaching, the nurse who starts a medical supply company.

Liz Ryan, founder of WorldWIT, says she hadn't noticed how common career hopping was among the professionals and small-business owners who belong to her organization until a university student at a campus retreat told her that that was what most struck her about them.

"It takes a fresh pair of eyes to notice things sometimes," Ryan says. "This girl told me that what she got out of the weekend was that not one of the 100-odd career women she talked to had had a straightforward business career, working her way up the corporate ladder, but zigged and zagged and veered all over the place. And I said, 'Wow! That's really true. That's true of everyone that I know.'"

It probably goes without saying that a negative indicator of the entrepreneurial personality is inertia. If an advertising salesman sits at the same desk for thirty years for whatever reason—fear of venturing into the unknown, lack of imagination, laziness, or, heck, a love of selling ads—he is not likely to start an Internet company. But the world needs advertising salesmen, and if he works hard and meets his quotas, he deserves our respect.

If he does start an Internet company, it will probably be short-lived. Cone, the Kauffman Foundation vice president, says almost all the failed entrepreneurs she has known showed a "stubborn streak," an inability to modify their ideas. In other words, mental inertia.

Entrepreneurs' innate agility contains within itself a paradox. They use it to outwit bigger opponents and therefore to increase their revenues and profits. But as their start-ups grow, they become more bureaucratic and more unwieldy and slower to react to challenges from upstart rivals. At that point, either they have to figure out a way to stay nimble or else they have to bail out and start another company (a common choice).

Bob Hillier devised a system to keep his architectural firm in Princeton, New Jersey, fast on its feet. He broke it into practice groups, which currently number thirteen. There is the health care practice group, the corporate practice group, and so on. Each is like a small firm, and each is responsible for going out and getting business. He puts entrepreneurial personalities in charge of each one, but of course the practices have the intellectual and technological horsepower of the Hillier firm behind them.

"The setup keeps us from becoming an unwieldy behemoth," Hillier said. "The practices are like guerrilla soldiers. Or to use another analogy, if a big corporation is like an aircraft carrier, our firm is like a fleet of PT boats, each with a captain constantly looking for work."

Actually, that format is becoming more common because it is the way accounting firms operate, but when he introduced it twenty-five years ago, it was unusual. From the beginning, it has had the triple advantage of making his firm leaner and meaner, attracting innovative types to keep it that way (twice, architects have come through Hillier's door to say they wanted to set up their own practice), and creating a wide mix of profit centers in a cyclical industry so that when business falls off in one area, it picks up in another.

Hillier has overcome a challenge that confronts every small-business owner at some point. As Kevin Plank, the founder of Under Armour Performance Apparel in Baltimore, puts it: "You spend so much when you're small trying to act big, and then as you get bigger you spend so much time trying to be small again."

Nimbleness is usually equated with quick, sudden movements: a bullfighter pivoting out of the path of a charging beast, a basketball player snatching a ball from an opponent, Jack jumping over a candlestick. But if you think of nimbleness as a talent for adaptation, then it can be stretched out over months or years.

In other words, you have to be able to play both a quick game of checkers and a long game of chess. Don't think you won't make the grade because you're the introspective, thoughtful type. The key is (a) to have an insight and (b) to apply it before a competitor does.

As we have seen, Alex Lidow, the CEO of International Rectifier, a maker of devices for converting alternating current to direct current, reinvented his company in stages over several years as he implemented two counterintuitive insights he gained from studious observation of the marketplace. The first was that International Rectifier would gain a competitive edge by abandoning its reliance on its core technology and "pulling in" other technologies to refine its products. The second was that people wouldn't pay for the energy efficiency that International Rectifier developed and that the company would therefore have to figure out ways to make buying it worth their while.

"We realized we couldn't create a silver bullet," Lidow says. "We had to reconfigure ourselves as a technology-pull company." As described in Chapter 1, that involved introducing a dozen new technologies and designing them to work together.

Implementing such a strategy takes time. But it also puts the company out in front and makes it more adaptable to changing circumstances. "The more you're organized around your technology, the less nimble you are," Lidow says. If you made the best buggy whips in the world in 1890, he points out, your days were numbered unless you had other technologies to fall back on.

•   •   •

If deep thought can be a form of nimbleness, so can asking stupid questions. Time and again, many of the people I interviewed practically bragged about their ignorance in the early stages of starting a business.

Why? Because once they had made it, in looking back they realized that asking dumb questions had put them in good stead.

Dot Smith and a partner started their pepper-jelly business with no notion of what a business plan was. When the general store owner who placed Pepper Patch's first order told her about regulatory requirements, "I thought he was talking Greek," she recalls. When the bank manager who was considering her request for a $1,000 loan told her to fill out a "pro forma," she had no idea what he meant. When her accountant tried to teach her the basics of bookkeeping, she thought he was speaking in tongues.

Still, she plowed ahead, always asking, "What does that mean?" She was a slow study. At the end of her first year, the accountant reviewed her finances and told her that Pepper Patch had been making 25 cents a case, not the $6 she had thought.

Every year after that, he would shake his head at her faulty arithmetic and ask her the same question: "Dot, is it really worth it?" But she blundered on. Her favorite story concerns an arduous journey to England to buy a $9,000 capper for creating a vacuum in her jars and sealing them. "I didn't realize it, but to operate a capper, you need a boiler," she recounts. "The engineer who came to install it said, 'Where's the boiler?'"

And so it goes: Vonfrolio of Education Enterprises asking a bank where she was supposed to get the business papers she needed to open a corporate account, Anderman of Ellie Mae making a pitch to insurance companies for a partnership "without quite knowing what I was talking about," Karl Eller of the Eller Company agreeing to buy a billboard operation for several million dollars and then asking himself, "What do I do now?" and Michael Huddy chatting with his blue-collar forest engineers at Crown Zellerbach about how to use a stereoscope "without tipping my hat that I didn't know what I was doing."

Dumb? Not at all. Winging it? Definitely. "OK, we may be a bit uninformed on some of the stuff, but what's important is to get out there and kick ass," says Luke Visconti of DiversityInc. "I've seen so many people mess around with business plans. They massage it like Kobe beef. You end up with analysis paralysis."

Winging is one of the purest forms of nimbleness. When Dot Smith and her partner started their venture in 1976, they waded in, cold-calling the Department of Agriculture to learn about labeling requirements, searching the back roads of Florida for a farm they had heard about that grew particularly lush peppers, and paying the driver of a refrigerated truck off the books to haul the peppers back to Tennessee with the rest of his cargo and drop them off at secret meeting spots. "I remember sitting in the church parking lot in the middle of the night, our flashlights ready to signal to the driver where we were," Smith recalls.

Another time, she tested a new line of cakes on her German shepherd, who was partial to Tipsy Cakes soaked with Jack Daniel's whiskey.

If you keep winging it, things often turn out just fine. After creating a buzz among athletes at the University of Maryland with his first T-shirt prototypes, Plank was ready for mass production. "I knew nothing about apparel, but I knew the center of the apparel universe was the Garment District," Plank says. "I hopped in my car and drove to Manhattan and parked at Thirty-fourth and Fifth. I walked around looking at all the fabric shops. I got a copy of *Women's Wear Daily* and found a list of contractors in the back. I went to one on Ninth Avenue and went in. I showed the guy inside a sample of my T-shirt. He asked which fabric I was using. I said I wasn't sure. He said, 'Where's your pattern?' I said, 'What's a pattern?' I was sent to a guy who did patterns. He said, 'Where's your marker?' I said, 'What's a marker?'"

He ended up with 500 samples, sent off thirty-five to players he knew, and carted off the rest to the Georgia Tech equipment manager, who said, "I'll buy 'em." Plank asked what his budget was. He replied, "Three hundred thousand dollars." And he was in charge of that budget? Plank asked. Yes, he was. Could he give Plank a list of all the equipment managers in the Atlantic Coast Conference? Sure.

A few weeks later, Plank got his first check, for $895, from the equipment manager at Georgia Tech for a shipment of eighty T-shirts.

Another time, he filled an order in four days for a product that didn't exist. The Arizona State football team asked if he could ship thermal undershirts for their Saturday game. No problem, he said, neglecting to mention he didn't have any. On Tuesday, he drove to the Bronx and loaded up his Ford Explorer with an elastic fabric he hoped would do the trick. On Wednesday, his contractor made the shirts. On Thursday, he shipped them to Oregon, where the game would be played. On Friday, they arrived. On Saturday, he watched 8–0 Arizona State beat Oregon on national TV, he says, "with my fingers crossed."

"I was wondering: 'Are the sleeves going to blow out?'" he recalls. "'What's going to happen to them? Are things going to tear?'" The equipment manager reported back that the players loved the garments, but that a few of them complained that it hadn't kept them as warm as they had expected. "I said, 'Well, actually, I sent you my all-season gear,'" Plank says. "'For my product line called cold gear, I can send that to you next week.' He said, 'No, we don't have any more cold-weather games this year.'"

The lesson he learned? "You have to roll with the punches. You have to be flexible."

Amar V. Bhide, a business professor at Columbia University, made the same point in an interview with *Inc.* magazine a few years ago. "A tolerance for ambiguity," Bhide said, "is a willingness to jump into things when it's hard to even imagine what the possible set of outcomes will be. It means going ahead in the absence of information and in the absence of having much capital and in the absence of having a novel idea."

Case in point: Vonfrolio, the nurse who launched one of her earliest businesses to calm down a colleague. The woman had gone into hysterics upon learning that the caterer for her daughter's wedding had just collapsed and died. Vonfrolio promised to solve the matter for her.

She called around but couldn't find a caterer able to handle 250 people on short notice. So she took on the job herself.

She enlisted friends, rented tents, tables, and chairs, went shopping at Pathmark, and cooked up tubs of dishes such as tortellini with fresh pears in a shrimp cream sauce. Everybody loved the food. So she started

Oh-la-la Caterers and did weekend events. Gays discovered her. Oh-la-la became hot. She made a bundle. "I did it. I winged it," Vonfrolio says. "And I found out that most of it was just plain common sense."

•   •   •

A lot of the scrambling that small-business owners do, of course, has to do with money. They can get really inventive when they are skirting disaster. Greg Herro, co-founder of the company that makes jewelry from cremated remains, tapped into the $25,000 credit line of a company he founded but no longer owned. He had retained the corporate name, Anything's Possible, however, and the line of credit that went with it. "Of course, the bank was not aware that I had sold the company," he said.

The hustle for cash can be never-ending. Plank got started on $20,000 in savings, then leveraged five credit cards for $40,000 and hit up every friend and relative who would listen to his pleas. Only after he got a $250,000 loan from the Small Business Administration did he give himself a salary, but kept it to $500 a week and canceled the paychecks when the bank account got too low.

When a National Football League representative called him to say he wanted to stop by his office, Plank claimed he was on the road because he didn't want him to see that Under Armour consisted of a desk in his grandmother's house. Instead, he invited the executive to lunch in a restaurant, then rushed to his bank to see if he had enough cash to cover the meal because he never knew whether his credit cards would work.

If necessary, entrepreneurs beg. They don't hold out a cup, but the message is clear enough: Could you please provide a valuable service for free?

After Joan Schweighardt published her own novel under a pseudonym to give the impression her GreyCore Press was gaining traction, she persuaded a beautiful friend to let her splash her photo on the jacket as the supposed author, a graphic designer to design the cover, an old friend to do artwork and create a company logo, and another old friend to create a Web site—all for free.

"I'm reaching out to all my friends and acquaintances and saying, *'Help!'* " Schweighardt recalls. (She also reached out to best-selling British author Fay Weldon in an e-mail and persuaded her to write a glowing blurb.)

The Meiland sisters set their sights even higher. After getting a quote of $250,000 from a professional photographer to do shoots of wedding scenes in their Manhattan bridal shop, Lisa Helene sent an e-mail to a photographer she had once known, asking him if he remembered her and telling him how much she loved his stuff—and, by the way, wondering if he might consider doing a shoot for her at a reduced price. "It was a shot in the dark," she says, but he did remember her and agreed to do the work for almost nothing. All he needed was a model. One of their friends agreed to do the job for a fraction of her usual fee and waived royalty payments.

One observation about the eight traits that make entrepreneurs tick: They overlap. You might find sections in any one of the eight chapters that would fit neatly into one or more of the other seven. That is because, with the help of some nationally recognized experts on the topic, I am dissecting into observable parts something that in reality can't be stripped apart: the human personality.

Here is an illustration of what I mean. Gary Doan, the founder of Intradyn, the maker of data storage and recovery devices, says he would never work for a big corporation. In part, his aversion reflects his desire to run his own show, but in part it reflects his love of taking the initiative. "The beauty of running a small business is that you can do course corrections quickly," he notes. "If you have a competitive product, you can never sit still, because the copycats will be on your heels."

Those two traits—the urge to be in charge and the fleet-footedness that lets you stay in charge—are so intertwined that they don't really exist separately from each other.

Similarly, agility often looks a lot like spotting and seizing opportunity, a trait discussed in Chapter 1. Dot Smith's circumvention of a town ordinance that restricted the expansion of her store to $5,000 construction jobs, by the simple expedient of adding three rooms, one at a time, that each cost $5,000, probably fits both categories. (Though you have to wonder if the town fathers weren't a bit dense.)

So does serial Internet entrepreneur Cameron Johnson's hiring of the winner of a national contest that Johnson had lost to collaborate with him on a new start-up.

So does Plank's decision—after seeing Mike Tyson at a postfight press conference wearing a hat with a company's logo on it—to send his sportswear to NFL players he had once worked with to try it out in public.

So does Peter Amico's method of going public by merging a shell company into his omnidirectional forklift business to avoid all the regulatory hurdles of going public, instead of the other way around. The maneuver also gave his company, Airtrax, liability protection that it wouldn't have had if it had merged into a shell company with hidden liens or lawsuits.

Now here is another aspect of agility that you might not have thought about before: the gift for keeping your ears open. At times you can do that only by keeping your mouth shut. Yes, plenty of the people in this book are gabbers. But never nonstop gabbers. And never boring gabbers. They are generally charming, smart, and bursting with enthusiasm. Gupta can't wait to demonstrate all the amazing features of his new BlackBerry to me over a cup of coffee, and a few minutes later he is eagerly scribbling a picture of a contraption he built half a century ago as a boy in India. Most endearing of all, at least to me, is how authentic entrepreneurs seem to be. Phonies and blowhards don't get very far in the small-business jungle.

But even while they are talking, they are scrutinizing your facial expression and body language. And when you weigh in, they listen carefully to what you have to say. Not only are they are picking up useful information and storing it away, but they are divining what makes *you* tick. If they want something from you, the people skills that come naturally to them usually produce the desired effect.

"Entrepreneurs constantly take input," says the Kauffman Foundation's Cone. "They talk to people, they tweak their product, they assimilate knowledge."

"That's the process," comments Sig Anderman of Ellie Mae. "You do a lot of listening and freethinking, and you can't be overly wedded to preconceptions or even to your goal." At a banking convention, a life insurance salesman was giving him a short history of the industry. At one point he mentioned that life insurance used to be sold at home mortgage closings but that now it was pitched mostly by mail. Anderman figured the shift had something to do with the fact that mortgage brokerage companies had replaced banks as originators of the loans. And that got him to thinking.

If banks had once sold life insurance to home buyers, why couldn't Ellie Mae's network of mortgage brokers do the same? He started talking with big life insurance companies. One year later, he reached an agreement with Royal Bank of Canada to distribute its life insurance products in return for a substantial investment. "I suspect hundreds of people walked by this insurance salesman at that convention and just said, 'I have insurance; no thanks,'" Anderman says. "I turned our conversation into something that I think will be a huge business for us."

Dot Smith, the housewife turned pepper-jelly peddler, is a talker who made friends easily and seems to have them everywhere. She called one at the Tennessee agriculture department to see if there was some way to cut through all the red tape for getting a permit to sell food to the public. She had found space in an unused corner of an old dairy barn that had been converted into an antique shop, she told him. No problem, he said. Hadn't the state already given its approval for the production in that same building of milk for sale to the public? It should be easy to transfer that right to homemade jellies, he assured her. His logic might have been a bit tortured, but the license came through.

Men in positions of influence seemed almost beguiled by Smith's clueless demeanor and moved to rescue her from her distress. Could that have been by her design? If so, was she really clueless? She once called General Foods to ask if she could buy a pectin product called Certo directly from the company to save money.

The man in the credit department questioned her about her business. All went well until he asked her to list its assets and liabilities. "I had heard those words but wasn't sure what they meant," she says. "I told him I thought they were equal."

There was a very long silence.

"Finally, he said, 'I'll tell you what, Mrs. Smith,'" she recalls. "'Someday, somebody will have to take a chance with Pepper Patch. And General Foods would like to be the one that does.'"

Later on, the Certo, repackaged in aluminum pouches instead of glass, failed to jell her mixtures and ruined 100 cases of them. General Foods paid for the damage and put her in touch with its pectin chemist in California. He adjusted her recipe, instructing her to cut the sugar content and use a rapid-set pectin. The changes worked magic. But that wasn't the end of their relationship.

"Every time I had a problem, I'd call Fred," Smith says. "They even offered to send him to Nashville."

When she expanded her product line to chocolates, she found a mentor at Nestlé. "He's wonderful. I can call him anytime," she says. "He'll say, 'Hi, Dot. What's your problem?' He's my guru in matters of chocolate."

(The flip side to such male solicitude back when Smith was getting started was male chauvinism. When she and her partner went to trade shows and talked up their products, men assumed they were flirting. Once, a banker asked them, "Do your husbands know what you are doing?")

•   •   •

Another manifestation of nimbleness is multitasking, a bureaucratic term for doing everything from working the phones to mopping the floor. You don't have much choice, of course, if you are a one-man show. "I was licking stamps, stuffing envelopes, billing, doing sales, writing copy, filing documents, everything," remembers John Heagney of his early days as a publicist.

Such juggling acts are not without their humorous side. While he ran his business out of his home, Heagney was also in charge of caring for his toddler daughter, putting her in an enclosed hallway that he separated from his office with a gate. If the phone rang and she started to cry, he would shut the door in her face. If he was changing her diaper, he would let the answering machine kick in and listen to his sonorous voice informing the caller, "John Heagney Public Relations. We're sorry; all our lines are busy right now."

Schweighardt, the one-woman publishing house, says she spends one-third of her time promoting her books, one-third of her time working on new titles, including copyediting, and one-third of her time acting as her own secretary and assistant, doing everything from sending faxes to packing books and carting them off to the post office.

The wonderful thing about doing everything is that not only does it require nimbleness, it makes you even more nimble in the process.

"Everybody talks about the transaction costs and long communications chains at big corporations and the thirty-two hoops you have to jump through to get a decision," says William J. Dennis, senior research fellow at the the National Federation of Independent Business's Research Foundation. "Is the logo right? Is the color right? Entrepreneurs don't have the resources for all that, so they move fast and by instinct. Plus they don't have to pay those costs."

The competitive advantage they gain just by being able to make snap judgments is incalculable, Dennis says. "You can locate the guy in charge and get his thinking on the spot," he notes. "At a big corporation, it is hard to find the right guy. And even if you do, the information you get can be skewed. Say the plan calls for a 10 percent increase in technology spending the following year. Say the company is no longer on track to reach that goal. It might take weeks or months to make the decision to modify it. Whereas the small-business owner will give you a straight answer: 'That figure is no longer valuable. We're in a state of flux. We'll probably have to ratchet it down.'"

If people running small businesses often find themselves *doing* everything, they also (unlike big corporations) have the ability to *drop* everything. After Herro's company made a technological breakthrough in producing diamonds from the refined carbon of human corpses, the press went wild. "It was a continuous three-month barrage," he says.

"There were days when we were doing twenty interviews a day. Every radio station in the country and the world was calling us." He and his partners put everything else on hold. Why? Because they realized the free publicity was worth millions of dollars and that letting it slip away would be the stupidest business decision they could possibly make.

Because they often have to scramble with meager resources against seemingly impossible deadlines, entrepreneurs tend to be adept in the art of subterfuge. They have to be willing to improvise. Think of how Plank promised nonexistent thermal T-shirts to the University of Arizona football team, or how Schweighardt put her gorgeous friend's face over a made-up author's name on the cover of her novel.

Instinct told Heagney that the door of opportunity swings open more readily if you tell a potential client that you can deliver what he is asking for than if you express doubts about your ability to do so. When the owner of a chain of organ stores asked him if he could design an oversized check for an awards ceremony, he said, "Of course I can," and rushed out to delegate the work to a graphic designer. When the retailer called back a month later to ask whether he had ever organized an awards banquet, Heagney replied, "Sure, we do them all the time," and after hanging up, asked himself, "What the hell do I do now?" He figured that out, too. The jobs led to more ambitious projects with the store chain, including the launch of a new product line, and eventually to an account with Steinway, the piano maker.

Likewise, Vonfrolio wasn't averse to making exaggerated claims to get deals done. When she came home from nursing duty one night exhausted and decided to start her own business, she wrote letters to E. F. Hutton and Merrill Lynch, advertising herself as a CPR instructor and sprinkling her prose with made-up statistics about death rates from heart attacks in high-pressure industries.

A few weeks later Merrill Lynch called, and Vonfrolio asked her roommate, "Do you know anybody named Merrill Lynch?" It sounded familiar, but she couldn't picture the face. Then she remembered the letters. She arranged to teach a class two weeks later. The next day, E. F. Hutton phoned. This time, she was ready with the crisp announcement,

"CPR Associates." When E. F. Hutton requested classes for 500 people right away, she said she was booked solid for several weeks but could set up an appointment after that.

Then the scrambling began. Vonfrolio took a two-day crash course to obtain certification to teach CPR. Refused a business loan by a male bank manager, she returned a few days later and talked a female manager into approving a $10,000 personal loan by saying she had just lost 150 pounds and needed $10,000 to buy a new wardrobe. She bought mannequins and other equipment, hired ten instructors, and got her business up and running with time to spare.

One of my favorite stories about skirting the rules is told by Visconti of DiversityInc. In his Navy days on Guam, he wheedled two decrepit truck trailers from the manager of a disposal plant, where they were supposed to have been demolished, so that his boss could use them as storage bins. When inspectors came to the base to poke around, he found a hiding place for one and instructed a subordinate who had a tractor-trailer driver's license to drive the other one around until the inspectors left.

That is thinking outside the box: helpful in any profession, but crucial for survival in small businesses. Ryan, the WorldWIT founder, showed the same knack in her days at Ucentric when she interviewed an IBM executive for a job—in the executive's own office. The candidate had always been too busy to make the trek to Ucentric, so Ryan made the trek to IBM.

Another time, she hired a hardware genius whose only condition was that a software engineer he knew be allowed to nose around the company for one day to make sure it passed muster in his specialty. At the end of the day, she hired him, too.

In her hiring tactics, she has nothing over Paul Brown, the founder of HearUSA. In trying to brush off an ad salesman who had cornered him in his office back in his MetPath days, Brown was so impressed by his deft riposte that he offered him a job on the spot.

"He was trying to sell me a page inside a new laboratory magazine," Brown remembers. "I said, 'Oh, this is just the first issue? Come back in a few months; I want to see how the magazine does.' He jumped up, leaned over my desk, and said, 'Mr. Brown, that is exactly why you *must* buy a page for this issue. *Everybody* is going to be reading the first issue, even if there is never a second issue.'

"I made him advertising manager. I wouldn't let him leave. I took him on a walk through the building. I said, 'What salary do you want?' He asked me to make him an offer. I said no, pick a number. He got flustered. Finally, he named a figure. I shook hands on it immediately. I used to do that all the time. He was flabbergasted. He was probably kicking himself for not asking [for] more."

Mark Hughes, founder of Buzzmarketing, pulled the same trick in reverse. He was trying to land the top marketing job at an Internet start-up, Half.com. When the founder called, he sensed from his first few words that the answer was going to be no, so before he could deliver the bad news, Hughes broke in with the spiel of his life.

"I said, 'Whether I get the job or not, I'm going to give you three ideas, and at least one of them will make you a lot of money,'" he recalls saying. "I can't even remember what they were. One of them had to do with Sheryl Crow. She had made some anti-Wal-Mart dig in one of her CDs, and Wal-Mart announced it was banning them from the store. So I figured he would be able to buy a lot of them on the cheap. He liked all of the ideas. He said to himself, 'I gotta have this guy.' To me he said, 'You gotta come.'"

• • •

Entrepreneurs also have an advantage in negotiating deals with larger companies: They can make decisions on the spot without consulting some higher-up. On more than one occasion, Brown has walked out on a transaction when the other party tried (unethically, in his view) to squeeze a last-minute concession out of him.

Years ago, for example, he went to Paris to sign an agreement to buy a laboratory for MetPath. The papers were drawn up, his certified check for $3.5 million lay on the table, and he was about to sign on the dotted line when the owner announced he had recently gotten some new accounts and wanted an additional $400,000.

"I said, 'That's great, Jacques. You just bought yourself a terrific lab.' And I picked up the check and ripped off my signature and left the room.'"

Another time Brown exploited his grasp of how corporate leaders think to structure a deal with Milan Panic, founder and CEO of ICN Pharmaceuticals Inc. (since renamed Valeant Pharmaceuticals), to the latter's liking.

Panic wanted $10 million for a lab, more than Brown thought it was worth, and he wouldn't budge on the price. So Brown offered to pay that sum out in three installments, $3 million immediately, $3 million after one year, and $4 million after two years—on the condition sales didn't decline in the second year, an impossibility given Brown's plan to squeeze out inefficiencies in the lab's operations.

"But he jumped at the deal," Brown said. "It added up to $10 million. His attitude was, 'Damn it, I demanded $10 million, I told the board I would get $10 million, and I won't settle for anything less than $10 million.' We ended up paying $6 million, but he was satisfied. At the end of the second year, he was probably thinking, 'Oh, that. That was two years ago. Now I'm prime minister of Yugoslavia'" (which, by then, he was).

In his 2005 book *Integrity Is All You've Got,* Karl Eller of the Eller Company recounted unorthodox gambits he has made over the years to close deals—gambits that it is hard to imagine a buttoned-down corporate bigwig attempting.

Once, only $50,000 apart on a deal, he sized up the man across the table as stubborn but free-spirited and suggested they flip a coin. The man jumped at the chance, and Eller won the toss. Another time, knowing that the owner of a TV channel he wanted to buy had a beachfront house in La Jolla, California, that he never used, Eller slipped in its transfer to him as part of a $75 million agreement. The man laughed and said it was a deal. On another occasion, figuring the owner of an outdoor advertising company he coveted to be a down-to-earth fellow, he deliberately went to his office at 7:30 A.M. and dozed off on his couch. When the owner arrived at 9 for his appointment, he woke Eller and, clearly liking the human touch, immediately began discussing terms.

And yet another time, Eller clinched a $1 million deal with a reluctant seller by tossing in four free tickets to prime seats at a Fiesta Bowl football game.

Of course, all that hyperactivity can wear a fellow down. Martin G. Klein, CEO of Electro Energy Inc., a developer of high-technology batteries, says he is getting a little weary of juggling so many balls—doing research, building test units, applying for government development projects, shopping around for a factory, and, most frustrating of all, raising money—for so many years that he can't wait for full-scale production to begin, probably in the fall of 2007. "It's like going from kindergarten through high school and now it's closing in on graduation day," he says.

Kirt Poss, co-founder of VisEn Medical, gets right to the point. "This has been quite a stretch for me, being five years of pretty much nonstop ambiguity and challenge," he admits. "I could definitely see myself wanting to take a little break and doing something a little more linear for a while."

One of the most difficult aspects of running a new company with a breakthrough product, Poss says, is the confusion of potential customers over what exactly the product does and whether they need it.

"How do you know whether you should grow piece by piece over several years or if you can raise $30 million and expand like crazy for two years to grab an opportunity that might not be there if you wait too long?" he asks.

Yes, precisely, says Carl Schramm, the Kauffman Foundation chief executive.

"What tolerance for ambiguity means is, 'No one here knows what is going on,'" Schramm notes. "So much of life is so complicated; managers have to operate in an amorphous space."

It has always been so, but Schramm says the issue is becoming more acute as the country becomes more and more a services society, where the product is intangible. "It's hard to say exactly what my foundation produces, or Ernst & Young produces," he points out. "They produce ideas, transformations, transactions. That talent for nimbleness becomes all the more important in a service economy where you're often not sure what the service is or what people like about it."

Jeff and Rich Sloan, the founders of StartupNation, offer free advice to help entrepreneurs start and run businesses. But they remember their first venture together, a product called the Battery Buddy that would prevent car batteries from going dead if the headlights were left on.

As they describe it in their book *StartupNation,* in 1989 they showed a prototype of the device to a company called Masco Industries in the hopes of licensing it. When a Masco engineer fretted that it looked too bulky, the brothers promised to come back in two days to show them a more advanced version. That night, they worked until midnight to improve the prototype, then spent the next day driving to car dealerships to snap photos of the apparatus attached snugly to the batteries of eighty models of cars and trucks in all. They got the film developed at a one-hour shop, put together a thick promotional binder with photos and explanatory material, and rushed back for their follow-up meeting. The Masco executives were impressed. It took more days of scrambling, but the Sloans finally cut a deal.

The lesson? "You don't walk into the office in the morning with a set of assignments: Do this by 3 P.M., do this before you leave for the day," Jeff concludes. "Any list takes second seat to what comes out of left field. That ability to make a snap decision and move on it quickly can make all the difference between total failure and huge success."

CHAPTER 5

Tenacity

Entrepreneurs never give up. They just keep charging along, full speed ahead. Damn the torpedoes, the impossible odds, the sudden crises, the skeptics, the exhaustion. High energy, drive, workaholism, hustle, restlessness, focus—all of these are manifestations of the same motivating force I call doggedness. But the glue that binds them together is tenacity.

Consider Paul Brown, founder of HearUSA Inc., the hearing-care chain, and before that of MetPath Inc., a laboratory testing company. "I took up karate at the age of fifty," Brown tells me. "The guy said, 'OK, we'll teach you old man's karate.' I insisted on real karate. He was shocked. I practiced for eight hours a week for a decade. I got my black belt. I kept going. I got my second-degree black belt. Then I was close to getting my third-degree black belt. I was fighting eighteen to twenty-five year olds. One day, my master wanted me to break a one-inch-thick slab of concrete with a front punch. I hesitated, but he kept goading me. So I did it. It was the highest point of my career. I knew I was lethal. I knew if I punched somebody in the chest, he wasn't going to get up. When my wife found out, she went berserk."

You don't want to mess with Brown. The image of a sixty-year-old man—whom not so long ago society would have written off as "elderly"—punching through a concrete slab is pretty compelling. But what captures my attention most is the fact that he put in eight hours of practice a week for a *decade*.

This is stick-to-itiveness of the highest order.

True, he finally dropped karate. Instead, Brown, now in his late sixties, does hand-to-hand combat. His coach is a 6-foot-4, 240-pound former Marine Corps captain and bounty hunter who runs a professional boxing school.

Karate is just punching and kicking without inflicting any real harm, Brown explains, but hand-to-hand combat is about disabling people without breaking their bones, if possible. It is a skill that appeals to the machismo so rampant in the business world. "I was at a meeting with a guy at Eagle Asset Management and told him about what I do," Brown says. "He got all excited and wanted me to show him my techniques. I had him on the floor for fifteen minutes."

Before I can quite conjure this image, Brown jumps up from his chair. "Here, let me give you some lessons," he says. Within seconds, I am bending over in pain. As guests at nearby tables sip coffee or talk on cell phones, he continues his tutorial. Here's how to thwart an attacker who has his hands around your throat. Here's how to knock the gun out of a thug's hand and send him sprawling.

"It's all about the throat," Brown explains. "It's hard to poke somebody in the eye, and the testicles are too small. People stop fighting when they can't get air."

Brown's training schedule demonstrates an elevated form of doggedness. To succeed, he says, you have to have patience, persistence, and perseverance. "Patience is discovering that you don't have the key to your house and so you wait for your wife to arrive. Persistence is circling the house and checking all the doors and windows to see if you can get in through one of them. Perseverance is removing the hinges from the door.

"That is the bulldog mentality," he says. "The entrepreneur has to have all three of those qualities."

The experts agree that tenacity is a defining characteristic of small-business innovators.

"The adrenaline flow they get from taking risks, from starting something from scratch, from competing in the marketplace almost becomes addictive," says Carl Schramm, the Kauffman Foundation CEO. He cites a famous saying by Theodore Roosevelt to the effect that it is far better to undertake great exploits and fail than to cower in the "gray twilight" of a humdrum existence. "What it means is, you've never lived if you haven't put yourself on the line," he says.

Gary Doan, founder of Intradyn in Eagan, Minnesota, is proof of that. Doan has endured endless setbacks in his entrepreneurial career but says he is driven to put in long hours by his belief in his product, buttressed by a compulsion to read almost everything he can get his hands on about the data archiving market.

Doan's battle with hepatitis C, the result of a blood transfusion in his youth, illustrates his powers of endurance. As the infection ate away at his liver, he took multiple drugs to keep the swelling down and beta-blockers to prevent his esophagus from exploding. He slept fourteen hours a day and was groggy the other ten.

In his waking hours, though, he didn't watch TV; he followed the markets, looking for trends and opportunities in the information technology business. It was during this period that he formed Intradyn, summoning software developers to his sickbed and putting together a business plan.

His liver transplant operation took place the week before Labor Day in 2001. Doan was in the hospital for eight days, not the two to five months the doctors had warned him to prepare for, but for several weeks afterward he was in near agony and got little sleep. Even so, he refused painkillers.

Intradyn was officially incorporated in October. "Within a few weeks, I was going full bore back at the company, mostly doing research, picking up on the trends," Doan says.

No wonder entrepreneurs are taking over the world.

•   •   •

The Kauffman Foundation's Judith Cone says that tenacity serves entrepreneurs best when they are undertaking the most difficult—but most necessary—task of all, raising money. "If you go to a banker and they tell you you're absolutely not bankable, do you quit? No, you go to another banker and another bank, or you find some other way. You engage in the daily struggle of pushing the ball up the hill. That's where perseverance comes in."

She recounts how Jack Stack and a group of fellow managers decided to buy International Harvester's remanufacturing factory in Springfield, Missouri, in 1983 to rescue it from shutting down. "He went on a quest to something like twenty-five banks" before he found one willing to put up the financing, she says. Their new company, the Springfield Remanufacturing Corporation, fought its way back into the game, and today it is prospering as part of the SRC Holdings Corporation, with Stack as its CEO. Stack wrote up some of the lessons he learned in his first book, *The Great Game of Business.*

Focus is what keeps tenacity in check. In his first year with the Liberty Mutual insurance company, Joe Macchia—who went on to start several insurance companies—quickly became one of the top salesmen in the country. His secret, he says, was to always tackle the toughest job first. While his colleagues were cleaning off their desks, he was making cold calls, starting at 8 A.M. sharp. "The nicest compliment I ever got was from a big auto dealer in New Jersey," he recalls. "After I closed the deal, he said, 'You're the most tenacious SOB I ever met.'"

Being tenacious means having to endure the stings of doubt from your detractors. "Other people looked at it and said it wouldn't work," says Peter Amico, founder of Airtrax, of his omnidirectional vehicle. "I looked at it and said, 'I'll make it work.'"

However, don't confuse resolve with stubbornness, Cone cautions. Resolve comes with an open mind—a willingness to listen to constructive criticism. The trick is to know how to separate the wheat from the chaff—to incorporate the smart ideas but reject the naysaying. That is not an easy task if you believe passionately in your product.

"When Ted Turner came up with the idea of live, on-the-spot reporters all over the world, twenty-four hours a day, people told him he was crazy, but he had this determined belief in his idea," she says. "But I'll bet he learned a lot from all the pushing back. That's one of the paradoxes, figuring out how to stay true to your concept and when to take in feedback and modify it."

Obviously, entrepreneurs have to have thick skins. If you are the sensitive type, forget it. When Karl Eller, chief executive of the Eller Company, was selling subscriptions to *Liberty* magazine and the *Saturday Evening Post* as a boy, he says, a lot of doors were slammed in his face. "I sucked up my gut and went on to the next door," he recalls. "If you want to sell, you have to keep going."

You might as well have fun in the process. Mark Hughes, the marketing consultant, says that when Steve Forbes, chief executive of *Forbes*, failed to return his phone calls, he bought a cell phone at Radio Shack for $100, activated it, and FedExed it to Forbes. "As soon as I got the receipt that the box had made it into the building, I started calling it," Hughes says. "I mean, picture it: 'What's that box doing ringing?'" Hughes finally did get through to Forbes and got what he was looking for—a plug for a book he had just written.

Heagney of Heagney Public Relations learned the payoff potential of resoluteness early on and has developed a method for unleashing it. He calls it the "tickler system": Every time somebody says no, ask if you can call back in sixty days. The person almost always says yes, figuring you won't bother. Then you do.

Years ago, as a freelance writer of ad copy, he tried the technique out on the creative directors of several ad agencies that he had sent fliers to. "Do you mind if I call back in sixty days?" he would ask. "Not at all," they would respond, eager to get him off the phone. When he did call back, they were surprised and favorably impressed—and more disposed than they previously had been to give him a try. "That lesson has served me so well for twenty-five years," he says. "Follow-up is God. The people who succeed in business are the ones who follow up. Follow up, follow up, follow up."

It is how he got his Steinway account, his big breakthrough. In planning a launch party for the Steinway-designed Boston line of pianos in 1992, his concept was to re-create the Boston Tea Party. The invitations mentioned only a very proper British high tea, staged in a large hotel banquet hall near Los Angeles and served by footmen wearing powdered wigs and carrying silver trays. A Steinway executive was in mid-speech when he was interrupted by the thunder of drums. Suddenly, the wall behind him opened, unveiling a huge merchant ship, with colonists hurling boxes of tea overboard while a fife and drum corps played.

"What an extravaganza!" Heagney recalls with relish. Then the anticlimax: "Steinway thanked us, and that was that. I didn't hear back from them. So I called them and asked whether they'd like to hire me to represent the Boston piano brand. They said no, they didn't have the budget. Here I had my foot in the door, but I couldn't seem to pry the door open.

"I asked if I could call back in sixty days. They said sure. So I did, but the answer remained the same: not this time. So I called back sixty days after that. And sixty days after that. And every sixty days for two years, and each time, the answer was no. I had gotten past disappointment. Disappointment has no meaning in business. What matters is follow-up, persistence. And I am the junkyard dog of persistence.

"Finally, after two years, we got the account for the Boston line. And later, in 1995, I got the Steinway account, our most prestigious ever."

• • •

Every small-business owner has a favorite story about how sheer tenacity won the day. Back when Luke Visconti of DiversityInc was an ad salesman at *Fortune,* he won back the IBM account after picking apart a *Fortune* marketing survey that others had ignored. Buried in it were data showing that *Fortune* readers had a much higher opinion of IBM than of its competitors. "It wasn't obvious if you didn't study it," he comments. "I was the only guy who broke the code."

Visconti believed there was a huge advantage for companies in having "extremely" satisfied customers rather than merely "very" satisfied ones. Yet *Fortune*'s marketing department had failed to use these survey results in trying to sell ad space to IBM. He soon landed a meeting with the son of IBM's general manager of advertising and showed him the results of the survey. By the end of the year, he was selling three advertising spreads an issue to IBM.

It took Visconti three months to fit the pieces of the puzzle together. But sometimes it can take a little longer. Alex Lidow, the CEO of International Rectifier, says he has been in litigation since 1986 trying to protect its patents. "Our claims have held up again and again through the courts, through the appeals courts, through the patent office, through reexaminations, through patent appeals, and all this kind of stuff," he notes. In the end, he collected more than half a billion dollars in royalties. "It was a long-term, very, very expensive and painful process, but it did work."

Perseverance isn't just how long you are willing to wait; just as important is how deeply you are able to dig. Just as success for a retail shop lies in location, location, location, so success in a venture requires research, research, research. Doan scours scholarly papers, patent applications, government reports, trade journals, and the Internet in his voracious quest for information.

"I can predict things," he says. "That comes from doing the research. Success has to do with vision, with looking at emerging trends, anticipating change, connecting the dots."

Entrepreneurs, says Mahoney of vFinance, have to wed their larger vision with the ability to deal with minutiae. Big-picture guys who are not detail-oriented can be angel investors, but people building a business have to be willing to delve into detail.

"Mozart had a grand vision, his concertos and symphonies, and then worked on the details, composing the music for the violins and the cellos and the clarinets and the flutes," he points out. "It's not the other way around."

Daniel H. Jara, a consultant and insurance agent who founded his company, Rimac Agency Inc., in 1977, doggedly fought to keep his business afloat despite his physical debilitation. In 1982, a botched back operation left him without the use of his legs. "I walked into the hospital and came out six months later in a wheelchair," he says.

While he was in the hospital, he ran his business, which he had built into three branch offices with a total staff of fourteen, from his bed. He soon discovered several employees were taking advantage of his absence, including a manager who was charging airline tickets for his personal use to the company account. Jara fired most of the staff.

But that was the least of his worries. "My whole life had changed; I became very depressed, facing this new reality," he remembers. When he finally got back home, he refused to go outdoors.

Eventually, though, he got his fighting spirit back. "I needed to keep my business and make it successful to pay for my special needs," he says. "I knew I would have to work harder than ever."

Now in his early fifties, Jara is working doing just that. He is the sole employee of Rimac now, and runs it out of his home. More involved than ever, he advises clients on the Hispanic market and trade with Latin America, and acts as a broker for commercial property and casualty insurance.

In addition, he is the president of the Statewide Hispanic Chamber of Commerce of New Jersey, which he co-founded in 1988. As a leader of the Latino community, he spends a lot of time organizing events, giving advice, and acting as an advocate. "I keep busy," he says. "I get up at 6 A.M. seven days a week and usually work until 11:30 P.M. or midnight."

•   •   •

If tenacity is the glue of doggedness, then boundless energy, drive, and restlessness are the pieces it holds together. Entrepreneurs often become quickly restless and bored with anything that resembles a daily routine. This can unleash their inventiveness, their unceasing search for new angles, their caffeine-fueled all-nighters, their need to take charge.

"An entrepreneur is somebody who gets bored easily," says Laura Gasparis Vonfrolio, founder of Education Enterprises Inc. "That's actually a key trait. There's the rush of starting a business, of making it grow, and then the boredom of running it and moving on. There's an itchiness to wear a different hat, to jump from business to business, to start a new business. New knowledge, new areas of growth. New, new, new!"

Most of the people I interviewed have just that sort of impatience flickering at the edges of their high-octane personalities. Lara Meiland and Lisa Helene Meiland say restlessness was already nagging at them as soon as they opened their Lara Helene Bridal Atelier in Manhattan. "We've mastered the basics and are feeling a little bit idle," Lisa says.

She turns to Lara. "If there were no more challenges, would you really want to sit here every single day?" she asks. "What would the point be?"

According to Lara, impatience is a strong indicator of whether people who are thinking about starting a business have the right stuff. Fellow students at Columbia University's business school who took a long time to make decisions never started a company. By contrast, "we were moving with urgency," she remarks. "I think if you are moving with urgency, the business propels itself along."

Frank Landsberger, the former MIT faculty member, recalls how restless he has always been. "Entrepreneurship is a form of addiction," he says. "I myself am an adrenaline junkie. I always want to be involved in something exciting, something new and untried. And if I don't get that hit, I don't feel fulfilled."

. . .

As I've said before, the eight attributes I have identified in this book are all aspects of a single personality as seen from different angles. As such, they blend into one another. The doggedness that drives entrepreneurs, for example, reflects their impulse to run their own show. If you are the guy in charge, you can stave off boredom pretty easily by launching new products, negotiating new deals, forming new alliances, or expanding into uncharted waters.

Entrepreneurs thrive on unpredictability, even turbulence. They seek out the unknown. Pete Newman, the founder of Gotham Software Inc., recalls how much he enjoyed working at a fish-freezing plant in Alaska, run by his cousin, after his sophomore year in college. "I was delighted because I didn't know anybody up there," he says. "I crave getting to know people. I crave change. Stability bores me.

"That's what I'm best at—adapting. And that was useful in founding Gotham, with so many changes coming at me."

Untold entrepreneurial personalities inhabit the corporate world, where they either carve out their own fiefdoms or else get restless under the bureaucratic machinery and go out on their own. Timothy Mahoney, founder of vFinance, did stints at the Computer Sciences Corporation, AT&T, and General Electric. But while he was still in his mid-twenties, he looked at what guys such as Steve Jobs were doing in personal computers, and he thought how much more exhilarating it would be to start his own company and make his own mark in the business world.

Joe Macchia, the founder of a Texas insurance firm, found himself fretting in his job as deposed chairman in early 2005. Having lost control to a group of investors, he hung on as a consultant in the hope of negotiating a severance package that would enable him to start yet another insurance company at the age of seventy.

"I'm getting my salary and waiting for a payoff," he said two months before the state of Texas put Reliant American into receivership. "I'd hate to walk away from $1 million. I'm hanging in the wings, but I'm getting bored. Being stalled in neutral takes some of the enthusiasm out of you. I want to get on with my life."

Not long after he spoke those words, he left Reliant and started the Macchia General Agency from scratch.

Impatience can sometimes push entrepreneurs to give up on a venture prematurely, but cutting one's losses early often opens the door to an even better opportunity. For example, dot-com artist Cameron Johnson gave up on one of his companies, Trueloot.com, after just one week because it wasn't making money fast enough. He reluctantly kept it going for three months, then sold it at a profit. Soon, he was on to his next project, a Web site to help car dealerships form closer relationships with customers.

And that is where all that boredom-induced restlessness leads: always to the next project. William Bygrave, the Babson College professor, says he has long puzzled over the proclivity for starting up one company after another.

"Every entrepreneur is a potential serial entrepreneur," he says. "In their minds, they usually have backup strategies even if they have never articulated them. Seldom do they get blindsided by something they hadn't really thought could happen. If the unexpected happens, they have a list of possible options in their brain for what to do next."

Not only that, he says, they are adept at switching from one field to another. "You can be a serial entrepreneur in the same industry, but eventually you don't do well because you probably know too much or you become stale."

Brown of HearUSA wants to stick to health care but has plans for a venture that would take him into new territory. He and his wife toyed with the idea of starting a company aimed exclusively at women years ago; with the number of female doctors growing sharply, he believes the time has come to act. The company would be called For Women Ltd. and have five divisions: health care, travel, education, babies and maternity, and general products.

Brown has tried his hand at several other companies over the years and believes he can resuscitate one that flopped miserably. It was called Kinetix, and it produced a handheld instrument, the Pulmometer, to measure lung function in patients with respiratory ailments, a potential market of 20 million people. Kinetix tested it; it worked, and Brown figured he had a winner.

Orders poured in—and only then did he spot the fatal flaw. Production required that a person sit at the end of the assembly line, manually testing each apparatus by blowing into it. The procedure was so laborious, he could manufacture only 100 Pulmometers a week. Brown realized the company couldn't produce enough to make a profit.

But he would like to start it back up now. "The technology to make it work wasn't available then," he says. "But it is available now."

•   •   •

Hillier, the architect and real estate developer, is working with his wife on a completely different sort of venture: a new magazine called *Obit* about celebrating life. Half the content will be devoted to obituaries of ordinary people who led interesting lives, and the other half to transitions people make, such as switching jobs or retiring. He got the idea, he explains, after observing the tears trickling down the cheeks of a woman sitting next to him on an airplane as she read an obituary of Captain Kangaroo in *People* magazine.

Martin Klein, CEO of Electro Energy Inc., says he is too engrossed in the intricacies of perfecting his batteries to be thinking about his next shot in the business world. But asked what he would do if by some unforeseen turn of events Electro Energy failed, he doesn't hesitate. "I'd start another company," he says.

The Meiland sisters have a master plan for expanding their Manhattan bridal shop into a national presence. First they plan to develop a wholesale line of gowns, then to open up retail shops in other cities. To publicize their products, they are thinking about writing a book called *For the Thinking Bride* to give brides practical advice on matters such as prenuptial agreements and wedding ring insurance. Eventually, they intend to launch their own fragrances, plates, shoes, and other upscale goods and go about creating their own brand. After that, perhaps, they will start a business that specializes in brand management and financial advice for European companies eager to break into the American market. Ultimately, they might even acquire other companies.

Nadine Thompson, the chief executive of Warm Spirit Inc., a network marketer of body care products, has an ambition of a different sort: replicating Warm Spirit in Africa as a nonprofit.

As she pictures it, she would build factories in countries such as South Africa and Ghana to make body lotions out of the shea and cocoa butters produced by local cooperatives. That alone would be a boost for the local economies, increasing the cooperatives' sales and creating jobs for unemployed local women. She even has hopes of recruiting some of the African American success stories at Warm Spirit to travel to Africa to act as mentors.

The more impatient types don't go into detail, but they, too, imagine themselves moving quickly to seize new opportunities. "If I fail in Cambodia, I will try somewhere else," says Herbert Jian, who just started an import-export business in that country. "When I'm no longer invaluable here, I'll find the next opportunity," asserts Kirt Poss of VisEn Medical. "If Intradyn were acquired, I'd start another business, absolutely," insists Doan, the founder of Intradyn. "I think I could start one or two companies a year." He adds that he expects his company to be acquired by mid-2006.

Most entrepreneurs who have been around for more than a few years have a track record of starting several companies. Doan's include Transition Networks, a maker of media conversion devices for computer networks, which he founded in 1987, and Neo Networks, a developer of a router to speed transmission of data over computer networks, which he left in 1998 to cope with his liver illness.

Peter Amico, founder of Airtrax, has trouble keeping track of all the companies he has run. He co-founded Martin Divisions Steel Products Inc. with his brother-in-law in 1968, sold his stake and started Ameri-Consolidated Steel Fabricators, started Centurion Securities Services with two partners in the early 1970s, launched Titan Detective Services on his own in 1978 and a helicopter-training school within the agency a few years later, and formed Airtrax through a reverse merger in 1997. "At some point in there, I started another small steel business," he says.

Charlie Horn, founder of the Promirus Group, has started nine businesses, beginning with a managed-care distribution company in Philadelphia that helped small- to midsized health maintenance organizations distribute their services to small businesses.

A subset of entrepreneurs just can't sit still long enough to actually run their companies, according to Judith Cone, the Kauffman Foundation vice president. Instead, they start a venture, build it up, lose interest, cash out, and go on to another one. "They love the creation process and don't like the operational side," she notes.

Entrepreneurs aren't just restless. They are motivated by the infectious energy I touched upon in Chapter 3. "Driven, driven, driven," Brown of HearUSA almost shouts to describe his state of mind in his early years as an entrepreneur. "I was on a high all the time. Driven! Driven! Driven!"

You can see that same energy in the frenetic pace of their lives. Johnson, who is running his father's car dealership full time while simultaneously cooking up new Internet ventures, recounted his schedule for one week.

"Wednesday I fly to Kansas. Thursday morning I give the speech [to a group of high school students]. Thursday afternoon I fly home and get back at 11 P.M. Friday morning at 6 A.M. I leave for New Orleans for an automobile dealers' conference, and then I come back on Monday. Monday I will be at work for a week and then I go back to Wharton to be with Nat [a business partner] for three days to try and work on launching this new company and just kicking around different ideas."

·   ·   ·

Many entrepreneurs coast along on a few hours' sleep per night. Visconti, the founder of DiversityInc, averages five hours but often gets by on three.

When James Poss started his Seahouse Power Company in April 2003, he says, he was up until 3 or 3:30 A.M. almost every night "refining business plans, sending stuff out, refining marketing, trying to calculate energy budgets, trying to figure out how to make everything work. I mean, I was a wreck for a little while." Now, his pace has slowed to a staid twelve hours or so a day—roughly 8 A.M. to 10 P.M., with time off for driving to the office and back and for dinner.

Vonfrolio of Education Enterprises travels two days a week to give seminars at hospitals and works out of her home when her infant twin daughters are sleeping, with her most productive hours between 10:30 P.M. and 1 or 1:30 A.M. The babies wake her at 5. "I'm good on four hours," she says.

Greg Herro of LifeGem knows all about sleepless nights. For eight excruciating months in 2003, he worked mostly twenty-hour days trying to put out a bonfire—a malfunction in the production of diamonds from cremated remains. The glitch wouldn't go away and was threatening to alienate the initial 200 customers LifeGem had lined up.

"This happened after we did a major media release that brought hundreds of thousands of people to our Web site requesting information about us," he says. "In a crisis like that, you don't sleep. You're up at dawn, you're up at midnight, you're up at 2 A.M., constantly thinking, 'How do we get this solved?' I've always liked a good cocktail, but this drove me to not drink."

Herro worked the phones, talking with the American scientists in charge of purifying the carbon, with the Russian technicians in charge of turning it into diamonds, with the families of the deceased to keep them informed of what was happening, "I was in extreme emotional distress," he says, which was made worse by the specter of financial disaster. Some clients demanded their money back, worsening a cash-flow crunch at the company. And because his wife had recently quit her paying job to help out at LifeGem, the couple were living at the edge of personal insolvency.

But he never thought of giving up. "That's what makes you a businessperson," he says. "That production problem was the big one, but stuff like this happens all the time. Boom, another one. There is no easy ride to the top. Anyone can make it through the easy stuff. If you're an entrepreneur, you'd better be able to make it through a predicament like that."

•   •   •

Of course, as you get older, more successful, and richer, you can afford to coast a little bit. But that just doesn't strike most entrepreneurs as an option. Hillier of Hillier Architecture was relaxing recently with his family at their compound on Nantucket. If the Europeans can turn their backs on the whole work thing for six weeks in the summer, couldn't Hillier at least enjoy a few days of repose in the sun?

He tried. But as soon as a call came through about a deal, he was on the first plane back to his Newark office.

Thompson of Warm Spirit Inc. recounts the never-ending string of road trips, speeches, meetings, late-night phone calls, and paperwork that enabled her to build her company from five freelance marketers to 10,000. She talks of the passion she felt about spreading the good news to women of color of the boundless opportunities that are theirs if they work hard enough to grab them.

"There's no time off on a Saturday," she says. "I probably put in eighty hours a week. I'm watching TV late at night and I have an idea for a product. The next morning, I write it out; I call a couple of vendors, a couple of perfumeries. I mix the perfume and the base. I work with our procurement person to choose the jars, the bottles, the caps, the labels, the design and concept. We have 350 different products, and I've had to do this for every one of them."

Amico sometimes puts in ninety-hour weeks (though to reward himself, he repairs to the lake by his house in the evenings with a fishing rod and a glass of scotch). Macchia, as the new president of the Early American Insurance Company many years ago, sometimes worked twenty-four hours straight. "My stomach turned glassy from all the caffeine I drank," he recounts. Joan Schweighardt of GreyCore Press spent fifty hours a week on her new publishing company plus thirty hours more as a public relations operative to pay her bills. To this day, she says, "I eat energy bars for lunch so I won't have to leave my desk." Liz Ryan once matched Schweighardt's fifty-plus-thirty schedule by putting in fifty hours a week on her consulting business and thirty on an amateur opera company she founded for young singers.

At Klein's first company—he was a partner—he did everything from sweeping the floor to writing research reports and doing all the hiring and firing. As a salesman at Xerox, Gyenes says, "I worked all the time. I worked weekends. I worked evenings. If I was out drinking until 2 A.M., I'd still show up at work at 8 A.M."

Do these people have lives? Yes—intense ones. Lisa Meiland says that when she worked for a corporation, "I was my business self at the office and then came home and took off my job clothes and became just Lisa." But now that she owns her own business, "This is my life. I don't have a job; I have a life. Everything is blended together. That is what entrepreneurs crave."

•   •   •

But they are human beings, too. Sure, adrenaline keeps him going, says Amico of Airtrax, but sometimes he feels overwhelmed. Now that everything seems to be coming together at his company, his schedule has gotten almost impossibly hectic. "I've been working sixteen-hour days most of my life. That I don't mind," he comments. "It's the eighteen-hour days that are getting to me."

Hyperenergy alone is not enough, of course. Another crucial component of doggedness is hustle, which is not the same thing. If energy is the fuel of workaholism, then hustle is the directing force. Both have to kick in to take you from point A, spotting an opportunity, to point B, seizing it.

According to David Weinstein, president of the Chicagoland Entrepreneurial Center, a nonprofit that helps small businesses find clients and financing, hustle defines the entrepreneurial spirit, and he should know.

After joining a small outfit that helped woman-owned and minority-owned businesses get access to capital, he installed new technology, then built it into information-tracking systems that the firm was able to sell to corporations and government agencies. As a result, from 1992 to 1995, the number of employees grew from three to twenty-five and revenue rose from $250,000 to $3 million.

Before long, Weinstein was appointed one of the youngest chief information officers in the Chicago city government, responsible for the $140 million Department of General Services, which managed the city's assets and facilities. He used some of these resources to build an easy-to-use computer system.

In 1996, he introduced Internet auctions to the city government. Until then, Chicago had sold parcels of vacant real estate through classified ads in newspapers, and a small number of savvy investors had usually bought them and flipped them for a quick profit. Weinstein's request to use city funds to market the lots on the Internet was turned down, so he put up $2,000 of his own cash to hire students to photograph the lots and to create a Web site to showcase them. He then held an auction and raised $7 million, twenty times more than they would have netted the old way.

A short time later, he met with Mayor Richard M. Daley to recount what he had done. "Daley turned to me and said, 'For bureaucratic reasons, you were told not to do this,'" Weinstein recalls. "'Yet you went ahead and did it anyway. This is the type of person I want working for me.' This was 1998. I was sizzling hot. My friends were all starting technology companies. I told the mayor we needed to compete with Silicon Valley. We created a council of advisers for the mayor made up of top technology companies in the area. I had the opportunity to meet with Bill Gates, Larry Ellison, Mike Kranszy—all the big names of high technology."

Hustling never has to end, either, as long as the entrepreneur is still breathing. Macchia started the Macchia General Agency insurance firm in 2005 on a $150,000 investment—a "scary" proposition, he says, given that he was seventy and knew it would take at least three years to build it into a going operation.

Richard Wellman still gets the same rush. Wellman, who has built several companies around airplanes and airplane parts, spends an hour on the phone describing how much fun he has had in his nearly five decades of wheeling and dealing.

One hour after the interview ends, he calls back. "I figured it out," he tells me. "All entrepreneurs are adrenaline junkies. They love the high of doing deals. That's it." And then he hangs up.

CHAPTER 6

Delusions of Grandeur

You gotta believe.

"I hope I can be the Henry Ford of this industry. This is going to be really big."

Those words were spoken by Peter Amico, chairman of Airtrax, which makes omnidirectional forklifts and other vehicles. But they express a sentiment that is nearly universal among successful entrepreneurs: Their venture is going to be really big.

In fact, a surprising number of entrepreneurs have no difficulty imagining that their fledgling business will earn a place on the honor roll of America's largest corporations, the Fortune 500.

Here is how Amico figures it: Material-moving equipment is a $20 billion industry worldwide, with forklifts accounting for $15 billion and scissors lifts $2.5 billion. And because of its vehicles' unique design, Airtrax will be a dominant player.

He sees Airtrax moving quickly into the top twenty forklift producers in the world and then into the top ten. "This is a big, big deal," he declares. "The potential for us is mostly vehicles with a lifting capacity of 3,000 to 5,000 pounds, which account for 40 percent of the electric-rider market. We could probably do 50 percent of the market in electric rider trucks, which is $4 billion. I think we can do that."

A long shot? So what? Kirt Poss has the same vision for his molecular-imaging company, which he projected would have $3 million in sales in 2005. That is 1/12,000th of the $3.6 billion in revenues that has put the Cincinnati Financial Corporation in the last spot on the latest Fortune 500 list, so VisEn Medical has a ways to go.

Poss isn't planning to pull the trick off overnight. In fact, he says, he might be long gone by the time it happens. But he believes so deeply in VisEn's technology and the expansion of molecular imaging in health care that the eventual Fortune 500 standing of a company like his seems preordained.

But not predestined. Human choice—his choice—did the ordaining. "In 2002, I could have said, 'Let's do imaging service for Pfizer,'" he points out. "And we could have been cash-flow-positive very quickly. But we chose a different course. 'Let's *not* be six people generating $500,000. Let's build along the path of developing technologies, developing products and scalable businesses, going public and being the leader. Let's spend significant money, get patents, scale the technology up.'"

By mid-2005, the company had raised $16 million and brought in an additional $7 million through deals and grants, even though it had reduced its staff from twenty-two to fifteen as it shifted its strategy to focus less on faster growth and more on research. Poss expects revenues to increase sixfold, to about $18 million, in 2007 and predicts VisEn could be in a position to go public by 2009, with his equity stake at around 5 percent—if he is still with the company, that is.

After that, he predicts, VisEn will continue to grow and grow and grow. "This could be very, very big," he says. "Am I a dreamer? Yes, by definition. I believe we can be a Fortune 500 company. That is my dream."

Not every entrepreneur harbors such a lofty ambition, of course. At least not publicly. In fact, quite a few set more modest goals, such as, say, a mere $100 million in sales followed by a sweet merger deal with a giant corporation that will enable them to push out in a new direction.

But whether they aspire to leave Microsoft in the dust or just create a nationwide chain of cheese shops, almost all exhibit an unshakable conviction that their product will take the world by storm. Yes, they acknowledge the possibility of failure, but that is usually a pro forma bow to the skeptics, even if they have failed before.

They believe. Ardently.

Paul A. Brown, founder of the company that today sticks needles into tens of millions of Americans every year, has been in the small-business landscape for four decades and has seen a shared quality among many of his thriving counterparts.

"To succeed, an entrepreneur absolutely must have delusions of grandeur," Brown says. By that, he amplifies, he does not mean a quixotic tilting at windmills, but rather an enthusiasm bordering on fanaticism about a product. He recalls the shaky beginnings of his first company, MetPath Inc., which he started just out of medical school in 1967 in a New York City apartment. "I was twenty-eight, a resident, I had $500 to my name, and my goal was to build a Fortune 500 company," he says.

He came close. After he sold MetPath to Corning Inc. in 1982 for $142 million, it was renamed Quest Diagnostics and ultimately made the grade, moving to number 366 in 2005, with $4.73 billion in revenue, up from number 391 the previous year.

That doesn't impress Brown. "It could have been a lot bigger," he says.

Coulda, woulda, shoulda. The only limit seems to be the entrepreneur's own estimation of how big the company can become. Luke Visconti figures his company, DiversityInc, will top out at maybe $100 million over the next decade. "Easily," he adds, enlarging the scope of possibility. "There is absolutely no doubt about it." He rattles off the reasons why. The circulation of the flagship *DiversityInc* magazine will grow from 150,000 in 2004 to 250,000 in 2006 and eventually to 350,000 or more. With ad revenues surging in a tough market for print journalism, revenues in 2005 were expected to double to nearly $10 million. The price *DiversityInc* charges per 1,000 circulation for a full-page ad— an industry benchmark—was $90 net, he says, an almost unheard-of premium. Unlike most publications in the throes of fast growth, *DiversityInc* will stay in the black.

Revenue will flow in from other sources, as well. DiversityInc.com's Career Center job search site alone will generate $6 million plus. He has linked up his job site with several big newspapers and expects to pull in dozens more, building a presence in every major city in the country. And opportunities in other fields abound. "We're not doing events yet," Visconti says. "The Conference Board makes a lot of money on them. I plan to do them, by 2006 at the latest. They should be a huge money generator, $2 million a year at least."

And what is to prevent him from providing consulting services to companies on diversity management? The market for those services will be boundless. With Latino and Asian populations in the United States exploding, immigrants pouring across our borders, white baby boomers retiring, and corporations realizing that to stay competitive they must recruit and promote minority talent, the momentum is building, Visconti insists. In the blink of a racially sensitive eye, every last company in the country with a grain of sense will be clamoring for guidance on how to adjust to this new workplace reality.

There are all kinds of other possibilities, he continues: joint ventures with other companies, education, TV, radio. "We'll be an irresistible force," he states.

*   *   *

Irresistible force. Unlimited potential. A good shot at being in every household in America. A cinch at capturing a piece of every home financing deal. That is the way entrepreneurs think.

"It is not a delusion of grandeur so much as a terminal optimism," says Kerry Sulkowicz, the psychoanalyst and corporate consultant. "It is necessary to have that grand vision. It is immensely motivating. It also breeds a kind of hope in the people you're dependent on. It inspires the people working for you to follow you."

Guy Kawasaki, the venture capitalist and author, considers this outlook the primary characteristic of a business innovator. "So many people will tell you it can't be done," he says. "If everyone took to heart those dire warnings, there would never have been an entrepreneur in the history of man. We'd still be rolling stones." Of course, many entrepreneurs do delude themselves; 99 percent of the time, he says, they fall flat on their faces. But without their delusions—their incurable optimism—there would never be that 1 percent that make all the difference.

Here is Nadine Thompson, the CEO of Warm Spirit Inc., holding forth on Warm Spirit's bright promise.

"We've triple-digit grown every year that we've been in business, which is amazing," she says. Revenue shot up 150 percent to $12 million in 2004 and was on its way to 100 percent growth in 2005 to $24 million, for example, and as she sees it, the next threshold is $100 million. Beyond that, she says, "I think the potential is really unlimited."

Hmmm. The target audience for Warm Spirit's soaps, lotions, and body treatments is black women, a large but not unlimited demographic niche. But nothing is carved in stone. Warily, Thompson talks about branching out to other women of color. And, heck, white women. And men. The introductory statement on the company Web site captures the emerging big-tent philosophy. "What hasn't changed is our commitment to serve women of color, all women and all people," it says.

The question would-be entrepreneurs should be asking themselves is whether they are thinking big enough. If you feel in your bones you're onto something big, if it is the chase after your dream more than the quick payoff that keeps you going, if you harbor dreams of building your $1 million ten-person firm into a $1 billion giant, if you brush off the question of whether it might make the Fortune 500 someday but can't bring yourself to rule it out, you are an entrepreneur.

On the other hand, if you are thinking about starting a coffee shop or Christmas tree farm because you think it might be a rewarding way to make a living, you might have a great future as a business owner, but you aren't an entrepreneur. If you are planning to open a Dunkin' Donuts franchise, you may end up selling millions of doughnuts, but you aren't really an entrepreneur. If you are hoping to amass a stable of a dozen Applebee's restaurants, you might make some serious money, but that will not make you an entrepreneur.

Entrepreneurs harbor grand ambitions. Sig Anderman, founder of Ellie Mae, a provider of software and Internet services to the mortgage industry, for example, makes the cut. He tackles the Fortune 500 question—will Ellie Mae hit the mark someday?—without nuance. "Absolutely," he declares. "I don't think I'm being completely delusional because the mortgage industry is so huge, the third- or fourth-largest industry in the country, somewhere between $2.7 trillion and $3 trillion in loans. That comes to 20 million loans, and about $2,000 to $3,000 is wasted in each loan." And it is Ellie Mae's ambition to squeeze out the waste.

How long will it take to reach the Fortune 500? "I'd say five more years," he predicts.

Five years, ten years. Somewhere down the road. Liz Ryan, founder of the professional women's networking e-mail community WorldWIT, hopes that a decade from now, "we'll be in the same category as a 401(k), as something employees expect from their company. We like to think job candidates will ask potential employers, 'Of course, you have a WorldWIT discussion group, don't you?'"

To illustrate the scope of her ambitions, she draws a chart showing "community listserv (e-mail)"—the technical name for her service—as the center circle, orbited by "weekly radio," "weekly HTML newsletter," "events," "surveys," and "conferences." She also draws a line at a 45-degree angle from the bottom of the page at the left marked "now" and the top of the line at the right marked "later."

No, WorldWIT probably won't ever be a Fortune 500 company, or even a publicly traded one, she says. On the other hand, it has already achieved a certain grandeur. Ryan claims it is "the largest e-mail discussion group on the planet," with 100,000 members exchanging thousands of carefully monitored e-mails a month as of August 2005—a figure she is confident will grow to at least 250,000 by the end of 2006—plus thousands more "bridge" members at corporate sites it plans to set up.

It won't make the Fortune 500, she repeats, but it *could* become a unit at a much larger organization, such as a publishing concern or dot-com conglomerate.

Is this all just fantasizing? That is the point. You can't reach the stars if you don't fantasize about it. "We think about expanding into new areas all the time," Ryan says. "Our plates are so full, but people always ask us: 'What about women in health care?' Oh, that could be interesting. 'What about alumni groups?' Oh, yeah. 'What about moms?' Oh, yeah.

"I am excited about this," she says. "There is kind of like no limit. You get people really using our community in really interesting ways that we wouldn't have thought of on our own. Like a person in Milwaukee posting to our European groups and our groups in Asia saying, 'Hey, I'm the room mom for my daughter's fifth-grade class. If you are involved in your school and our kids are roughly the same age, what about setting up an international scholastic pen pals association?' How easy would that be? The miracle of e-mail."

Speaking of e-mail, Gary Doan has no doubt that he will capture a slice of this fast-growing pie. His company, Intradyn, makes backup systems for companies' e-mail. The data protection market is probably already close to $10 billion, Doan notes, and the e-mail archiving market, while now a small part of that, should grow at more than 50 percent a year to $4.5 billion in 2009.

Intradyn's basic Rocket Vault has a target market of several million small businesses. And while the Compliance Vault is aimed at a much smaller group—a few hundred thousand small brokerages, investment banks, and other firms—he foresees a rush of orders as they come to realize that they must store the data on nonerasable tape to meet federal regulations.

"As more and more companies buy it, there will be a chain reaction," Doan predicts. He projected a fiftyfold increase in sales of the Compliance Vault alone to somewhere between $50 million and $100 million by 2007. By then, he expects, it will have been acquired by a big corporation—and he will be on to his next project.

Greg Herro's target market is much bigger. Today, 26 percent of the 2.5 million Americans who die each year are cremated, ranging from 15 percent to 20 percent on the East Coast to 60 percent in many places on the West Coast. The national average is expected to hit 55 percent by 2020. On top of that, 98 percent of the people in Japan are cremated, as are 70 percent of the people in the United Kingdom, two markets that hold great promise. Add to all that the fact that most of LifeGem's customers buy two or three diamonds, and you have a formula for growth.

"Our mission is to be the primary reason people choose cremation," Herro says.

. . .

It helps to have a vast potential market, especially if you have a unique product or one that competitors can't match. As you will see later in this chapter, entrepreneurs almost universally believe they have one or the other. While that confidence can sometimes delude them into making lofty assumptions about their growth prospects, it also helps keep their spirits up when they go through rough patches.

Michael Huddy, chief executive of International Barrier Technology, is sure that the market for the Blazeguard wood panels and other fire-resistant building materials the company makes with its patented Pyrotite compound is huge.

Like Herro, Huddy likes to indulge in statistical analysis about how huge. Tens of millions of homes will have to be built in the United States by 2030 to accommodate a burgeoning population of 350 million and to replace all the aging homes that will be torn down between now and then. Not to mention all the dwellings destroyed by ever-more-destructive hurricanes such as Katrina and other natural calamities. With land becoming scarcer in urban areas, the houses will be constructed closer together, and fire protection will take on a new urgency.

"The prospects for building are extraordinary," Huddy comments. "From our standpoint, the market is basically almost limitless." Which is not to say International Barrier will become a colossus bestriding the housing materials market. It is to say that Huddy is optimistic about capturing niche markets where the advantages of its technology are apparent. Already, it has pulled in some revenue supplying roofing for commercial modular buildings used for portable classrooms and the like. By seizing opportunities such as that, Huddy predicts, International Barrier's revenues will surge to $100 million over the next decade (from $4.4 million in fiscal 2005).

"The market for fire-retardant products is probably 50 billion square feet a year," he says. "We're right now at about 8 million. We haven't even scratched the surface. There is a huge market out there for us to grow in."

Martin Klein, chief executive of Electro Energy Inc., a maker of high-technology batteries with 2004 revenues of $6.7 million, predicts it will be a $500 million company someday. In a growing $50 billion industry, it might surpass that, though he doubts it will ever make the Fortune 500.

Alex Lidow harbors no such reservations about his International Rectifier, a $1.2 billion maker of power management semiconductors. Power management, the key to energy conservation, will blossom into a $70 billion industry by 2013 from $15 billion today, he predicts, and there is "no question" his company will outpace the general growth. "We're chewing it up right now because our unique strategy of technology pull is hard to imitate," he says.

Joe Macchia, a newly minted septuagenarian, sees plenty of earning left in his future. "There's $175 million in business out there that I could get my hands on—I just know it—in a slightly high-risk corner of property and casualty insurance, commercial auto/garage," he says. "That includes parking lots and garages, auto repair shops, used-car lots. I know that sector like the back of my hand. There's also a lot of business to be had selling general liability business to small contractors." In early 2005, in fact, he started the Macchia General Agency insurance company.

Though sales of his Seahorse Power Company's solar-powered compactors were a modest half a million dollars in 2005, James Poss says, "There is absolutely no limit to the opportunity out there." A lot of compactor and appliance manufacturers are showing interest in the contraptions as an extension of their product lines and could open up their distribution channels. He is in early talks with Japanese companies about possible licensing agreements and also has his eye on China, Korea, and Western Europe. Eventually, he would like to use the expertise in circuitry and power management that he is gaining for other applications, including water desalination in the third world.

Pete Newman, who sold Gotham Software Inc. when he realized a deeper-pocketed start-up was aiming for the same market, thinks his next project could be as modest as creating a new board game or writing a screenplay. Even so, he was thinking big when he was in charge of Gotham. If only he had gotten the funding he needed, he says, "We would have built the product and launched it and either grown aggressively and made millions or been acquired by a big financial company someday for $50 million or more." It could have gotten even bigger than that, he says, except his plan all along was to bail out and "go fly-fishing" once a certain size was reached.

•   •   •

Some limit their aspirations for temperamental reasons, such as the restless drive that is discussed in Chapter 5. The Meiland sisters, for example, hope to expand their Manhattan bridal shop into a chain with stores in New York, Beverly Hills, Texas, Palm Beach, Chicago, and maybe London, and extend into jewelry, accessories, and other related products. But if they become bored with their start-up, they will sell it and move on to something else.

Some say that focusing on the size of a business misses the point. Cameron Johnson considers the Fortune 500 question irrelevant. "That is just going to happen if it happens," he says. "Bill Gates was a nerd. He built Microsoft just because he wanted to write languages for computers. He didn't have any idea that he would become the richest man in the world. That wasn't his goal. That was just one of the benefits."

Ross Levin, president of Accredited Investors Inc., concurs. "Size is a poor measure of success," he asserts. "The real gauge is: Are we doing what we are supposed to be doing?"

It goes without saying that some business owners have a faith in their product that can defy logic. And that is not always a good thing. I once went to a trade show in Pittsburgh, sponsored by one of those invention marketing firms, where would-be inventors from all over the country came to display their wares. I strolled past hundreds of booths behind which eager designers proudly showcased the products they hoped would capture the hearts of consumers everywhere. There was a Christmas tree stand that one inventor was certain could hold any size trunk with ease and would last forever. So what if it weighed about forty pounds? There was a wooden apparatus that could be glued to a kitchen cabinet to hold a ketchup bottle upside-down, eliminating forever the risk of throwing out one's shoulder trying to shake the last few drops out of the bottle. So what if it was ugly? There was a balloon-activated bubble blower. So what if the chances were 1 in 10,000 that the cheap plastic device could be sold at a profit, and 10,000 to 1 that if it was, a big toy company would steal the market away with a more attractive knockoff?

But I couldn't help noticing the glint of the true believer in the eyes of these hopefuls.

I say all this to differentiate the real entrepreneurs from the lightweight enthusiasts who might display a single entrepreneurial trait—delusions of grandeur—and none of the others.

Successful entrepreneurs have those other hardwired traits—a knack for seizing opportunities nobody else has noticed, an unrelenting drive that keeps them in the game when things start falling apart, a genetic predisposition to start moneymaking ventures, a feverish desire to be in charge that keeps them on top of all aspects of the business, a knack for navigating shifting circumstances, and a hard-nosed pragmatism—that, taken together, give justification to their vision for their products.

"You have to believe in your product," says Herro of LifeGem. "If you don't believe in it and it's not a life goal, if you don't think that it is something that you can sink your heart and soul into, it's never going to amount to what you think it can. Flip side: If you do sink your heart and soul into it, it's going to go beyond your expectations."

•   •   •

As I've said, entrepreneurs believe in both the uniqueness and superiority of their products. They can sound a bit like proud parents carrying on about the extraordinary intelligence of their toddlers. Indeed, it's impossible to miss the affection in their voices when they talk about their creations. Listen to Peter Amico describe one of his omnidirectional forklifts:

"The vehicle basically has no parts. It is a very simple machine. It will go up a flight of stairs. For somebody to move a big machine around in a crowded place with tight spaces can take hours. We can do it in seconds. Take the example of a twenty-foot bar sitting against a wall in a twelve-foot-wide corridor. Our forklift could just move sideways down the corridor, pick it up, and move sideways back. A traditional forklift couldn't even get at it. People ask us, 'How wide is the narrowest aisle you can operate in?' The machine is 84¼ inches wide. So the answer is 85 inches.

"We recently conducted tests and found that this vehicle is twice as safe from a stability standpoint compared with standard forklifts. In certain stability tests, most competitive truck lifts will fall over at a 27- or 28-degree angle, ours only beyond a 45-degree angle. Our lift truck has a low cowl and no steering wheel or hydraulic levers, giving it the best visibility in the world in its category."

He could go on, and he did. But you see my point.

The adulation that such people show for their products is usually well placed. They are smart, they have done their research, they have studied the competition, they have taken out patents, they have taken their lumps and bounced back.

They have earned their bragging rights. Take Sig Anderman, the self-described "arms dealer" to mortgage brokers. Within months of the founding of his company, Ellie Mae, he says, twenty other companies were trying to imitate him, including General Electric, Fannie Mae, Microsoft, and a slate of dot-coms.

"Everybody said they had the definitive system," he points out. "But today, we are the dominant player in the business of connecting mortgage brokers with appraisers, title companies, wholesale underwriters, Fannie Mae and Freddie Mac, flood reporting companies, and so on. Of 40,000 mortgage companies in the United States, 23,000 use our E-Pass Platform. We now have 190 employees and expect revenue of $30 million in 2005." That compares with $18 million in 2004.

He's not tooting his own horn; he's just reciting the facts.

The bottom line, he believes, is that Ellie Mae has solved the maddening inefficiencies that have plagued the mortgage industry since its inception.

It is a claim that entrepreneurs make again and again: Their product is simpler, easier to use, a breath of fresh air in an increasingly complicated, convoluted world. And they are onto something. The market value of simplicity came home to me years ago when I was reporting a story about the nation's biggest retailer of electronic organs. Bob Fletcher, the owner of a Florida chain of shopping-mall stores called Fletcher Music Centers, told me that slumping sales in the mid-seventies had pushed him to the verge of closing up shop when he realized why the Japanese organs that had become the only game in town were losing their appeal to the elderly, his main customers. They were too complicated, with endless buttons and tiny letters inhospitable to arthritic hands and failing eyes. So he started his own line with big, easy-to-use buttons, and sales took off.

The mass of Americans who have trouble using their microwave ovens or can't figure out how to turn on their cell phones know what I am talking about.

Doan of Intradyn does, too. Doan touts the elegant simplicity of his Rocket Vault data storage system, calling it the perfect alternative to the bewildering machines that most small-business owners and managers just don't have the time to master. "It is simple to use," Doan boasts. "You just plug it in. It's automated. It's simple to operate. You don't have to have an IT staff. Even technophobes can learn how to use it in less than one hour. The price starts at $1,500, a one-time investment, and you own both the hardware and the software."

Newman, founder of Gotham Software, sings the same simplicity tune. Though he was forced to cut his venture short, the software that he was producing for the financial services industry was designed to let people collaborate in the most efficient way.

"Everybody wins," he says of the vision he had. "The issuer gets a lower cost. The banks may end up with lower fees, but by streamlining and speeding up the process, our software enables them to do more deals. It also keeps them in regulatory compliance. Some banks skirt the rules, plead ignorance, and pay fines. That opens a niche for me to get in there and say, 'Hey, you're not being ethical.'"

*   *   *

Throughout this book, you have probably detected passion in the voices of entrepreneurs as they speak about their companies and their products. That is another element of their delusions of grandeur, or perhaps just another name for it. They believe, passionately. They are the holy rollers of the business world.

Not only that, but they know they have passion and, being pragmatists (a tendency that will be explored in Chapter 8), they leverage it to their advantage. Or rather, they display it and watch the magical effect it has on those around them.

"My employees buy into the vision and the plan because I get so passionate about things," says Anderman of Ellie Mae. "They are inspired by my unwavering belief that we can be successful."

You also have to be passionate about your product. The Meiland sisters' father once stopped them short by asking them whether they were passionate about their plan to start a pastry shop in Manhattan. No, they replied, they weren't, and they realized with a start that that was the reason why the project seemed to be going nowhere.

"If you want to start a company, you have to have passion," Lara Meiland affirms.

Lidow of International Rectifier says his long affair with semiconductors was love at first sight. He had gone to Cal Tech as a scared seventeen-year-old with the intention of studying to be an aeronautical engineer. But on his first day, he attended his first class in applied physics, the foundation of semiconductors. "I fell in love with it instantly," he says.

Within five years, he had his Ph.D. in applied physics from Stanford. "I rushed through because I just couldn't wait to get out there" and apply his learning to the business world.

Vonfrolio, the nurse who runs Education Enterprises, gets right to the point. "The only entrepreneurial trait that is universal, in my view, is passion," she says. "I've met smart entrepreneurs, stupid entrepreneurs, compulsive entrepreneurs, laid-back entrepreneurs, but they all had passion. Some go into it for the fun, some to make money, some to prove a point, some because they don't want to work for anybody else, but the successful ones all have passion. Some are decisive, some are scattered. I've had nurse entrepreneurs call ten times a day in a panic, asking, 'What should I do?' But they have passion."

According to Ross Levin, founder of Accredited Investors, the actual product is almost irrelevant. "You could build a business with anything, as long as you can find something you can be passionate about," he comments. "I could have been a minister; I bet I would have built a thriving congregation."

Small-business visionaries have to have the confidence to overcome the naysayers. "Everybody is going to tell you you're wrong," says Doan of Intradyn. "'Why do you think that when nobody else does?' I've heard that so many times."

The more unusual your product, the higher the degree of skepticism you may encounter. Overcoming people's doubts requires a healthy overdose of optimism, and entrepreneurs do not disappoint. Bob Hillier, the architect and property developer, says their optimism is typically "insatiable." It suffuses their vocabulary, as when Schweighardt says a new book "could be the breakthrough I've been waiting for" or Amico declares that, beyond just believing in his product, he "*knew* it would work," or Anderman describes himself as the most optimistic person he knows, or Brown says his hearing care company "is at a major crossroads."

Charlie Horn, chairman of the Promirus Group in Tucson, Arizona, and a recent entrepreneur in residence of the McGuire Entrepreneurship Program at the University of Arizona's Eller College of Business, has come to a somewhat philosophical conclusion about entrepreneurs' upbeat nature.

"They believe in creating a future possibility that they can achieve, often something others don't believe is possible," he remarks. "This trait has to do with having the ability to ignore the past." He elaborates: "By the way we're brought up, we've become conditioned to what's not possible, from the time we start to walk and talk. As we get older, the realm of the possible becomes narrower and narrower, and we develop compensations for what's not possible. I believe entrepreneurs develop the ability to ignore the past and break loose from that mind-set."

For sheer, exuberant optimism, talk to Richard Wellman. He merrily discusses the failures and setbacks he has endured over the years, from which he has always managed to bounce back. After making $4 million in a deal with American International Group Inc. to restore damaged airplane parts, he says, "I took all that money and started my own airline, Custom Air Transport, and pissed it all away." Today he keeps busy with sundry projects but figures opportunity is just around the corner.

"People are always asking me what I'm doing," Wellman says. "I'm doing what I always do: I'm a phone call away from the next $1 million deal."

• • •

What I most remember about the protagonists in Albert Camus's novels, such as *The Stranger* or *The Plague,* that I read in my college days was that they were always trying to leave their mark on the world—their "scar." Camus's existentialist theory was that the authentic hero revolted against the absurdity of the universe by means of bold action that would leave its imprint for posterity to ponder. It was a way of shaking your fist at cruel fate.

Don't we all want to do that, leave our mark in one way or another? That current is especially strong in entrepreneurs. They don't just want to run their own show, though that is what throws them into the race. Once they are running, they decide they want to change the world.

We've already seen that clearly enough. Amico thinks his omnidirectional vehicles will fundamentally redirect the construction industry. Doan thinks his data storage systems will sweep the small-business world. Huddy feels an obligation to get his company's fire-retardant technology onto the market because he is convinced it will save countless lives. Klein believes the superefficient batteries he produces will help lower pollution and reduce America's dependence on oil. Lidow says his company is at the forefront of solving the world's energy crisis and claims that its variable-speed-motion and lighting technologies could slash the world's annual energy consumption of 404 quadrillion BTUs by 30 percent. "I feel so strongly we have to change that I get overly passionate," he declares. James Poss, whose company makes solar-powered trash compactors, says he is extremely passionate about energy saving and is on a mission "to stop the bleeding."

Innovation also has a human face, and Herro tells this story to prove it. His first commercial order for a diamond came from a man named Bill Sefton, whose twenty-seven-year-old daughter was dying of Hodgkin's disease. She had fallen into a coma and had only a few days to live when Sefton learned about LifeGem and contacted Herro.

The young woman had written a letter to her family, telling them she wanted each member to take some of her ashes with them whenever they traveled and to sprinkle them on the streets and beaches and in the parks and woods so that she could say she had been there. "If I catch any of you putting me on your mantel, I will come back and haunt you," she had scolded them.

"So she got it—she got the LifeGem concept of keeping your loved one with you as you go forward in life," Herro says. "Everything up until this point has been about the end. How do we bury the body, how do we get rid of the body, how do we make the body small enough to put it in the closet, how do we do that? We came along and said that's wrong. What it is about is remembering your loved one and making something beautiful that you can keep with you and go forward in life.

"Bill's daughter was a diamond when she was alive and she's a diamond when she's gone," he sums up. "That's what her family said again and again."

Entrepreneurs see themselves in benevolent roles. Their delusions of grandeur spread out into a grand vision of doing good. They want to create a better world. They will tell you so, and they will advertise the fact to the public.

True, it is in their self-interest to strike that pose. It polishes the corporate image and might even burnish the bottom line.

But, generally, they are sincere in their idealism. Some want to change the world, as we have seen; others hold more modest hopes about improving a corner of it. Thompson wants to empower women—especially African Americans, but really all women who have been beaten down in a patriarchal society—and in recruiting them to market her company's body care lotions, she preaches the virtues of "grasping our part of the American dream." As described elsewhere in this book, she also hopes someday to start network marketing companies in poor countries, creating jobs for women in places such as South Africa and Ghana.

"I'd love to see a woman who says, 'OK, I can make another product with this or I'm going to use the money from Warm Spirit to open my own spa in South Africa or my own hair salon,'" Thompson says. "I don't think Warm Spirit is the end of the road. I think Warm Spirit has to be a doorway."

Horn cites thousands of people who have told him that the money they have saved from using his company's ScriptSave card helped them pay the rent and afforded them access to medication that otherwise might have been beyond their reach. Anderman calculates that his company saves more than 75,000 trees a year by eliminating so much paperwork in the mortgage industry. Hughes, the small-business consultant, says he has a "Robin Hood agenda" to reach out to help people fix their troubled companies. Mahoney decided to run for Congress in 2006 in part, he says, to save the Democratic Party from its "disarray." Levin says he recently visited an elderly client in her home not to offer investment advice but to help her deal with "emotional issues" such as whether to sell her house. Reading aloud a note she sent him thanking him for his "depth of understanding," Levin declares: "That's why I'm in this business!"

Often, entrepreneurs trace their idealism back to their youth. Hillier remains proud of his role as a student at Princeton University in leading a revolt against the anti-Semitic eating clubs of the day. He says he got a diverse group of jocks, thespians, and class leaders to band together to demand an alternative. "It rattled the university," he recalls. "The trustees said no, but our action eventually led to change."

•   •   •

This raises an interesting question: What is more important to the entrepreneur: making a positive contribution to society or just making money?

The received wisdom is that making money is not that important, really; what counts to a true believer is the challenge, and money is for the most part a barometer of success. There is a lot of truth to that, but it isn't necessarily that simple.

Still, it is the prevailing view. Judith Cone of the Kauffman Foundation says that getting rich is "absolutely not the core motivation" for most successful entrepreneurs, but rather is an agreeable by-product of their efforts. Granted, she says, a lot of people start companies to make a mint—they came out of the woodwork in the dot-com boom—but they don't succeed over the long haul.

A lot of entrepreneurs echo that view. "I really don't care that much about money," Plank says. Herro calls making money a sideline, not the principal goal, and adds, "If people see a dollar sign on your forehead, you'll never succeed. But if they see what you really want is to find a solution, you will."

Levin says he frequently passes up chances to make a quick buck, such as his decision to allow software makers to use his Wealth Management Index for free and his readiness to cast off obnoxious clients. He also advises clients to stop focusing so much on money and more on what they want to do with their lives.

"I had a client in today who has way more money than he needs yet always asks his wife for receipts from her shopping trips," he mentions. "We told him, 'You need therapy.'" He advised a corporate muckety-muck to chuck his $250,000 salary and pursue his dream of writing a novel. "His income has fallen to about $25,000," Levin says. "And he just wrote me a note: 'Thank you for giving me the courage to do this and making me believe in myself.'"

Hillier, the owner of an architectural firm, is in the money-is-secondary camp, but not 100 percent. "I had dinner the other night with an entrepreneur and I asked him about his business, but all he could talk about was the money," he says. "That's not true entrepreneurship."

On the other hand, he says, he really gets a kick out of making money. Recalling how his friends helped him put on a puppet show when he was seven, then grabbed the $2 proceeds afterward, leaving him without a penny, he says, "The experience taught me a great lesson: Greed drives everybody."

No kidding, say the money-matters folks. As someone who has made a lot of money, lost it, and made it back, Eller of Eller Media says he considers himself an expert on the subject. "The potential for making a lot of money is a main driver," he says. "To say it isn't is BS."

Others are equally blunt. Brown: "You have to want to get rich." Gyenes: "I have always been oriented to being successful, for a combination of reasons, of which money is a big one. I care about money because I want a lifestyle that requires money." Mahoney waxes lyrical about freedom of action as the "greatest gift" of running a business but adds: "Part of creative freedom is having working capital."

But do they mean it? "I think that is how they rationalize it," says Tim Faley, managing director of the Samuel Zell and Robert H. Lurie Institute for Entrepreneurial Studies at the University of Michigan's business school. "They think, 'I'll tell the world I'm doing it for the money and somehow I won't seem so crazy.'"

Newman of Gotham Inc. recalls his disillusionment with jobs in corporate America early in his professional career, and, after getting dismissed from one of them, his delight in teaching inner-city kids.

"I believe idealism is a driving entrepreneurial force," he says. "That's all you have to hold on to when it's 2 A.M. and nothing's going right and nobody has been returning your calls. It sustains you through the darkness."

CHAPTER 7

Wait a Minute: Will This Work?

It is tempting to view entrepreneurs as somehow stuck in adolescence, bursting with energy and driven by grandiose dreams the way we all were once upon a time. In truth, their lofty ambitions are often accompanied by a firm pragmatism that keeps them grounded in reality.

To be a true entrepreneur, you've got to keep asking yourself questions such as: Wait a minute—will this really work? Does anyone really want what I have to offer? For every optimistic message from the right side of your brain that tells you to reach for the stars, there has to be a cautionary one from the left side of your brain that beseeches you to see the writing on the wall.

The evolution from romantic to realist can take time, but it has to happen if you are to achieve success. James Poss tinkered in his basement from the age of eight, coming up with increasingly sophisticated gadgets: a crossbow, a rocket from a kit, a battery-powered fan. But only when he did research to see if anybody had taken out patents on his ideas did he begin to address the practical question of whether anything could come of his inventions.

As discussed in Chapter 1, Poss came up with an idea in college for making an energy-efficient clothes dryer with a vacuum chamber, but after digging up ten patents that covered the process, he realized you can't patent a concept, only a *method* for utilizing it.

He did more research and learned that nobody had marketed a vacuum dryer. He realized *he* could get a patent for making a vacuum dryer, as long as it was distinct from the other ten that had already been patented.

"It was at that moment, I think, that I got the entrepreneurial bug," Poss says. "I was suddenly connecting inventions to the marketplace."

He was still—and is still today—in thrall to an ideal: to help create a better world by increasing energy efficiency. But he was beginning to understand that you have to be practical in order to make it happen.

At first, he resisted advice from his older brother to spend time working as a corporate manager to learn how the industry worked. But eventually, he realized his brother had a point: hands-on experience matters.

Out of college, he did a stint with Disney World, helping to make a motor for its new motorcycle ride; with Saturn and Ford, to help them develop hybrid motors; with Solectria, to sell electrical vehicle components; with a San Francisco company that made plastic molded sailboats. Then, at his brother's recommendation, he applied to Babson College business school's entrepreneurial program, partly to learn the basics and partly to gain credibility as a serious contender in whatever venture he dreamed up.

That tug again, between passion and pragmatism. On the one hand, Poss says, "There I was, writing business plans for grandiose products like a geothermal-energy project and a floating windmill farm." On the other hand, "From working at Solectria, I knew how to put together a powerful drive system to drive a compactor, a solar vehicle that goes up and down."

Dot Smith, founder of gourmet foods producer Pepper Patch Inc., made a similar journey from wide-eyed to hard-nosed. "I learned not to produce a jelly or jam just because it sounded good," she says. "You might want to do some market research."

In her early days, she discovered, she was unwittingly serving as a research kitchen for a lot of other companies. If she created a jam or jelly that became a big hit, Smuckers or some other industry player would immediately hit the shelves with a similar, cheaper product. For a time, she was selling her pumpkin-and-sweet-potato butter to Disney World. Though Smuckers held the franchise for Disney World, the amusement park could carry Pepper Patch's butters because Smuckers didn't make those flavors. "But guess what?" Smith notes. "They make them now."

Smith has come a long way from the days when she had to ask someone to explain the difference between assets and liabilities. She laughs at her former naïveté and recounts what her experience has taught her. "The temptation is to just go out there and get huge sales and then think about how you are going to fill the orders," she says. "But then they beat you down on price and you learn what margin is. You have to know where you are in different distribution channels: wholesale accounts, business-to-business sales, catalogue sales, the Internet, retail. Don't ever try to compete with wholesalers."

Her advice to people new to the small-business world: As you expand, focus on financing above all else. The best products, she says, are almost always made by newcomers to the business who haven't yet grasped the sanctity of the bottom line.

But regardless of how good their jellies or jams are, she says, if they don't get their financial house in order, they will hit their production ceiling. They will no longer be able to meet demand without building a facility (which means taking on debt), bringing in an outside investor (which can lead to a loss of control), or getting a co-packer that makes the product using your recipe (which can compromise quality, as they often substitute cheaper ingredients for the original ones).

. . .

In contrast to Americans such as Poss and Smith, Umang Gupta, the CEO of Keynote Systems, was an utter realist about his career from his elementary school days.

Though Gupta loved to assemble gadgets, including a magic-lantern slide projector and a paddlewheel boat, he never made the connection between his inventiveness and the marketplace. Growing up in a middle-class social milieu in India that shunned business and finance, he never thought that his imaginative tinkering would lead to a career in business.

Three paths lay open to him, he believed: the military, engineering, or politics. He rejected the military as too constricting and engineering as too prosaic, and considered politics by default. Observing that he was better than almost anyone he knew at getting things done, he concluded he should be a manager, but not in government because the pay was too paltry. "So I decided my future lay in business management," he says.

And thus began his passage to American entrepreneurship.

Rather than seeking admission to a prestigious American engineering institution, as most of his college peers did, or attending the newly founded Indian Institute of Management in India, he went directly for a management degree in the United States, which nobody from his college had ever done before.

Rather than pay a small fortune (by Indian standards) in application fees to a lot of schools, he sent his résumé only to those that waived them, even if it meant studying on a little-known campus.

And rather than racking up debt, he chose the school that offered him the best financial package. Kent State gave him a full assistantship, and that is where he went.

In his first job out of business school as a systems/financial analyst at a steel company, realizing he would win over the floor workers more easily if he didn't speak like a British aristocrat, he trained himself to Americanize his accent.

He decided to switch to the computer industry because that was where the future was. He got a job at IBM in sales and marketing because that would be a quicker road to a leadership position than software engineering.

He then gave himself a crash course in the basics of business and finance.

"I really did not understand the fundamentals," Gupta says. "I had gone to an American business school. I had worked at an American steel company. But to really, really understand how an American banker makes money was something I had no clue about, and here I was selling them computers and trying to show them why computers ought to be good for them."

And so it went, a rigorous, disciplined excursion down the path of pragmatism.

After taking a leave of absence from IBM to return to India, Gupta came back to the United States and rejoined the computer giant in San Francisco. He got a promotion, but he also began laying the groundwork for starting his own company.

"I'm securing my base, getting myself financially ready," he recalls. "Evenings, I'm starting to learn the microprocessor business on my own as a hobby. I get together with a couple of Indian guys who were quite interested in the same subject and we actually form a little shell corporation. The personal-computer revolution is unfolding in front of me much the same way the Internet revolution will unfold twenty years later. I keep working away on this idea and even put together a little business plan. I have transformed myself from being this sort of executive type to wanting to be an entrepreneur."

He made a final decision: He would start a company in America, not India. And the springboard would be Silicon Valley, not IBM. So he left IBM, but he didn't quit the corporate life cold turkey. He prepared himself for independence by joining a hot Silicon Valley start-up called Magnuson Computers as the director of marketing.

A year later, he was ready and left Magnuson to start his own business. He hooked up with a partner, a database software geek, and started a small company "with the idea of getting venture capital and building a huge computer called a database computer." His plan, he says, was to "make this very, very specialized machine that could process databases 100 times faster than ordinary computers such as Magnuson or Amdahl could. A lot of people had written papers on database computers at the time. I devoured every one of them. I learned a lot about what was involved and I tried to find venture capital for it."

But then he failed. He failed so completely that he can no longer remember, exactly, the name of his fledgling venture. But he remembers why he failed. He had covered his bases on hardware (he knew it cold) and software (his partner knew it cold), but not venture capital.

With Silicon Valley start-ups in arcane new technologies sprouting like mushrooms, venture capitalists often had trouble understanding the products or services that they were financing. As a result, they put their trust not in the breakthroughs the founders promised, but in the management teams that had been assembled to carry them out.

Gupta and his sidekick did not a management team make. Neither had ever been the manager of so much as a print shop. Where, the potential investors wanted to know, was their CEO? While Gupta stalled them, he continued networking with people in his field and hit it off with a guy called Larry Ellison who headed a company that later became the Oracle Corporation. Ellison offered him a job, and he took it. "So I first became a consultant for him, with basically the charter to write the first formal business plan for Oracle, and soon after that joined as a full-time employee," he says.

For years, Gupta had been methodically priming himself to be an entrepreneur. And now here he was, a high-priced flunky for somebody else once again.

"All I knew was I had to learn some more," he says. "So I spent the next three years at Oracle both working on the sales and marketing side but also learning the entrepreneurial ropes, and learning the technology."

He persuaded Ellison to make him general manager of his first personal computer business. But he concluded that Oracle, which excelled at making software for mainframes, was heading for a stumble in the PC world. Most customers preferred smaller, nimbler competitors in the PC software business, he says—upstarts such as Microsoft and Lotus.

In 1984, Gupta left Oracle, joined forces with a former Oracle programmer named Bruce Scott, and launched Gupta Technologies with a 60-40 ownership split.

The dream was realized. He was finally an entrepreneur.

• • •

What is the lesson? It all comes down to the Greek adage to know thyself. If you have the right stuff—self-confidence, a sharp eye, drive, an overwhelming need to be in charge—you still have to be able to be *practical*. You have to show a steely resolve to stick to the game plan and to resist impulse.

William J. Dennis, the head researcher at the National Federation of Independent Business, compares entrepreneurs to musical geniuses such as Beethoven. What sets them apart from the crowd are their unusual insights, he says, but what transforms the insights into products is organizational aptitude.

Kenneth Smith, economics professor and former dean of the University of Arizona's Eller College of Management, speaks of those two mutually supporting qualities as "quotients." The "idea quotient" is the percentage of people within an organization who come up with the insights, he says, and "the innovation quotient" is the percentage of that group who know how to seize the commercial opportunity.

That is where his school's entrepreneurship program comes in. It links University of Arizona engineers, scientists, and others who have hit upon great ideas with can-do types who know how to commercialize them.

For example, he said, a group of optical scientists created a product that could look into the retina of a baby and determine whether it had been a victim of shaking. An undergraduate team of students worked with the scientists on a business plan and created a company called Optica.

"It all comes down to organization," says John Heagney of Heagney Public Relations. "An entrepreneur has to be really self-centered. You want to be in control. You're constantly thinking, 'It's my company. I run the show. I'm the boss. Me, me, me.' But that means you have to know yourself. If you don't examine your strengths and weaknesses, you're going to fail."

A cardinal rule for avoiding that trap is to hire somebody who is willing to stand up to you—somebody who is smart, independent-minded, and skeptical, with no compunction about questioning your latest harebrained scheme.

Outside consultants can play that role, too. Heagney has identified some common failings among small-business people, including not paying enough attention to public opinion. The wrong way to deal with a potentially troublesome turn of events is to hide it from public view, he says, a tactic doomed to failure. As in the case of a local developer who found the bones of a woolly mammoth, he points out, "the news will leak out, and suddenly there will be a feeding frenzy of paleontologists saying you are destroying Florida's natural history. You'll have cameras outside your office building."

This developer did it the right way. He contacted local paleontologists and several state agencies, got permission to remove the bones, and donated them to a local museum, with favorable press coverage and a plaque commemorating his generosity.

"If you mishandle the early stages of a situation, you put yourself below zero," Heagney concludes.

While it is important to have grand ambitions, an oversized ego can crowd out smart thinking. Kevin Plank, Under Armour's founder, says taming your self-importance is crucial for success. Keep second-guessing yourself, he advises; if new information makes a decision you just made suspect, back-track.

"I've made wrong decisions, but I've never stood on a mountaintop and said, 'Here's what we're going to do and here's our direction,'" Plank says. "You can't let pride and ego dictate the terms. You need to know where you're going, but if all of a sudden I-95 North is backed up with traffic, maybe you've got to take another route."

Not only should you consult colleagues you know will give you an honest opinion, he says, you have to do something that is much harder. "You have to realize you're not going to make all the decisions anymore," Plank said. "You have to delegate responsibility."

For Michael Huddy, CEO of International Barrier, that is a nobrainer. Yes, it was a shock to his ego to surrender a piece of his authority to a number two, and yes, he was so reluctant to take the step that he instructed her to do nothing for the first thirty days except talk to people and learn the ropes. Don't make any decisions, not yet, he instructed her.

But finally, he let go, and it was a lot easier than he thought it would be.

Sharing power with corporate partners has been crucial for the growth of International Barrier. For example, to break into the modular home industry, Huddy teamed up with a company that knew all the players and purchasing agents, lines and points of distribution, and ins and outs of the market. "You jump on the train and take off," he said. "It saves years."

The ultimate test of pragmatism is knowing when to get help, whether it be by hiring a CEO, taking a partner, or selling out altogether.

•   •   •

Kirt Poss used all the resources at his disposal to get where he is today. His starting point was to pursue a "challenging" career, possibly in medicine. As a college student, it only made sense to hold summer jobs at medical device companies to test his interest in the field and to study the products they made. After college, resolving to become a doctor, he moved to Boston to take science courses that would prepare him to apply to medical school. He also landed a laboratory job at the Massachusetts General Hospital's Center for Molecular Imaging Research and published papers with Ph.D.'s.

As his expertise grew in the interlocking fields of medicine, technology, and health care, he began to see a future for himself in business. The next logical step was to enroll in the F. W. Olin Graduate School of Business at Babson College, famed for producing entrepreneurs. After that, his plan was to work at a big health care company for five to ten years or so, and only then start his own business.

That is pragmatism for you. But there is more.

Two weeks before business school classes started, Ralph Weissleder, the head of the Center for Molecular Imaging Research and a big name in molecular imaging, asked Poss to join him in starting a company.

Poss, however, was practical as ever. He asked the world-renowned expert a lot of questions. He spelled out his reservations. He said he would have to think about it.

Six months later, Weissleder called again. This time, Poss outlined a business plan, and the two men talked through the idea for a second time. Again, Poss wanted to think about it.

"I had a lot of contacts in the health care and health science fields," he says. "I went to them with it. I asked, 'Is this real or imaginary?' My mind-set was not to do it—to do it only if the concept was so compelling that I had to do it. I strongly believe you better start with something that is really good."

Again, Poss demurred. He continued in his business school coursework. He had worked in imaging for three years, and he understood the technology; now he wanted to explore the business applications.

"Part of my reason for being so pragmatic was that I had just gotten married," he notes. "I knew that after I graduated from business school I could get a good job in Europe or the West Coast and really enjoy myself. Why throw that away?"

Finally, Weissleder won him over, and the two men incorporated VisEn Medical in the summer of 2000, between Poss's first and second years at Babson. As always, Poss was determined to get it right. He limited his appeals for money to angel investors—wealthy individuals who back promising start-ups—with expertise in health care. "I wanted people to ask tough questions and hold my ax to the grindstone," he says. "If they were willing to give me money, I figured, we really had something." He set a financing goal of $500,000. He garnered $1 million.

He exceeded the bar he set for himself and since then has surpassed his projections in building the company. He allows himself a self-congratulatory pat on the back. "This endeavor is going to be very, very good for me" if it is successful, he exults.

But he does know that all good things eventually come to an end. "I'm very pragmatic," he says. "Steve Jobs got fired by his board at the age of thirty. It happens all the time. I see it. I know I'm not immune from it. It has to be a match, and that may or may not be the case as things grow."

.   .   .

If pragmatism is a hallmark in the corporate world—where the bottom line rules and angry investors call for the CEO's scalp if the stock price dives—as well as at start-ups, it sometimes goes AWOL at nonprofits. Of course, nonprofits (and for-profits with a socially responsible bent) have to carefully balance idealistic goals with nitty-gritty business practices such as cost controls and strategic planning.

Nadine Thompson, who preaches empowerment to the African American women she recruits to sell her Warm Spirit body care products, views her larger mission as teaching business basics to idealistic young people. Her message to them is that the most noble cause will go nowhere unless it is carried along by a strong tide of pragmatism.

At a workshop in Boston, she asked a young woman what her "compelling vision" was. The woman replied it was to open a community center for black girls where they could read, learn to use computers, and pair up with mentors. Thompson prodded her to spin out more details of her dream, then cut her short with a simple question: What would the rent be?

The young woman thought about that and said maybe $2,000 a month.

How many staff would she need to hire?

Perhaps three.

What would she pay them?

Around $10 an hour.

What supplies would you need?

"We spent half an hour with her and we put a whole business plan together—I had somebody writing it out," Thompson says. "It turned out she would need about $70,000 for the first year."

Where would the woman get that kind of money? She had no idea. No bank would lend it to her, that much she knew.

"If you did Warm Spirit and you made $5,000 a month, you could bank $70,000 in less than a year and a half," Thompson pointed out to her. "Can you live on the money you're making at your full-time job now?" The woman said she could. Well, then, Thompson told her, if she walked into a bank and showed a lending officer a savings account of

$60,000, she could probably get a small-business loan to supplement her capital.

"All of a sudden, you could see it click" on her face, Thompson says.

There are practical benefits to engaging in socially redeeming activities. Luke Visconti, the founder of *DiversityInc*, a magazine and Web site that educates corporate America on the competitive advantages of attracting and promoting minorities, knows there is profit to be made in do-goodism.

Visconti cheerfully acknowledges that his Diversity Stock Index of the fifty most diversity-friendly publicly traded companies was created for marketing purposes. He goes on to say that one reason he is so generous with employee benefits is that it gives him the moral authority to fire nonproducers. "If they can't measure up, they have to go," he says.

Visconti appreciates the marketing potential of his commitment to social justice. Doing the right thing connects you with your community and customer, he has found. Joining the board of Bennett College, a school for African American women in Greensboro, North Carolina, was the right thing to do. It also helped solidify his friendship with the Reverend Jesse Jackson, a friendship that was bound to be noticed.

"When I go to the Rainbow-PUSH event, Jesse Jackson pals around with me," Visconti says. "Once, he ran across the lobby of a hotel and hugged me. Everybody there—IBM, GM, all the big corporations—noticed."

Youthful dreams of changing the world sometimes need a healthy dose of pragmatism. Many a college sophomore shuns the business world, envisioning a glamorous future on Broadway or digging up the ruins of a lost Inca kingdom. Happily, the almost inevitable reality check can flower into a business success.

Right after college, Greg Herro insisted on pursuing a career in music. For three years he kept at it, slowly beginning to appreciate the business side of the profession even as he grew to realize he would never see his name on a marquee. He threw in the towel, moved back home, and got into computer consulting, eventually starting his own company.

CALCULATED RISK

As we have seen, risk taking is an entrepreneurial characteristic. Some might say it is the opposite of pragmatism, but in fact it is disciplined, with close consideration of the cost-benefit ratio. Certainly, it has a gambling element, but it is never reckless gambling.

To be sure, risk is risk. Entrepreneurs are willing to bet a lot of time and treasure on their dreams. They can be excruciatingly cautious. But when the time comes to bet all their chips on what looks like a winning hand, they do it.

Herro's initial investment in LifeGem was the classic risk-it-all gambit. Each of the four partners put up $25,000, but he was the only one who didn't hold on to a paying job. He sold his consulting firm and his house in the suburbs, piled himself, his wife, his dog, and his cats into two cars, and headed into Chicago to live off savings until they were down to $2,000.

He was taking a risk, but it was a calculated one. He had spent a decade searching for the right outlet for his imaginative energy and had finally found it. He wasn't about to let financial apprehensions paralyze him now.

The reaction of the funeral industry amused him. Risk-averse (maybe burying cadavers will do that to you), they ignored his appeals for joining forces—until they saw he had a winning hand. Then they came calling.

"That's human nature," Herro says. "Most people aren't risk takers. They are not going to go out on a limb."

He tells this story of how taking a smart risk can make all the difference. LifeGem had finally made its big breakthrough. A crematorium had extracted carbon from human remains for the first time by using a special lower-temperature, reduced-oxygen procedure, and a laboratory had turned the carbon into extremely pure graphite—weapons-grade graphite, in fact. All that remained was the export of the graphite to Russia, home of the only specialists he could find capable of turning the graphite into diamonds.

The only problem was that the export of weapons-grade graphite would have involved all sorts of permits and forms and delays. So a Russian-speaking associate carried the compound through customs in a sealed plastic bag without declaring it. "It was legal, but the red tape would have taken forever," Herro says. "So we just took the chance of walking it through."

Entrepreneurs are audacious. They are willing to make huge bets and to suffer the consequences of losing. But their daring has nothing reckless about it.

"It isn't that they are risk takers so much as that they are extremely good at managing risk," says Smith of the Eller College of Management. Dennis of the NFIB puts it this way: "They don't roll the dice. They don't pursue wild schemes. They take calculated risks. They know they can't get 100 percent of the information they need, but they can get 90 percent. When ordinary people think of risk, their expectations of failure are high. When entrepreneurs do, their expectations of success are high."

Frank Landsberger knows about risk. In 2004, at age sixty, he led a dogsled expedition through the frozen wastes of Greenland to lay claim to the discovery of the world's northernmost island, which had been recently liberated from the sea ice by global warming. But Landsberger, a former venture capitalist and university professor and most recently an investment banker, says entrepreneurs are actually risk-averse: "They study a project to death in an effort to minimize risk."

Put another way, they don't leap out of bed in the morning and exclaim, "I'm going to take a risk," says William Bygrave, the Babson College professor. Rather, "they get out of bed and as they are in the bathroom shaving, they are thinking, 'Who in the hell can I get to share that risk with me?'"

And they almost always find someone to share it, he says, because their passion for their production is so infectious.

Of course, being a motley crowd of individualists if there ever was one, they show varying degrees of tolerance for risk. In general, experts say, they are more willing to take huge risks when they are young and have little to lose (and all the time in the world to make a comeback) than when they are getting on in years and in no mood to jeopardize their hard-earned wealth and reputations.

Not only that, but in the population at large, the tolerance for risk can increase as economic circumstances change either for the worse (as when a laid-off corporate manager opens a consulting firm) or the better (as when a retired executive dips into his savings to start a winery).

"The question is: When are people ready to take risks?" says Carl Schramm of the Kauffman Foundation. "I know somebody who worked as a bureaucrat at the Social Security Administration until he was fifty, then started his own company. And why not? He had a government pension to fall back on."

· · ·

A stark example of taking a make-or-break gamble because you have no alternative is Peter Amico's decision to put all his chips on AC-powered motors for his omnidirectional forklifts. Another one is Michael Huddy's $125,000 bet back in his Weyerhaeuser days that could have cost him his job.

At the time, he was being groomed to be an entrepreneur at Weyerhaeuser and had been sent to Wasau, Wisconsin, to turn around the money-losing Eastern hardwood operations. A nearby Mennonite community with a state-of-the-art sawmill soon came calling with a proposal. If he would lend them $125,000 to buy a beautiful stand of old-growth trees from a farmer who was demanding a cash payment, they would harvest them and then repay him in full, plus let him have the first truckloads of logs at a steep discount. It was a great opportunity, but his controller told him Weyerhaeuser would never go for it.

So he cut the check without informing Weyerhaeuser. Headquarters wouldn't find out until the end of the quarter, by which time the money would be replenished and he could show a good profit. He won the bet. Prices went up, so his division made even more money than he had anticipated.

"It was a big risk," Huddy says. "If there had been a forest fire,

I'd have been looking for a job. But it proves my point: Big companies are not good at taking advantage of sudden opportunities; small companies are."

Even huge risks are eminently pragmatic, because the events leading up to them have a momentum that can't be easily broken, he believes. "You are locked into this thing," he says. "You end up so far in it you don't have a choice. You've already spent everything you had and you leveraged everything, so you get to a point it's just kind of like adding a little more fuel to the fire. As long as you can last, there is always hope."

Hope is what drove Herbert Jian, the onetime Maoist Red Guard who went on to start a furniture store in California and, more recently, the US Import & Export Company in Phnom Penh, Cambodia. As a youth, Jian says, he "gradually took on the mentality of risk taker" because it was the only escape from the dreary totalitarian society that was crushing his spirit.

When a visiting American journalist asked him to set up interviews with ordinary people in the neighborhood and to act as translator, he immediately agreed, even though he knew he would be breaking the law that required a government official to be present. But he took the risk because he saw the American as a door to a world of opportunities.

"I thought up an alibi on the spot," he says. "If the police came after me, I would say I was just practicing my English. I would also say I was praising the government to the skies."

He became even more daring and more wily, sneaking two American couples through fortified gates into the forbidden territory of his college campus. He instructed them to wear cheap Chinese clothes and raincoats with hoods and to keep their heads down as he squeezed them into a group of students he had recruited and sneaked them past the guards.

As the ringleader, he could have been kicked out of school, but he knew he could count on his collaborators to stay mum.

Gupta, of Keynote Systems, almost always affixes the adjective *calculated* to risks he has taken, including the first one of any significance: shunning a military career that could have guaranteed him a life of status and comfort (he had placed third in the country in the entrance exam for India's equivalent of West Point). It was calculated, he said, because it was not a spur-of-the-moment decision but one he had mulled over for many months. His pragmatic conclusion: He would be miserable taking orders from anybody.

That need to be in charge is, of course, a trademark of the budding capitalist, but Gupta says he didn't really believe he was a bona fide member of the community until he took his first huge risk as the CEO of Gupta Technologies in 1987.

His biggest, and for a while sole, customer at the time was the Lotus Development Corporation, accounting for more than $1 million a year in revenue. Upset when Gupta Technologies began selling its software to his competitors, Lotus's CEO, Jim Manzi, gave Gupta an ultimatum: Sell us your company for $10 million or lose our business.

"I figure if Lotus is willing to pay me $10 million, five times my annual revenues, that validates I've got a great business," Gupta says. "That just gave me the heart and courage to go out and get venture capital." It was, he says, a calculated risk. And it paid off.

It's not just Gupta, actually. Most entrepreneurs describe their risk taking as carefully thought out. As a result, they don't let failure bother them. They made the right moves, they figure; they just got unlucky.

"I do make risky moves, but I don't make stupid moves; they are all calculated risks," Cameron Johnson says. In October 2004, for example, as the car dealership he was running for his father began taking delivery of 2005 Fords, he went out and bought about 100 2004 models from other dealers because huge rebates had made them suddenly hot.

"Some people would say I was crazy for putting $3 million in inventory like that, but to me it was not a risk at all," Johnson says. "People wanted the '04's." He sold them all and made a very fat profit. His advice to people who are just getting started: Take risks! Take them now, when you can roll with the punches.

Lisa Meiland, who like Johnson is in her twenties, agrees. "Most people subconsciously pair the concept of risk with failure," she says, whereas entrepreneurs pair it in their minds with reward.

Her sister Lara chimes in, "I don't think of myself as taking risks. Risk implies failure. I think of myself as a potential success maker. I don't have aversion to risk because I don't even see it." And one of the reasons both sisters think women make better entrepreneurs than men is that they are more willing to take risks. (Others are that they are better listeners, more adept at multitasking, more curious, and more focused.)

*   *   *

Of course, even in calculated risk taking, luck is still involved. Entrepreneurs talk about how strokes of good luck or bolts of bad luck changed the course of their business careers. Often a chance meeting can lead to good fortune. A wealthy woman Thompson was lucky enough to meet in an evening class took a liking to her, invited her to dinner, and implored Thompson—then a twenty-seven-year-old, recently divorced social worker with a mountain of credit card debt—to go to graduate school and become an accredited psychotherapist. Thompson demurred; her new friend persisted. Thompson said she wasn't smart enough; her friend told her she was highly intelligent. Thompson doubted she had the credentials to gain admission to a good school; her friend pulled strings to get her into Smith College, one of the best in the field of clinical social work. Thompson said she had no money; her friend said she would handle the cost.

So Thompson went and, within three years of earning her degree, landed a job as dean of multicultural affairs at Phillips Exeter, the elite prep school, where she met her future benefactor and partner in Warm Spirit.

In what Thompson regards as yet another amazing twist of fate, just as she was coming to an entrepreneurial crossroads, wondering if she should keep moving forward or turn back, she came across a postage stamp honoring Madame C. J. Walker, a daughter of former slaves who rose from doing fieldwork on a Louisiana plantation to become the most successful African American businesswoman of the late nineteenth and early twentieth centuries. For Thompson, learning the story of how Walker put together the country's first network marketing company, just as she was hoping to do, and how she had done it all alone, on her own grit, was an inspiration.

Until that moment, she had been unable to shake her doubts: Was the concept viable? Was she smart enough to pull it off? What did she really know about sales? Could she be the next Mary Kay Ash (the founder of the nation's number-two direct seller of beauty products that bears her name)? No, she could not, she kept thinking.

The postage stamp changed all that. "I'm like, 'My God! This is exactly the kind of concept I had,'" Thompson says. "'It must mean something. This must be real.'"

Luck probably does play a role in creating a successful small business, in the view of Craig Aronoff, founder of the Family Business Consulting Group in Marietta, Georgia. "Every entrepreneur talks about it," Aronoff says. "They say, 'If such and such hadn't happened in just the way it did, my business wouldn't be here today.'"

He cites the case of two clients in the metals trade who had been limping along for years and were thinking about shutting their businesses when, almost overnight, steel prices soared, and both made more money in one year than in the previous ten years combined.

Of course, bad luck can strike as suddenly as good. Two fatal crashes within five weeks forced Amico, founder of Airtrax, to shut down his helicopter training school, even though his pilots had done "everything by the book," he says. Huddy says his experimental hardwood-growing project out West for Crown Zellerbach had finally attracted the company's interest, but just as he was on the verge of winning a commitment for a major investment, Crown became the target of a hostile takeover and pulled the plug.

And Newman of Gotham Software thought he had made a financial breakthrough at an investment fair at the Hilton in New York in early September 2001, where some big names in the banking world expressed interest in his project. "I was starting to see the light at the end of the tunnel," he says. "Then 9/11 happened."

But usually, tales of happenstance have happy endings, even if bad luck is encountered along the way. Alex Lidow, the CEO of International Rectifier, says that for his father, who arrived in America in 1937 with $14.50 in his pocket, the circumstances of International Rectifier's beginnings were truly serendipitous. The father had gotten an offer to work for an inventor in California who was developing an automatic film-developing system using photoelectric cells. He took a Greyhound bus across the country, but when he arrived, he was told the inventor had died. The widow didn't know what to do with all her deceased husband's equipment, so he made her an offer and bought it. He was soon making rectifiers for warships.

Plank recounts how a seeming act of Providence bailed him out of his worst funk ever. Two years into his apparel business, everything was going wrong, and for the first time he was having doubts about the wisdom of keeping it going.

He was at home, and he was hungry. He looked in his wallet; it was empty. He had no money in his checking account, and all his credit cards were maxed out. He searched his pockets, then his car, for spare change but found none. "I was literally broke," he notes. "I said, 'Oh, man, did I pick the wrong thing, going after this T-shirt idea.'" He drove to his mother's house for a bite to eat, then checked his post office box.

"Sitting in that box was a check for $1,000, and I was right back on my way," Plank says.

Sometimes, an offhand comment can change the course of an entrepreneur's history. When Visconti was producing advertising sections for *Forbes* and *Fortune,* one of his employees noticed the articles always covered industrial subjects and wondered why they never explored personnel issues. He considers her offhand comment as the genesis of his interest in diversity in the workplace.

Then another fortuitous encounter occurred. Visconti was visiting Publishers Press in Louisville, which specializes in small magazines, and while wandering through the factory, looking at hundreds of magazines, "most of which looked like ransom notes," he happened to spot two that were very attractive. It turned out both were published by the same company in Connecticut, Image Mark.

"I called the CEO of Image Mark and asked, 'Who does your design?'" Visconti recalls. "He said, 'We do.'" Visconti met with the designer, who produced a cover that he loved. Visconti believes this was one of the main reasons for the magazine's successful launch.

Even so, most entrepreneurs acknowledge that they make their own luck by virtue of hard work, deal making, and networking. As Jeff Sloan, co-founder with his brother Richard of StartupNation, a multimedia company aimed at helping budding entrepreneurs, puts it, "You have to put yourself into a position where you can grab the luck that comes your way."

"We call it the gefilte fish philosophy," he says. "We had a golden retriever who would put his head right on my foot under the dinner table. One day I dropped a piece of gefilte fish—and it landed, literally, right in his mouth. That dog created his own luck."

CHAPTER 8

Failing Upward

Entrepreneurs, as we have seen, view the world as a muddled, unpredictable place. Forever expecting the unexpected, they are adept at shifting course at a moment's notice.

Entrepreneurs are always on the move, always ready to take a risk, always thinking of the next project. They are driven, impatient, high-energy hustlers.

Entrepreneurs spot opportunities almost everywhere they cast their restless eyes and move quickly to seize them.

And occasionally, these traits cause them to fumble. But there the paradox kicks in: The missteps and occasional fiascoes are a key ingredient in the entrepreneurs' recipe for success. Successful entrepreneurs analyze what went wrong and figure out how to leverage their mistakes to their purposes.

They fail upward.

Sig Anderman, founder of Ellie Mae, the provider of Internet connections to the mortgage industry, is very familiar with the phenomenon. "In every venture I've been involved in, you somehow come up with an idea and a business case for it, but either the product or service or the approach just isn't quite right; it doesn't click," Anderman says. "So you have to look at it and say, 'OK, is it the product or service? Is it really something anybody else would recognize as a valuable product or service other than yourself? Are we delivering it right, are we pricing it right, is the message right, is the value proposition right?'"

Simply stated, you take stock of the mess you have created and fix it. Peter Amico did. You might recall from Chapter 1 how Amico, desperate to make his omnidirectional forklifts affordable, hit upon the solution of using AC motors because they were cheaper than DC motors. True, the motors didn't work, but Amico figured that with improved technology they soon would. "My attitude was: AC motors are the only way this is going to work, so let's assume they'll work," he says.

Talk about setting yourself up for failure. And fail he did, for a while. He miscalculated how soon "soon" would be by a couple of years. But in time, the AC batteries indeed lived up to his expectations, and failure begat success, with the added bonus that today, his engineers are the most knowledgeable in the world about AC technology.

Entrepreneurs know—they *just know*—that they will reach the prize that they are pursuing. For them, setbacks are not failures but rather markers that warn them to change their course.

"They never think of themselves as failing at all," says Guy Kawasaki, the venture capitalist. "Vince Lombardi once said the Green Bay Packers never lost a game; they just ran out of time. Entrepreneurs never fail; they just run out of money."

After Greg Herro's LifeGem made its technological breakthrough in producing diamonds from cremated remains, he and his partners started calling funeral homes to enlist them as partners. Like many small-business innovators, they don't do market research. Why bother? This revolutionary new way of sending the dead off to their final reward would be a huge new opportunity for the undertakers who took LifeGem up on its offer. It ought to be a no-brainer for them.

They called 500 randomly selected funeral homes throughout the United States to gauge their interest. Not one showed any.

They followed up the calls with letters and got the same number of replies: zero.

To my mind, that is failure. Writers are used to rejection slips, but 500 of them? Herro, however, viewed the debacle as a business bargain in disguise. For just a few hundred dollars in phone bills and postage stamps, plus a few days of spinning his wheels, he had extracted a piece of wisdom for which a consulting firm might have charged thousands of dollars: Go directly to the consumer.

Which he did, with happy results. "We contacted a PR firm, and when I told them what we were up to, their jaws dropped," he says. They knew it would make a great headline, and they quickly sold the story to the *Chicago Tribune* as a page-one exclusive. At 5:45 A.M. on the day it ran, Herro was in bed, listening to the radio and savoring the thought of reading about himself in the newspaper. He gave a start: The announcer was alerting early risers to a weird little company called LifeGem that was profiled that morning in the *Tribune*.

His phone rang. It was a reporter for a news agency. As soon as he hung up, it rang again. All morning, all afternoon, all evening, it just kept ringing. "Are you the Greg Herro that's in the paper? Are you the Greg Herro that is involved with creating the diamonds? Are you the Greg Herro . . ."

Until then, LifeGem's Web site had gotten a total of 100 hits. Suddenly, it was getting 6,000 an hour. "We were on Howard Stern," Herro marvels. "We were on the *Today* show. Jay Leno did a monologue piece on us. Kelly and Regis did a thing on us. Interview requests were coming in from Australia, South Africa, Japan."

Going directly to the public worked. Orders trickled in, and suddenly funeral homes were signing up to do the processing. Some failure.

* * *

Luke Visconti, co-founder of DiversityInc, puts it this way: "You gotta figure out the angles and use them for maximizing what you can do. I don't stick to one thing foolishly. If it's not paying off, cut loose and move on."

In that sense, he uses failure as a tool for creating his future. For example, he started DiversityInc as a free Web site. But he soon realized that if his company didn't get other forms of revenue, it wouldn't survive. So in 2000, it started charging for the site. He got angry messages, accusing him of exploiting ethnic diversity for profit.

He didn't care. A free Web site was a mere miscalculation. The real failure would have been to dig the hole even deeper. "That circulation revenue kept us alive when the Internet market tanked and advertisers slammed on the brakes," Visconti says.

Specialists say that failure is not only inevitable, it is often positive. Frank Landsberger, the former Cambridge professor, likens it to "booster shots against the flu." He points out that in biotechnology, one of his specialties, laboratory researchers who consistently fail are much more likely to achieve a blowout breakthrough.

Charlie Horn, founder of the Promirus Group that provides discount prescription drug card programs, uses the same analogy. "I have learned that setbacks or 'failures' need to be addressed head-on and thought of as nothing more than feedback," he says. "It's like a scientist experimenting—does he have failures or test results that help him adjust and refine the next phase of testing?" Successful entrepreneurs study the feedback, make adjustments, and test again, he says.

"If you want to be the master of the universe, failure is the price you pay," remarks Judith Cone, the Kauffman Foundation vice president. "It relates back to that quality of tenacity."

Or grandiosity. Schramm, Kauffman's chief executive, believes that people who see problems as opportunities are the people who move civilizations. "They have an almost religious mission—'I am here to do something'—and accept the notion that they will stumble along the way," he says.

It helps that in the United States, unlike most of the rest of the world, nobody holds it against you if you fall on your face. Not only do Americans take setbacks in stride, Cone notes, but "in certain regions, like Silicon Valley and Boston, failing is almost a heroic accomplishment."

It is not uncommon, in fact, to hear entrepreneurs recount their bloopers with a "can you top this?" bravado. Consider David Weinstein, president of the Chicagoland Entrepreneurial Center.

"The most important and ultimately most gratifying experience in my life to date was failing, and failing miserably," Weinstein declares. "I love to talk about it. I was one of the key Internet failures in Chicago." It is not a confession; it is a boast. But where is the upside? "I believe men become great when they are humbled," he says.

Here is what happened. At the age of twenty-eight, Weinstein left a high-level job in the Chicago mayor's office to help start Blue Meteor, a company that built back-office computer systems for large corporations. He promptly raised $30 million from venture capitalists in Chicago, New York, and California, and almost overnight, Blue Meteor went from three people to 110, its revenues from zero to $5 million.

But it was a tottering edifice. "The initial mistake I made, and it was a doozy, was raising $30 million without a sales plan," Weinstein recalls. "Can you believe it? I understood the market and I positioned the company well. So I told myself. And from the time I raised the money until we had a wind-down and asset sale, we struggled unsuccessfully to find a sales plan."

He had raised a ton of money; he had snagged blue-chip customers such as Levy Restaurants, an upscale Chicago restaurant chain; he had gotten positive press in national publications including the *Wall Street Journal*; he had created a charge-ahead culture. But Weinstein just didn't have what it took to manage the fast-growing company he had created.

Part of turning failure into success is knowing when to bow out. For Weinstein, this moment came early in the game.

"I should have moved over and brought in somebody smarter than me to move it to the next level," he says now. But he didn't have time for such trifles. "I was too busy going on local talk shows like *HotBox* to brag about my company," he explains. "I didn't focus on sales. I didn't focus on operations. I got too caught up in myself. The money came so easily, it was as though I was ordained to win. I stopped working as hard as I had been. I didn't pay proper attention to details.

"Things fell apart quickly. They usually do; I believe they fall apart at twice the rate they climb. My failure was stark and very public. I take the blame for it."

So what is the moral of this story? Weinstein says it is simply that going into business for yourself means making mistakes and learning from them. You have to fail; it is a rite of passage that humbles you and stiffens your spine for future battles.

·　·　·

Paul Brown, founder of HearUSA Inc., has blazed a long trail of failures that turned into success. And he loves to talk about them. At his first company, MetPath, which did blood tests, he leveraged the occasional failing grades his lab got from the federal government (amongst mostly A's) by publishing them in his promotional brochures. Physicians were so shocked and impressed at his honesty that many sent their business his way.

In the mid-1980s, Brown learned another lesson: Do feasibility studies. This start-up made a small plastic device that snapped onto a wrist cast in a way that allowed the thumb and forefinger to move freely. Researchers at the Tufts University Department of Orthopedics loved it and said anyone with a wrist cast ought to have one. Brown sank $150,000 into the venture for a 45 percent stake. It flopped. The company had neglected to do market research to see whether people would actually pay money for a cheap-looking piece of plastic.

The blunders and miscalculations continued at HearUSA, including two botched acquisitions "One person said to me once, 'I never saw anybody wipe egg off his face faster than you do,'" Brown remarks. "I'm like those battery-powered cars that cruise across your living room. When they hit a chair, they don't just keep pushing against the chair in futility; they instantly change directions and keep moving."

If anybody can do Brown or Weinstein one better in the goof-up department, it is probably Pete Newman, founder of a company that never got off the ground. Newman quit his job at a nonprofit to start Gotham Software Inc. in April 2000. His plan, as he puts it, was to "slap together a business plan, put together a couple of million bucks, and be off and running."

As anyone who has ever launched a start-up can tell you, it is the second of those three steps that is most likely to throw a wrench into your plans. Newman persuaded friends and relatives to put up $100,000 and sweetened the pot with $20,000 of his own savings. He worked on Gotham full time for three years on a shoestring.

Even though he barely managed to raise one-twentieth of his stated goal, Newman continued to act as though the big payoff was just around the corner. His headquarters were in his Brooklyn home, but he went out looking for office space, held discussions with a software developer, researched the market, and refined his business plan to a "rock-solid" fifty-five-page blueprint.

Not only did he not have enough money to back these plans, he spent what money he had unwisely. He paid an accountant $10,000 to do financial projections that were at best expensive guesswork and to make introductions to investors who never materialized. He won a spot at a venture-capital conference on Long Island (sponsored in part by the accountant) only to find that half the people who stopped by his booth were either job seekers, competitors from other booths, or lawyers looking for business. "Nothing came of it, except it helped me hone my business pitch," he says. "I guess it was pretty comical."

He hired a smart intellectual-property attorney, which would have been a good move if his company had taken off, which it never did. He spent $70,000 on legal advice, whereas $40,000 would have been enough. "I invested in heavyweights, both because I needed their help but also to impress potential investors," he says. "But many of them were playing me. They didn't come up with the contacts I had expected."

He also kept fine-tuning his software prototype, more than was necessary, at a cost of $80,000.

It became almost farcical when a group of supposed investment bankers, recommended by a financier Newman's lawyer had met at a conference, *stole his identity.* Claiming to be specialists in start-up funding and software development, they were in fact operatives for a criminal enterprise. After Newman sent them his business plan, his Social Security number, and other personal information for a business loan, he got bad vibes and asked them to return the documents, but they were too busy racking up $70,000 in debt under his name to comply. He is still pursuing them legally (along with the FBI) in the hope of putting them behind bars.

"I've got the paperwork to prove these guys stole my identity," he says. "It's not that I wasn't being cautious. I was, all along. Yet, you're also always desperate as an entrepreneur. I learned a lesson: People know you're desperate. Also, a Web site can pretend to be anything, and there's no clear way to tell a fraudulent from a legitimate business. I met with them and their financier, and they seemed like honest business people."

Failing upward? Newman can take solace in knowing he did the best he could with the cards he had, a strong three of a kind. How was he to know that a rival company named i-Deal, backed by some of America's biggest corporations, would come out of nowhere and knock him out of the game?

And yet he was still able to break even. In exchange for his DealTrack software, i-Deal gave him an interest-free loan to pay off his $250,000 debt and offered him and his partner jobs with good salaries, stock options, and a percent of the profit from their product. "We avoided bankruptcy," he says. "Now, we run a sort of start-up within a bigger company. We have office space, support people, and, most important, instant credibility with hundreds of financial services firms. I'm still an entrepreneur, and the benefits of being one within a corporation are that I can get more support for more ideas."

If anything, the self-confidence and drive that got him into the game are stronger than ever. His frustration at never having run a business, of never having hired employees, and of never having filed a tax return that reported a business profit nag at him, but those regrets only spur him on. "When the time comes, will I become an entrepreneur again?" he asks. "Absolutely. There is no doubt about it."

Gary Doan is no stranger to setbacks, either. In his first venture, in 1977, making speaker hangers, his mistake was "selling them way too cheap. People didn't want to hang $1,000 speakers from $29 hangers." Lesson learned.

Doan later stumbled in a computer networking venture he founded called Transition Networks that he launched in 1987. After clashing with directors, he resigned in a huff in 1996 and was forced to relinquish stock options that would have made him rich had he stuck around for just a little while longer.

After that, Doan left another startup, Neo Networks, missing out on an opportunity for a cash bonanza to support his family in the event he succumbed to the hepatitis C that was ravaging his liver. (He has since had a successful transplant operation.) After Neo Networks went bust, he suffered the added indignity of realizing he had made the right bet on the future of router technology but had lost his company anyway, while his rivals who had made the wrong bet had prospered.

"People laughed at us at first, even though our model became the triumphant one," he says. "I thought I had a home run, but I did all the wrong things. A lot of other people made a lot of money." (He notes ruefully that two of his vice presidents at Neo Networks later founded NuSpeed Internet Systems in late 1999 and sold it seven months later to Cisco Systems Inc. for $463 million.)

Did that discourage him? Not a bit. In the business world, new problems are constantly cropping up as technology and markets evolve, he says. It is up to entrepreneurs such as Doan to identify them and grab them before anybody else does. That requires decisive action and the willingness to fail.

In fact, he described his early fiascoes as springboards to his current project, Intradyn, a maker of data storage and recovery devices for small businesses that was ranked by an industry group as one of the best products of 2003. In 2004, Intradyn bought another niche software maker, and by late 2005 had increased its revenue to a projected $2.5 million.

And if Intradyn, too, flops? He shrugs off the question. "All you need is a problem to solve and the logic to solve it," Doan says. "I could do this several times. In fact, there are several other opportunities out there right now."

•　　•　　•

Several other opportunities . . . sound familiar? We looked into that deep well of faith in Chapter 6 when we talked about delusions of grandeur. As I have pointed out elsewhere, the eight traits of successful entrepreneurs are facets of a single personality that are bundled together, as it were, and that act on one another. Thus, the capacity for failing upward derives from all the other core characteristics. Even when they are crashing and burning, entrepreneurs still scan the horizon for other opportunities and are prepared to tap into their reservoirs of energy, doggedness, self-confidence, optimism, and inventiveness to get the next project going.

Kevin Plank, the founder of Under Armour Performance Apparel, for example, made a crucial discovery while selling flowers in college to fellow students: Never deal with a live product that can die on your shelf, especially if you buy it on the cheap. His senior year, he ordered 1,500 dozen roses that, at 25 cents a stem, were not the cream of the crop. Customers were soon calling to complain that the flowers had wilted or that the wrong color had been delivered. One guy said his girl-friend had broken up with him because she had received yellow roses, the color of friendship, instead of red, the color of love.

So Plank was forced to come up with creative solutions to increase the appeal of his product. One was tier pricing. He offered flowers in a gold box with a cellophane window for $40, compared with $25 for flowers in a plain white box, and to his surprise got a lot of orders. The gold boxes cost him 50 cents instead of 25 cents, so he made $15 on every 25-cent investment.

He also learned to increase profits by broadening his product line (he sold vases for $60) and tacking on fees (such as delivery) wherever possible. Plank eventually sold 1,176 roses and discovered some valuable business lessons in the process.

"I learned I was good at putting teams together, and good at working towards a goal," he says. "And I learned the importance of presentation."

In another venture, he found that acting quickly can avert disaster. At a Grateful Dead concert, he sold only twenty T-shirts out of his stock of 400. So he went straight to his girlfriend's house, and the two stayed up all night tie-dying the remaining 380. The next day, he went back to the show and sold them all.

Today, as the CEO of a $240 million company, his earlier dalliances with failure have given Plank a sixth sense for what will and won't work. "There are things I walked away from, whether it's marketing campaigns or product lines, where I've got it all the way to the point where we're about to pull the trigger, and I say, 'You know what? That's not right for us.'"

In July 2002, for example, he pulled a women's line of garments at a cost of $600,000 even though the company had healthy advance orders for them. Why? An instinctive perception that it didn't "live up to the standard that we built for our brand"—and the belated recognition that he hadn't gotten input from actual women about whether they would wear the clothing.

"I don't regret [my decision] at all," Plank says. "It hurt like heck at the time, but it didn't hurt my customers. I wanted to make sure that the first experience a woman would have with my brand would not be a negative one. We came back the next year and rolled out a great product, eleven styles that were rock-solid, and from that we were able to build our women's business up to where it's about 18 percent in 2005."

Similarly, Scott Cook, the founder of Intuit, a provider of personal finance and small-business accounting software, realized that spotting mistakes early on can stave off disaster. His company was falling short in two ways: making its QuickBooks software a one-size-fits-all product and disregarding a class of users who were crying out for a more sophisticated version. He says a smart rival could easily have come in under the radar and grabbed a piece of the market. But by spotting the gaps quickly enough, he was able to plug them in time.

"We found out that small and medium-sized businesses don't say, 'I'm a small business' or 'I'm a medium-sized business,'" he points out. "They say, 'I'm a medical business' or 'I'm a real estate property manager' or 'I'm a framing contractor' or 'I'm a jeweler.'" In each case, their work flows are dramatically different.

A contractor, for example, has no permanent inventory and no credit cards, and worries mostly about invoicing and job estimates, he says. Likewise, consultants, retailers, nonprofits, and manufacturers all have their own concerns and procedures. So Intuit began tailoring the software to each category.

Also, while most of the companies that used it were small, a few were larger. Cook and his top managers at first thought that was an anomaly and ignored them.

Then somebody from Intuit went out and talked to them and reported back that they loved QuickBooks but wanted something with more features and greater speed.

"We were stuck in a mental rut," Cook recounts. "We had to make a mind-set change. We came up with QuickBooks Enterprise," tailored to the needs of the larger companies. "It is much better and cheaper than rival brands."

Intuit had also initially erred by allowing its tax software to get more and more complicated in the face of overwhelming demand by the public for greater simplicity. "We should never have let that happen," Cook says.

But the company quickly realized this mistake and embarked on a campaign to create easier-to-use products. It soon launched a simplified, user-friendly version of QuickBooks called QuickBooks SimpleStart that can be set up in fifteen minutes and that uses easy-to-grasp language such as "money in/money out" rather than "accounts receivable." It also issued SnapTax, a software designed for the IRS short forms that allows the forms to be completed in eight minutes.

Asked to list the key traits that make them tick, most people put ability to handle failure toward the top. Ross Levin of Accredited Investors ranks it number one.

In an article he wrote in 2002 for the *Journal of Financial Planning*, Levin called failure "a necessary component of the trifecta of meaning— risk, failure and success." That is because entrepreneurs view setbacks as vehicles for moving their ventures to a higher level of performance.

In his mind, failing upward is largely a matter of compensating for your weaknesses. At his first job at a financial planning company in the early days of the industry, Levin usually struck out in prospecting for clients. So he teamed up with a gregarious colleague who could easily snag the customers for him and concentrated on his strength, selling investment strategies.

He made a similar move a few years later when he took a job as president of another financial planning company. In this position, he had to pacify the owner and deal with financial planners instead of clients, and he wasn't particularly adept at either task. So he hired a chief operating officer and took on the more cerebral role of strategist, at which he excelled.

At Accredited Investors, the company he founded in the mid-1980s, one apparent blooper he committed was switching to fees from commissions. Revenues sagged immediately. That is where tenacity and self-confidence made all the difference. He stuck to his guns in the conviction that fee-based services would build a more solid client base, and in time that is what happened.

"Every so-called failure I have committed actually caused me to become better at what I was doing," Levin says.

Monumental failures can hone survival skills to a samurai-sword sharpness. Alex Lidow's father learned this in the early 1960s when he veered from his power-management business into the pharmaceuticals market. He dreamed up the ill-fated diversification after a conversation with a staff chemist about the high cost of prescription drugs. The chemist, who had worked for a pharmaceutical company, told him about generic drugs, which were a fairly novel concept at the time. Soon, the elder Lidow created a company, Rachelle Labs, which produced the generic drug tetracycline for pennies per pill instead of dollars.

The company did reasonably well for a while, but in the end it had to be shut down. Lidow explains that his father hadn't correctly gauged the competitive landscape and had failed to anticipate that an upstart like him would never be able to steal business away from the pharmaceutical giants.

"They were extremely powerful," Lidow said. "It takes an awful lot of money to compete against those companies, and there is an awful lot of litigation. So we were involved in huge lawsuits for long periods of time and eventually realized this is just a distraction and decided to refocus on power management."

Stick to your knitting, and never underestimate the competition.

Pretty simple guidelines, but when an entire company goes belly up because you flubbed one of them, you learn not to make the same mistake twice.

Lidow's experience with the drug company engendered a policy of being aggressive about obtaining and enforcing patents for International Rectifier's new product, HEXFET, the first broadly commercial variable-speed drive. International Rectifier's patents on those speed drives, or power MOSFETs, have brought in more than half a billion dollars in royalties so far and, more important, have protected its turf against deep-pocketed rivals.

That is not the only good that can come out of the ruins of its pharmaceutical misadventure. Recognizing a broader competitive threat, International Rectifier poured more than one-third of its research and development budget into quality control and reliability improvements throughout the 1980s to achieve what it calls "absolute perfection" in its products.

. . .

There is another upside to failure that you probably won't read about in the business literature: It forces you to take stock of your values. Entrepreneurs can become so caught up in the exultation of building a business that they neglect their families, their friends, and their own emotional health. Witnessing their business go up in flames, painful as it is, can jolt them out of their workaholic trap and open their eyes to what really matters in life.

It happened to Umang Gupta. In 1984, he started Gupta Technologies, a provider of the world's first client/server database software and tools for personal computers. A few months later, his first son, Raji, was born. Within three months, Raji started to have epileptic seizures, and Gupta and his wife, Ruth, were told that he was profoundly developmentally delayed. Before he turned three, Raji died. "It was a very difficult time in our lives, but in order to get through it, I doubled and tripled my energies on Gupta Technologies," he says. "The company became my way of ensuring I would make enough money so Raji would never have to be institutionalized. During that period, I was never far away from the utter terror of not being able to look after Raji financially when he grew up. Becoming financially self-sufficient was all that mattered to me during those three years."

Wanting a sibling for their firstborn child, Clare, but fearing that Raji's disability might be genetic, in 1988 the couple adopted Kashi, "a big, healthy, wonderful-looking newborn baby." Two years later, in 1990, they learned that he was developmentally delayed, too, though not as severely as Raji.

"That just really broke us for a while," Gupta recalls. "I kept asking myself how this could happen. We survived intact as a family purely due to my wife's patience and perseverance. I was building Gupta Corporation, and for the second time I doubled or tripled my energies to the point where I neglected home, family, and a lot of relationships for the next few years."

In other words, he transferred his emotional commitment to an inanimate entity.

The company went public in 1993, and for a short period it was worth more than $400 million, which made his personal share worth $100 million. Gupta was elated. He had nurtured his company and watched it grow as though it were his own child that he had lost.

It didn't take long, though, for giants such as Microsoft and Oracle to go after his market—or for newer players such as Powersoft to nibble at the edges. "So we were a hot company in 1993, and a pretty hot company in 1994, but the seeds of our demise had already been sown," Gupta said. "I should have recognized at that stage that it was a no-win situation for me and I'd be better off selling out."

Oracle made an offer of something like $13 a share, well over the market price, but Gupta held out for more, not because he wanted the money, he said, "but ultimately because I didn't want to sell my baby. That was a mistake."

The company began losing money, the stock tanked, and by 1995, Gupta saw the writing on the wall and resigned as CEO. The game was over. "I sat down and asked myself the question: 'So what went wrong, and what do I want to do next?'" he says. "I realized that, basically, I had moved the pendulum too far toward work and professional success but neglected the family." In 1996, he took a long family vacation and soon after that cashed out his shares in Gupta Technology.

Later, in 1997, he made a small investment in a company called Keynote Systems that measured the performance of corporate Web and wireless systems. Within months, he was asked to run it. He anguished over the offer. Should he take the plunge back? Would he fall prey to his old addiction to work? He had long talks with his wife.

"We made a collective decision," he says. "I said to her, 'You know, I've learned a lot, I don't know if I can apply what I've learned, but I believe I can. I'd like to try again.'" She agreed.

Since then, he has built its revenues to $54 million from $200,000 in 1997, taken it public in 1999, and, for a few heady days of the technology boom, watched Keynote's valuation grow to almost $5 billion and his personal stake in it to over $400 million—"on paper," he reminds himself. Despite the bursting of the dot-com bubble and the loss of a significant part of the company's customers and revenues, he has painstakingly nurtured it back to financial health, and his stake in the company still remains around $40 million. But his real achievement, he believes, has been to strike the right balance between work and life outside the office.

"The most important thing this time around is that I don't define my success as just that of the company, how much it's worth, how much we're worth—none of that," Gupta emphasizes. "It really comes down to how good our family life is, and how proud I feel for Keynote and its people. That is my touchstone for success."

Joan Schweighardt learned a valuable business lesson from another man who, like Gupta, gained a sense of renewal as a result of his misfortunes. Schweighardt's little publishing company, GreyCore Press, had been struggling for years. Her first three books, all novels, got positive reviews, she says, but first one distributor, then a second, went out of business, taking a lot of her money with them. "So there I was in July 2002 with commitments to three additional books and no distributor, no money, lots of debt, still working thirty hours a week as a freelancer for a public relations company to pay the bills," she recalls.

Nevertheless, she was able to keep her company afloat after publishing the story of a man who lost a leg in a car accident and went on to become a world-class triathlete. But it almost didn't happen. She had gotten money from an angel investor to produce the book, *One Man's Leg,* by Paul Martin, but, suddenly fearful that she would botch the job, tried to fob it off on a fellow small publisher. When she told Martin about her decision, he lit into her.

"He basically said, 'If I can run, swim, and bike in a triathlon on one leg and come in the top 20 percent with all the two-legged freaks, you can get your company running again,'" Schweighardt remembers. Her spine thus stiffened, she threw herself back into the task, and made a success of the book. She has since linked up with a first-rate distributor, put together a loyal staff, and marketed a big seller.

"Paul Martin told me that losing his leg was the best thing that ever happened to him," Schweighardt says. "It made him realize how failure can open up a new vista of opportunity."

•   •   •

Some feel that failure can be a cathartic, even positive, experience. Karl Eller, CEO of the Eller Company, says he learned the three cardinal rules of his trade from botching so many deals over the years. They are: Listen to the customer; get a yes or no out of him quickly, with no dilly-dallying; and finally, once an agreement is reached, "get the hell out of there fast, before the guy changes his mind."

"You have to be willing to fail," he says. "Look at Henry Ford and Thomas Edison. How many times did they fail? Failure is a good thing."

In fact, he believes a smart boss gives his people a long leash so that they can fail and figure out for themselves what they did wrong. The more pressure you put on people, the less creative they become, he believes, while the less oversight you exercise, the more resourceful they become.

Peter Gyenes, the former chief executive of Ascential Software, says a failed $600,000 deal he blew back when he was a salesman at Xerox taught him the perils of overconfidence (he had been boasting of his imminent coup) and the importance of teamwork (he had thought he could pull off the deal on his own).

From his many other failures, he says, he has also drawn these conclusions:

- Take responsibility for your goofs.
- Never pin the blame for them on somebody else, even if he or she deserves it.
- Never be ashamed of them.

You have to fail to succeed, Gyenes says. He uses a sports metaphor: If you don't fall down while skiing, you aren't trying hard enough. Another oft-quoted sports metaphor is apt as well. "I've missed more than 9,000 shots in my career," Michael Jordan once said. "I've lost almost 300 games. Twenty-six times, I've been trusted to take the game-winning shot, and missed. I've failed over and over and over again. And that is why I succeed."

Here are some other lessons that entrepreneurs say they have drawn from their struggles to overcome the mistakes they have made.

Know when to fold 'em. Bob Hillier, founder of the Hillier Group, says he blew $2.5 million to develop a wireless light switch, for which he still holds seventy-two obsolete patents. The product never took hold, but Hillier says the failure didn't bother him in the least. "We were on the right track," he says. "We just ran out of money."

Try harder next time. Fear of failure is a positive force because you redouble your effort not to let anybody down, Hillier says. Take Paul Brown. After he sold his stake in his first company, MetPath, he tried even harder with his next major venture, HearUSA, and made it a success.

Stick to what you know best. "Anytime we stray from our core strengths, publicity and dealing with the press, we run into trouble," said John Heagney of Heagney Public Relations. Likewise, Richard

Wellman, who has done deals all his life involving airplanes and airplane parts, sank $40,000 into a time-share project in the Dominican Republic that quickly went wrong. "You have to realize that the mechanics that make you successful in your line of business don't necessarily apply in another line of business," he says.

Make pleasing customers your number-one priority. Herro of LifeGem says he became overextended at Anything's Possible, the computer consulting company that was his first business, and began neglecting some of his old customers to handle all the new business coming in. They picked up on his neglect right away, he says, and bad-mouthed him to the skies. He has never repeated that mistake. Similarly, Lara Meiland and Lisa Helene Meiland, co-owners of the Lara Helene Bridal Atelier in Manhattan, discovered that as much as they like minimalist chic in wedding dresses, most brides don't. "The girls have been waiting all their lives for this, and they want something to die for," Lara says. They realized that when it comes to the sale, it is the bride's taste that counts.

Analyze what you did wrong. "I look at setbacks analytically and try to decipher them," says Martin Klein of Electro Energy Inc., a maker of high-technology batteries. "I always try to list a series of options and solutions. I engage in free thinking. Don't restrict your thinking. Look at all the pluses and minuses and filter your course of action."

Maintain your self-respect. Newman worked for a public relations company that came apart after the founding partner's sexual escapades drove clients away. He worked for a law firm that discarded him after it no longer needed him. From both employers, the message he got was that he was expendable. But he didn't care. "I felt my work ethic and my values were better than senior management's at both places," he said. And, in fact, at his next job as a broker and analyst at a small brokerage firm, he flourished because he respected himself, and soon gained the respect of his clients as well.

Keep a lid on spending. That is a refrain you hear again and again. James Poss, president of the Seahorse Power Company, which makes solar-powered trash compacters, says he spent $100,000 for twenty prototypes of the original version of the machine, whereas ten at half the cost would have been plenty.

Expect no sympathy for your snafus. When Lisa Meiland worked at J.P. Morgan, she made a bad call and the trade went against her. "I learned that 'we' is when the trade goes well and 'you' is when the trade goes badly," she notes.

Don't assume that all publicity is good publicity. Vonfrolio of Education Enterprises says her biggest mistake was spending $66,000 "to print and mail the ugliest brochure imaginable—so ugly that I thought it would be a real attention grabber and pull in a lot of business." She was wrong. The response rate was close to zero.

Realize that success isn't as important as being in the game. The Meiland sisters laugh about their failed business concepts, which include a screwable heel for shoes, a Danish pastry shop, "chic but cheap" children's clothing, and yellow patent leather suits (whose legs, alas, stuck together). "As long as we feel we have thrown ourselves into this every day and wrung every last bit out of it, then we're happy," Lara says.

•　•　•

What is their secret? What enables entrepreneurs to move so effortlessly from failure to success? We've mentioned their drive, their tenacity, their agility, and their optimism as factors. But the one ingredient most central to this ability is the fuel that propels the faltering innovator up the ladder to the next challenge: self-confidence.

"I have never known an entrepreneur who didn't have confidence in himself and in what he was doing," says William J. Dennis of the National Federation of Independent Business.

A caveat: Self-confidence doesn't always come easily. Some people confess to being plagued by self-doubt, even to fears that they will eventually be exposed as frauds for tricking the world into believing they are smarter than they really are. It is known as the impostor complex, and it afflicts highly successful people in any field.

"I often have this feeling that one of these days somebody is really going to figure me out and realize that I'm not all I'm cracked up to be," says Anderman of Ellie Mae.

The caveat, however, rates no more than a mention. Insecurity, anxiety, and self-reproach are universal human sentiments. But entrepreneurs wrestle those qualms to the ground. For a long time, Levin of Accredited Investors says, he has lived with a paradox: "I have great self-confidence but also great insecurity."

However, like most successful entrepreneurs, Levin has learned to keep the insecurity at bay and ride the self-confidence to achievement. "Therapy allowed me to go from being outwardly motivated to being inwardly motivated," he says. "I was with a group of people and we talked about stuff that forced me to pull up the window shade and allowed me to be vulnerable."

Similarly, Gyenes, the former chief of Ascential Software, recalls the dread he felt at Xerox many years ago when he made his first cold calls to potential customers. Locking himself in a room with a pack of cigarettes so nobody could see him sweating, he would dial the phone and pray that nobody answered.

It took him a while to figure out that his seemingly self-assured colleagues also got butterflies in their gut. He came to a couple of other realizations, too. The gift of gab—"effective presentations," in his words—was crucial for rising to a leadership position, so he methodically worked on improving his speaking style, and in turn gained even more confidence as his improved speaking style led to more sales.

It is a virtuous circle: The more you succeed, the higher your self-confidence. The higher your self-confidence, the more likely you are to enjoy even more success.

When he was working for WTNJ, Heagney of John Heagney Public Relations marveled at how easily he could sell airtime to businesses that had never heard of the radio station. "I'd leave the shops wondering, 'How'd I do that?'" he says. He hated making the pitches, but his success at it built up his self-esteem.

At one point, he grasped that what he was really selling was himself. It was a revelation that sealed his professional fate. "There was no other product I knew so well, no other product I believed in so much, no other product where I could control the quality so fully," he says. "I realized I had been an entrepreneur, screaming to get out of my fear of rejection and failure, all my life."

Herro of LifeGem had no idea how good a salesman he had become at a little computer-consulting firm until he went out on his own and took a large number of clients with him. The ease with which he pulled it off built up his confidence even more. "I said, 'Hey, I can do this on my own,'" he says. "That is one of the core traits of an entrepreneur, that realization. You have to have that inside feeling, 'I *know* I can succeed.' Once I had it, there was no turning back."

Index

ABOUT THE AUTHOR

BRENT BOWERS was a business editor for *The New York Times* for ten years, and before that a reporter and editor for *The Wall Street Journal*. He lives in Brewster, Massachusetts.